Greek Pottery in the Bronze Age

Plate I. Late Minoan I storage jar from Pseira

Greek Pottery in the Bronze Age

A. D. LACY

METHUEN & CO LTD

First published in Great Britain 1967
by Methuen & Co. Ltd,
11 New Fetter Lane, London EC4
Copyright © 1967 by A. D. Lacy
Printed by Butler & Tanner Ltd,
London and Frome

Distribution in the U.S.A.
by Barnes & Noble, Inc.

Contents

Illustrations

Acknowledgements

The author wishes to express his special gratitude to the following:

The Director and Staff of the British School of Archaeology in Athens for the use of their library.

The Librarian and Staff of the Library of the Hellenic Society in London.

The Staff of the Library of the Victoria and Albert Museum in London.

Mr John Boardman and Dr H. W. Catling of the Ashmolean Museum at Oxford.

The Librarian and Staff of the Fogg Museum, Harvard, Cambridge, Mass., U.S.A.

Mr J. N. Coldstream and Mr R. A. Higgins for kindly reading the manuscript and making a number of useful suggestions.

Mrs Wace French for her views on pottery styles of the Mycenaean Periods.

Mr M. Cardew and Mr J. Leggett for their information on ceramic processes in Northern Nigeria.

Mr H. Wakefield of the Isles of Scilly Pottery for his many informative letters.

Mr Ernest Welsman, whose inspiration enabled me to visit so many Bronze Age sites in Greece and the islands.

The author and publishers are grateful to the following for permission to use illustrations. The plate and figure numbers are those for this book:

American School of Classical Studies, Athens, Figs. 2c; 70a, c; 74d, f; 76d; 84c.

American School of Classical Studies, Princeton, N.J., Figs. 69f; 74e; 76b.

Antiksamlingen, Nationalmuseet, Copenhagen, Figs. 72e; 77a; 90d; 91a, b; 94e.

Archaeological Institute of America (*American Journal of Archaeology*), Figs. 31c; 44e; 76c.

Ashmolean Museum, Figs. 8e; 12c; 17b; 67c; 85c.

Professor Carl W. Blegen, Figs. 2e, f.

Monsieur A. Bon, Lyon, Fig. 41e.

Trustees of the British Museum, Figs. 9d; 31a, b; 37e, f; 59b; 65c, d; 67e; 72a; 83e; 84a, d; 98a, d; 101a, c; 103b.

The Managing Committee of the British School of Archaeology at Athens (Volumes of the *B.S.A. Annual*), Pl. IIa, b, c, d; Pl. IVa; Figs. 11d; 17d; 18b; 21c, e; 22c, d, e; 23a, b, c, d; 26e; 56a, b, c, d; 57d, e; 58c, d; 63d, e; 85a; 91d; 110a, b.

Professor John L. Caskey, Figs. 65b; 102a; 103a.

The Clarendon Press, Oxford (*Scripta Minoa* by Sir Arthur Evans), Fig. 55.

Mr Piet de Jong and Mr M. S. F. Hood, Figs. 44f; 51c, d, e, f.

Editions Cahiers d'Art, Paris [(*a*) *L'Art de la Crète* and (*b*) *L'Art des Cyclades* by Christian Zervos], (*a*) Figs. 1a–e; 2a, b, e; 5a, b, f; 6a, b, d; 8b, d; 12b, d, e; 18a, d; 33e; 34c, d; (*b*) 96a–e; 98b, c, e, f; 100a, b, d, e; 101b, e; 102b, f; 106a, c, d, e; 108c; 109.

Trustees of the late Sir Arthur Evans (*Palace of Minos*), Pl. IVb; Figs. 18c; 22a; 26a, b; 31e; 33a, b, f; 39a; 47a; 48d, e, f; 49c, d; 53d, e, f.

Dr A. Furumark (*The Mycenaean Pottery*), Figs. 71, 75, 79, 87, 95.

Messrs Hannibal, Greece, Pl. IIIb; IVc; Figs. 53b; 76c, e; 78a; 83a, d; 90a; 94d.

Holle Verlag G.m.b.H., Baden-Baden (Matz: *Crete and Early Greece*), Figs. 5c; 65a.

Istituto Poligrafico dello Stato, Libreria dello Stato, Rome (*Palazzo Minoico di Festos* (Banti and Pernier), *Annuario della Scuola Archaeologica in Atene; Bolletino d'Arte*), Figs. 25d; 26d, f, g; 27d, e; 28; 29; 78c; 91e.

J. M. Meulenhoff Uitgever, Amsterdam (Devambez: *Greek Painting Compass History of Art*)), Pl. IIIc.

Dr Ernst Meyer, Berlin, Fig. 66.

Professor Luigi Morricone, Rome, Figs. 94a; b.

Monsieur le Conservateur, Musée d'Archéologie, Marseille, Fig. 44a.

Monsieur le Conservateur, Musée du Louvre, Paris, Figs. 63c; 78b; 85a.

National Archaeological Museum, Athens, Figs. 74b; 94c.

The Director, National Portrait Gallery, London, Fig. 4.

Mr Cas Oorthuys, Amsterdam, Fig. 32a.

Mrs J. D. S. Pendlebury (*The Archaeology of Crete* by J. D. S. Pendlebury), Figs. 3; 7; 10; 13; 19; 20; 24; 28 (pt); 29 (pt); 36; 45; 46; 52; 64.

Miss Josephine Powell, Rome, Figs. 6c; 9a, b; 21a; 37a; 39b; 40b.

Römisch-Germanisches Zentralmuseum, Mainz (*Pitharades* by Hampe and Winter), Fig. 32b.

Professor Doro Levi, Director, Scuola Archaeologica Italiana di Atene, Figs. 78c; 90e; 91e.

Society of Antiquaries of London (*Archaeologia*), Figs. 44d; 48a, b, c; 49a, b; 53c; 57a, b, f; 58b; 67a, b, f, g; 69b, c, d, e; 70b, d; 72c, d, f; 73d, f; 74a, c; 77d; 83c; 91c.

Society for the Promotion of Hellenic Studies (*Journal of Hellenic Studies*), Figs. 27b; 47b.

Messrs Thames and Hudson Ltd, London (*Crete and Mycenae* by Spyridon Marinatos), Pl. IIIa, d.

The University Museum, University of Pennsylvania (*Excavations on the Island of Pseira*, Seager), Pl. I; Figs. 21d; 31d; 33d; 39c, f; 40d; 42a; 43b, c, d.

Chronology

M = Minoan
H = Helladic
Myc = Mycenaean

The periods accepted for Cycladic periods are virtually the same as the Minoan.

The dates shown are subject to constant minor rectification with new discoveries, but within reasonable limits are those generally accepted. Precise dating of any phase of Minoan, Mycenaean or Cycladic pottery is, in any case, a refinement which our present knowledge does not justify.

BC	CRETE (Minoan)	MAINLAND (Helladic and Mycenaean)
before 3100 3000	Neolithic	Neolithic
2900 2800 2700 2600 2500	EM I	EH I
2400 2300 2200	EM II	EH II
2100 2000 1900	EM III	EH III
1800	MM I	MH I
1700	MM II	MH II
1600	MM III	MH III
1500	LM I A B	Myc. I
1400	LM II	Myc. II
1300		Myc. III A
1200	LM III	Myc. III B
1100		Myc. III C
1000	Sub-Minoan	Sub-Mycenaean

Simple vase forms. Polished at first, then incised and later picked out
in white gypsum. Suspension lugs.   *End of Neolithic Age.*

Beginning of Bronze Age.

Burnishing superseded by slip.
Range of shapes enlarged including chalices.
Some suspension lugs still in common use.
'Urfirnis' ware.

Minyan ware.
'Teapot' and 'sauceboat'. 'Vasiliki' mottled ware.
Beautiful stone vases.
'Pictoglyphic' script.

Hole-mouthed jars. Decoration matt white on dark ground.
Introduction of slow wheel. First palaces built.
Ionian migrations into Greece begin.

Barbotine ware. Introduction of quick wheel.
Kamares ware. Linear A script in use (probably non-Greek).

1st destruction of palaces (probably by earthquake).

Palaces rebuilt. Achaean migrations into Greece from North begin.
Shaft graves at Mycenae. Very early Tholos tombs in Thessaly.

Floral style of decoration in Crete. Beginning of Mycenaean civilisation.
Marine decoration, Crete. Large Cretan pithoi.

Stirrup jars. Palace style of decoration.

2nd destruction of palaces (earthquake or tidal wave and Mycenaeans).
Treasury of Atreus at Mycenae built. Introduction of Linear B script.

Achaeans in Cyprus. Trojan War.
Dorian invasions. Destruction of Mycenae and Tiryns.

End of Mycenaean civilisation.   *End of Bronze Age.*

Beginning of Dark Age.   *Beginning of Iron Age.*

Foreword

Nearly all popular works hitherto written on the subject of Greek pottery are confined to vessels produced during the thousand years before the Christian era, starting with the period of the Dorian invasions which marked the beginning of the Iron Age. This period begins about 1100 BC. It is, however, only the later and better known period of Greek ceramics. The two thousand years preceding the Iron Age constituted what is known as the Bronze Age. To bring such a period into focus, we have to go back in time from our own day to the birth of Christ. When we look at this Aegean Bronze Age we should bear in mind what Sir Arthur Evans said in the *Journal of Hellenic Studies* half a century ago, that the scientific study of Greek civilisation is becoming less and less possible without taking into constant account that of the Minoan and Mycenaean world that went before it.

For nearly four thousand years before the Bronze Age we have the Neolithic Age. During this vast period – for excavations begun in 1962 at Chatal Hüyük in Asia Minor have unearthed pottery of neolithic style which the excavators date to about 6600 BC – pottery was made in Greece which by 3000 BC had reached a wonderfully high standard in fabric, in form, and even in decoration.

Of the two principal collections of ceramics in Greece, the one in the National Archaeological Museum in Athens includes hardly any specimens of Minoan pottery, while the one in the Archaeological Museum in Herakleion is confined, as is natural, almost entirely to pottery discovered in Crete. Together, however, they shelter the most representative collection of Minoan and Mycenaean ceramics in the world.

The British Museum in London has a magnificent collection of classical pottery, but only a comparatively meagre selection of Minoan and Mycenaean ware.

The collection in the Ashmolean Museum at Oxford, although nowhere near the size of the other three, covers in a wonderful way the whole two thousand years of Minoan, Helladic, and Mycenaean ceramics. This Bronze Age collection was begun in 1900 and enriched for forty years by Sir Arthur Evans. At his death the rest of his collection was, by his wish, given to the University of Oxford, with the result that the Ashmolean now houses the finest collection of Cretan antiquities outside Crete itself.

There are a number of smaller provincial museums in Greece, both on

1

the mainland and in the islands, which house collections of Neolithic and Bronze Age pottery, but with some exceptions they lack both catalogues and pictures of their most interesting contents, a feature which seems to characterise many larger museums in other countries.

In the task of selecting illustrations for a work of this nature, one is presented with a number of conflicting problems. On the one hand we have the beauty of photography, such as the splendid coloured plates of Max Hirmer which illustrate that grand work, *Crete and Mycenae* by Professor Marinatos.

On the other one cannot but feel a sense of admiring awe for the enchanting plates reproduced from water-colours and pencil drawings executed with loving care more than half a century ago such as illustrate the massive tome on Minoan vases in *Gournia* by Harriet Boyd-Hawes, or the *Palazzo Minoico di Festos* by Pernier and Banti, or Evans's *Palace of Minos*. Thanks to the courtesy of those to whom grateful acknowledgement is made on pages xi–xiii, it has been possible to reproduce examples of both kinds.

As for illustrations in black and white, owing to the immense strides made recently in photography, we are able to enjoy not only excellent photographs of specimen vases of every period, but also to compare them with black and white drawings such as illustrate the noble work on Mycenaean vases by Furtwängler and Loeschke, where one can see them through the eyes of the artist.

The drawing sometimes has an advantage over the photograph, particularly where the fugitive colour of the design on the vase has been partly obliterated by the action of damp and time; but which the artist has so carefully and skilfully reconstructed from the faint traces that were still visible.

In assigning Minoan vessels to a particular chronological period, we have relied principally, as is only natural in the case of Minoan ceramics, upon the allocations made by Sir Arthur Evans. In the case of Mycenaean ceramics, Furumark's chronology has been used as the most generally accepted, but without his complex sub-divisions. In the case of Cycladic ware, grateful acknowledgements are made to Professor Ch. Zervos for his fine work, *L'Art des Cyclades* and to the authors of *Excavations at Phylakopi in Melos conducted by the British School at Athens*.

It has not been found practicable to show the relative size of vases, nor has any attempt been made to include a scale in photographs or diagrams. Not only are scales ugly but they are not often of much use.

'It is an obligation', says Professor Carl Blegen in his great work *Prosymna*, 'of every excavator to set forth in plain terms the results of his work.' Due to a neglect of this rule by some excavators in the past much knowledge of Bronze Age pottery is still hidden from us, or even irretrievably lost to posterity by the hazards of war or the destructive action of earthquakes.

As regards Cyprus, no attempt has been made to deal with native styles of Cyprus pottery during the Bronze Age, apart from vessels of Mycenaean style made in that island, or of Minoan and Mycenaean vessels imported into Cyprus. In this connection may we look forward to a new work by Dr Karageorghis on the artistry of individual Mycenaean vase decorators?

The excavations now taking place in Asia Minor prompt a short digression to suggest that some interesting results might reward a comparison of objects found in Aegean excavations of the Bronze and Iron Ages with those discovered further east upon the Asiatic continent.

During the third and second millennia, a period which coincided with the Aegean Bronze Age, some shapes and decoration of early Chinese ware bore a strong resemblance to Late Neolithic and Early Minoan vessels. Not only is this true in a general sense but also in matters of detail.

What a strange likeness is to be found between the chamber-tombs on the hillsides below the fortress of Mycenae and those built even to this day on the sloping sides of the hills in south China. Both seem to be sited in the same manner; both are arranged in groups belonging to people of the same clan; both are furnished with earthenware articles for the service of the dead in the next world; from both it would seem that on occasions the bones, after the lapse of a certain interval, were transferred to burial urns covered with a lid.

Even the beehive tomb has its counterpart in China, except that here the stones of the dome are arranged in the form of a spiral, the old Chinese symbol of eternity. This is perhaps not the place to pursue this matter, but other and equally striking examples of similarity are to be found.

What is the origin of the link that seems to have united in the remotest antiquity two races separated by half the world?

Among all the remains which may help us out of the darkness of the unknown in the study of pre-history, the most abundant and the best preserved are those of pottery, and among all the arts to which Crete made an original contribution, pottery was certainly the most flourishing. Thanks to the vast number of specimens which were made throughout the centuries of the Bronze Age in Crete and on the Greek mainland, we have been able to mark the successive stages of the Minoan and Mycenaean civilisations.

The historian of pre-classical antiquity has no guide so reliable to enlighten him where literary sources fail, no more trustworthy evidence to confirm his usually scanty information than the remains of ancient ceramics. There is no country where the Greeks lived, no place with which they traded, which does not yield immense numbers of vases.

To the Greek potter the vessel he made was not produced solely as an object of beauty or solely as an object of utility, but he always strove to reconcile utility with beauty; and it may be said that however much the Greek vase was made to serve the needs of daily life, it is never without its artistic value.

Even in neolithic times the primitive Cretan artisan was proud of his work, and took advantage of every rudimentary means at his disposal. Even in those very remote times he had an innate sense of shape and design. By baking in the open air he was able to smoke his vessels which he then polished to a high lustre. Then a little later he filled with a white pigment the lines he engraved upon the clay.

The creative impulse which showed itself in all branches of art and industry was particularly noticeable in ceramics, an activity which was still further stimulated by the introduction of the potter's wheel. The potter was even able to compete with the metallurgist in the thinness of his walls. In his imitation of the colour and patina of bronze or the texture and veining of marble, even the dead were deceived by the vessels which were placed beside them in the grave. It is these apparently fragile clay vessels which have best survived the wreck of successive Greek civilisations and it is they alone which enable us to follow step by step the rise and fall of Greek art.

CHAPTER ONE

The Neolithic Era

6600–3000 BC

The Cretan Bronze Age is represented at Knossos, the Minoan capital of Crete, by deposits some seventeen feet deep, but below these Bronze Age deposits are the debris of successive Late Stone Age or Neolithic settlements twenty to twenty-six feet deep. These deep deposits represent an immense tract of time. They carry us far back into the mists of antiquity to the beginnings of human activity in the Greek lands.

Long before the first pyramid in Egypt was built, a settlement was already in existence upon the hill known today as Kephala, where later was built the famous palace of Knossos. This enormous depth of neolithic deposits from virgin soil up to the first layer of the Bronze Age represents a disintegration of clay platforms, and of wattle and daub huts of long generations of neolithic inhabitants, and we see that Knossos was already a thickly populated site at a remote prehistoric date. It was upon these very neolithic remains that the first palace of the early Minoan kings was built, for almost all traces of the Early Minoan periods disappeared when the summit of the hill was cut away at the beginning of the Middle Minoan epoch to form the necessary level space for the construction of the first palace.

We know little of the origins of these neolithic people. Anthropologists were inclined at one time to the view that they were immigrants from North Africa, and the time of their coming could not even be surmised. In a lecture to the British School in February 1963, however, Professor John Evans reported that the earliest pottery in the second neolithic level at Knossos associated with houses entirely of mud-brick, suggested settlement from Asia Minor, and that a radio-carbon date for the original encampment gave 6100 ± 150 BC (see *Archaelogical Reports for 1962–63 by the British School at Athens*, p. 29).

Thus recent excavations in these deep levels have yielded finds that take us back to the sixth millennium BC or even earlier, so we see that the site of Knossos, capital of the Bronze Age kings, was occupied by a stone-using people for thousands of years before copper reached Crete.

Stone vases cannot unfortunately be used as evidence for dating, for they may remain in use for hundreds of years after they were made. In fact, protodynastic Egyptian stone vases were found at Mycenae in a

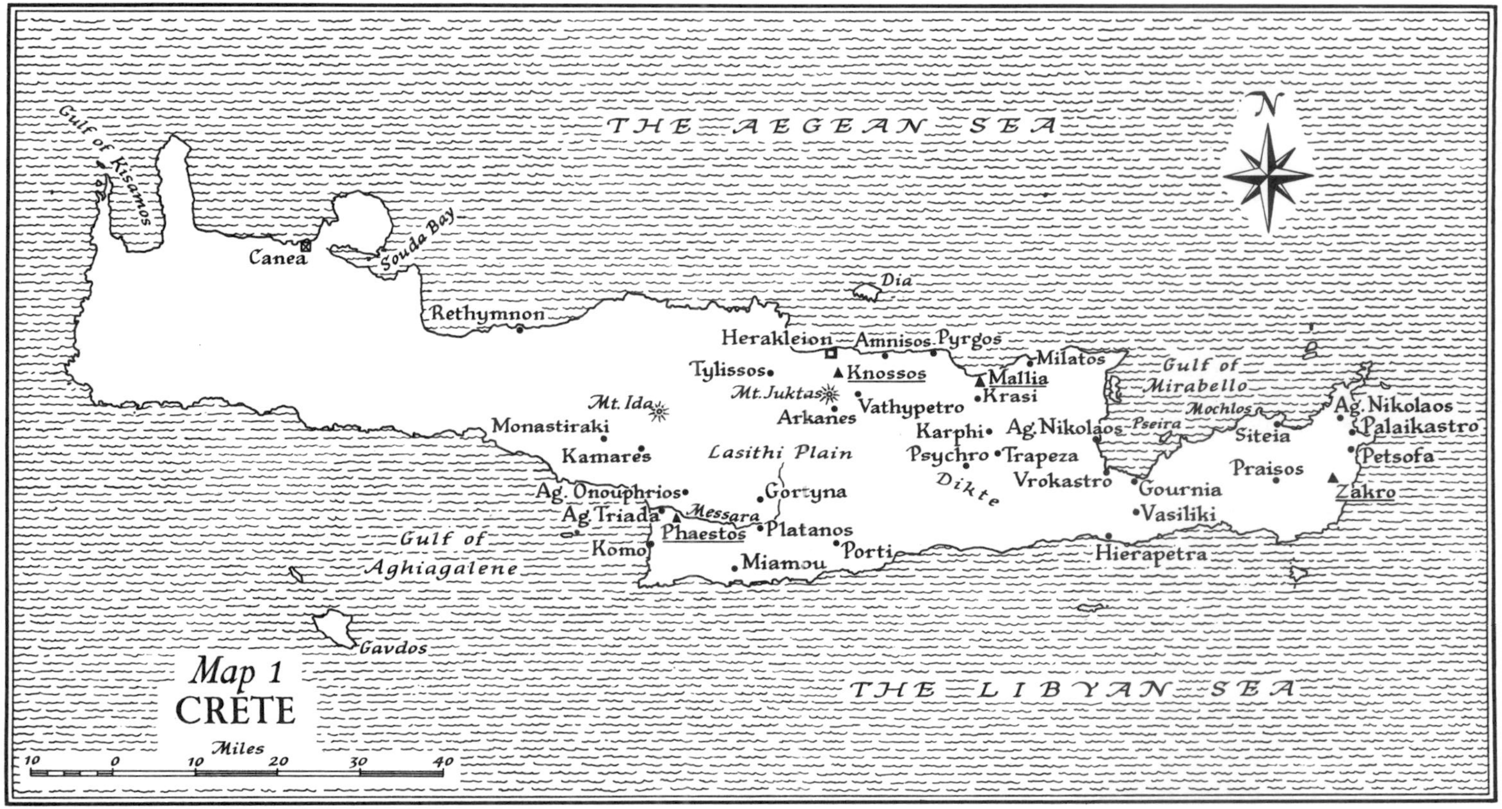
THE AEGEAN SEA
N
Gulf of Kisamos
Canea
Souda Bay
Dia
Rethymnon
Herakleion
Amnisos
Pyrgos
Milatos
Tylissos
Knossos
Mallia
Mt. Juktas
Vathypetro
Krasi
Mt. Ida
Arkanes
Karphi
Ag. Nikolaos
Pseira
Mochlos
Gulf of Mirabello
Siteia
Ag. Nikolaos
Palaikastro
Monastiraki
Kamares
Lasithi Plain
Psychro
Trapeza
Petsofa
Praisos
Ag. Onouphrios
Gortyna
Dikte
Vrokastro
Gournia
Zakro
Ag. Triada
Messara
Phaestos
Platanos
Vasiliki
Gulf of Aghiagalene
Komo
Porti
Miamou
Hierapetra
Gavdos
Map 1
CRETE
Miles
10
0
10
20
30
40
THE LIBYAN SEA

Map 1. Crete

tomb of the Mycenaean II period, and at Asine in the Peloponnese in a
tomb of Mycenaean III – intervals of over a thousand years in both cases.
This is not to say that domestic utensils were all made of stone before
the advent of ceramics, nor that all early domestic pottery was derived
from stone originals.

The excavations in 1962 at Chatal Hüyük in Asia Minor emphasise
that before the introduction of pottery about 6600 BC domestic utensils
were made of wood or of baskets, for remains of these have been found
in the lowest deposits there.

It does, however, mean that weapons and axes and other implements
were made of stone and not of metal. Obsidian blades and arrow-heads
have been found which show that this material was imported, probably
from the island of Milo, for obsidian is not native to Crete.

Peoples in a primitive state of civilisation remain in that state for long
centuries till some revolution in their ways starts their minds working
along new lines and a remarkable development occurs. This was the
case in both Egypt and Crete in the third millennium BC when the use
of metal became known to both countries at almost the same time. Until
this moment arrived, Cretan culture had been almost static for thousands
of years.

That this holds true even today is demonstrated by an article in the
Illustrated London News of 18th August 1962, which describes a community of potters in Northern Nigeria who are producing earthenware
pottery by methods which differ little, if at all, from those employed by
the neolithic Cretan of 3000 BC. Potters' wheels are not used, and all
traditional vessels are made by hand. There are no developed kilns, and
glazing is unknown.

This is remarkable enough, but even more striking is the fact that
vessels are also being made today in Crete, Cyprus and the Peloponnese
under the same conditions as they were more than four thousand years
ago, as we see from the most interesting books recently published by
Professor Hampe (see Bibliography).

It was the advent of metal which revolutionised men's minds and
caused a striking change in material culture.

Except in the case of Egypt, pottery is almost our only guide in studying the neolithic civilisation; objects of leather and wood and clothing
have nearly all disappeared in the destruction caused by damp and
weather and the lapse of time. Only the implements of bone and stone
and terracotta vases have remained.

Up till recently, neolithic dating, especially in the absence of pottery
with a distinctive style, has had to be estimated largely by the depth of
deposits, but a new method is now under trial. This is the radio-carbon

test, which is based on the fact that every plant contains a given quantity of radio-active carbon in addition to ordinary carbon. Since all living creatures absorb plant constituents directly or indirectly, radio-active carbon is found in men and animals, particularly in their bones and teeth. While they are alive, this substance is continually replenished, but naturally when they die they no longer absorb radio-carbon, and the amount in their remains becomes reduced through continuous radiation. After 25,000 years it disappears completely, leaving no trace at all in organic remains. Up to this length of time, the percentage of radio-active carbon in a body or in its skeletal remains can tell us with a very considerable degree of accuracy when the body's metabolism had ceased, thus establishing the age of the bones. This method was discovered in 1950 by Dr Willard Libby, an American.

Modelling and design found their first expression in pottery, and by means of this we can follow the progress of mankind in its first steps towards civilisation.

Even so, a slow but sure development took place throughout the Neolithic Era, for exploration of the deep strata at Knossos has revealed a progressive advance from bottom to top with the introduction of white-filled decoration on its pottery.

In one or two instances, fragments of what has been described as pottery have been found in pre-neolithic deposits, but no finished article has so far been discovered.

Most clays contain a small quantity of iron salts, and if firing takes place in the presence of air, these oxidise and produce a red colour. If, however, the air is absent when the clay is fired, the colour is usually black or grey.

The early potters soon learnt to use a 'slip'. The pot was moulded out of comparatively coarse material and then, just before firing, was dipped into a mixture made of refined clay and water. A thin veneer of this mixture thus covered the pot to form a smooth outer surface over the coarser material from which the main body of the pot was made.

We may conveniently regard the Neolithic Era in the Aegean as extending from 6600 BC to 3000 BC, and the stratigraphic divisions as Early, Middle and Late for this era of three thousand six hundred years. The size and distribution of the neolithic population of Crete has not yet been accurately determined, but enough sites have been excavated to make it possible to say that, although smaller, it was spread over an area as wide as that occupied by the population of the Bronze Age.

The lowest of the neolithic layers at Knossos, for a depth of about three feet from virgin soil, contains a quantity of fragments of clay vessels. During this Early Neolithic period it was only the most essential

household vessels, fashioned by hand out of imperfectly cleansed clay
and burned in the open fire which were produced. They were not dipped
in a slip of finely ground clay, but the surface was usually polished both
inside and out. The effect of this burnishing was probably to make the
vessel less porous. The surface clay was hardened by pressure of the
tool, so that a kind of outside skin was formed.

There was no resemblance to the pre-dynastic pottery of Egypt. Forms
were limited to rude cups, bowls and basins, some with lugs at the sides
pierced for suspension with holes which were usually horizontal but sometimes vertical (Figs. 1 and 2). These early vases were rarely ornamented,
and they were monochrome, ranging in colour from red through brownish
or grey to jet black.

Perhaps the most representative selection, illustrating the principal
types of neolithic pottery similar to the Cretan, as well as some of the
common household implements, ornaments and figurines, is to be found
in the museum at Corinth. There are groups of deep rounded bowls,
ranging in colours from red through buff and grey to jet black found in
a cave near Nemea not far from Corinth. Somewhat later are the vessels
coated with an orange or reddish brown lustre which were found at
Corinth itself.

The second layer of about five feet from the bottom at Knossos contains the same type of pottery as the first, except that certain rare specimens are decorated with a few simple linear designs (Fig. 2). The potter
had begun to trace zig-zags, triangles and chevrons with the point of a
bone or stone.

In the third and fourth layers, six to twelve feet above the bottom, the
number of these incised fragments increases, although very slowly; in
fact, the proportion of incised sherds to the total number found does not
amount to more than about three per cent. With few exceptions of Late
Neolithic date, the patterns were always incised before firing.

With the passage of time, some of the incised vessels contain a white
substance in the incisings. The use of this white pigment so as to produce
a light design on a dark ground marks the beginning of a new style of
ornamentation destined to have a long history, for the white-filled incising later suggested the use of white colour applied with a brush. The
range of ornaments used increases with the introduction of hatched triangles, chequers, diamonds, and rough geometric figures made out in
dots.

The shapes of the Middle Neolithic period did not differ much from
those of the Early Neolithic period.

The early incised decoration consisted entirely of straight lines, and in
fact curved linear decoration was rare during the Neolithic Era. This

a.
Knossos

b.
Cave of Eileithyia

c.
Knossos

d.
Cave of Eileithyia

e.
Knossos

Fig. 1. Neolithic vessels

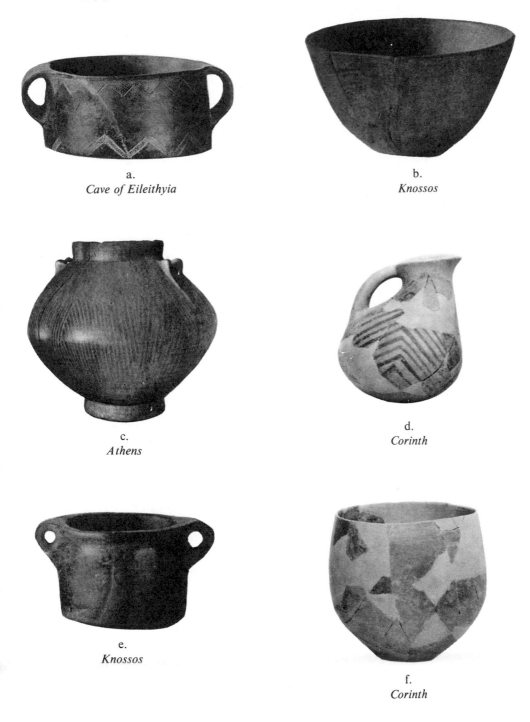

a.
Cave of Eileithyia

b.
Knossos

c.
Athens

d.
Corinth

e.
Knossos

f.
Corinth

Fig. 2. Neolithic vessels continued

style of pottery decorated with white-filled incised lines appears in a large number of countries in the latter part of the Neolithic Era, not only in the eastern Mediterranean, but also in Asia and western Europe. During this period the better sifted clay took a brighter polish on the black surface which distinguishes even the undecorated vases from those of the preceding period. These black burnished vases are sometimes called 'Black bucchero' or 'Bucchero'. The word is Italian on account of the large number of such vessels found in Italy, particularly in Etruria.

The neolithic potter found that natural clay alone was not sufficient for his pottery, for as it lost its moisture in drying, it contracted. Some substance had to be mixed with the clay to render it sufficiently porous for the steam when formed to escape and prevent the vase from cracking in the oven. He discovered that powdered charcoal made from wood or bones added to the clay served this purpose. This accounts for the blackness of much of the neolithic pottery. In northern Nigeria today we find the same result achieved by the use of finely cut hay or grass digested by donkeys.

The oldest neolithic vessels are of globular form or have the base only slightly flattened. Even at the present day, many primitive peoples use spherical pots which stand upright more easily when placed upon uneven ground. Gradually, the clay was more carefully purified, was more evenly baked, and was polished. It is believed that this brilliant polish was obtained by the use of rounded pebbles or bone.

However this may be, it is as well to remember that an immense quantity of splendid pottery is made today by the natives of northern Nigeria under neolithic conditions, and before speculating on neolithic processes of manufacture in the early Greek lands, it would seem possible to solve some of the problems by examining the interesting processes used by the African potter.

In the deposits of the Late Neolithic period, the civilisation is shown to differ considerably according to locality, and one class of incised vases introduces a new principle of decoration which combines curvilinear decoration with rectilinear.

With better firing, the pottery became less pervious, so that burnishing was not essential, and much pottery was simply wiped with a cloth leaving striations visible, although burnishing was retained in use for smaller vessels for aesthetic reasons until it was replaced by glossy paint.

The advanced quality of the pottery and of other objects found even in the lowest neolithic strata at Knossos proves that some considerable degree of culture had already been achieved by the time the settlement was founded. Men were not savages before the introduction of metal.

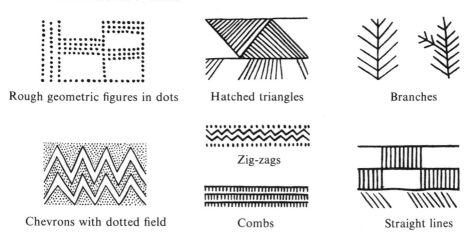

Rough geometric figures in dots	Hatched triangles	Branches
Chevrons with dotted field	Zig-zags Combs	Straight lines

Fig. 3. Patterns on Neolithic pottery from Knossos

They made beautiful pottery of fine quality. The neolithic settlement at Knossos must have been quite extensive, for in it have been found besides pottery, stone axes, maces of serpentine, knives of obsidian, but no trace of metal. Yet at the very bottom on virgin soil, the finds do not represent the really crude neolithic culture such as existed, for instance, in Britain.

A remarkable characteristic of the early periods is the large number of small clay figures that have been discovered: animals, birds with incised wings, even little female statuettes presumed to have been used in connection with their religious rites. Sometimes these statuettes are standing, sometimes sitting and sometimes crouching. The early peoples of Crete seem to have worshipped a great goddess.

As to the origin of the neolithic population in Crete, speculation is still rife. The figurines strongly resemble some of those found in Asia, and a striking likeness has been observed between the ceramics of Crete and the early ones of Anatolia. The early pottery of Megiddo is indistinguishable, except in the absence of incising, from that of the later neolithic strata of Knossos, while some of the early pottery from Byblos is not only incised but has the white filling. It rather looks as if there had been a very early immigration from south-west Anatolia.

CHAPTER TWO

The Minoan Era

3000–1100 BC

In 1905 at an archaeological congress in Athens Sir Arthur Evans put forward his first classification of the Minoan civilisation of the Bronze Age into three periods and nine phases, a classification admittedly formal, but which nevertheless corresponded with the facts and has since needed surprisingly little modification.

The term Minoan is simply a picturesque name equivalent to the whole Bronze Age of Crete, and was chosen because Knossos, the capital of King Minos or of the Minoan dynasty, was inhabited from the beginning to the end of that era, and has provided a more complete range of data for the study of its development than any other site. This Minoan Bronze Age began at the end of the Stone Age with the introduction of copper, continued with bronze for weapons and tools, and ended with the incoming of iron, which replaced the softer metal. During this long period of about two thousand years, whether it be spears, daggers or saws, nails, fish-hooks or kettles, they were of copper or bronze and never of iron.

Civilisation in the various parts of the Aegean during this time developed along parallel but not identical lines. To make a distinction, the three chief divisions of the Bronze Age in the Aegean Islands are known as Early, Middle and Late Cycladic. On the Greek mainland they are known as Helladic, although the Late Helladic period is commonly called Mycenaean after the chief centre of political, economic and military power at that time.

Little is known of the origins of the Early Helladic and Cycladic cultures, but it seems probable that somewhere about 3000 BC the islands of the Cyclades were settled, most of them for the first time, by immigrants from Anatolia, who brought with them a highly developed Bronze Age civilisation. Some of these people moved on to settle on the mainland of Greece, where they mingled with the neolithic inhabitants to create the Early Helladic culture.

About 1900 BC, when both Helladic and Cycladic cultures had reached an advanced stage of civilisation, they came to an end; the Early Helladic as the result of immigration and destruction by Ionian tribes, and the Early Cycladic possibly as the result of annexation by Crete.

For the non-specialist, it is not always easy to memorise the periods

14

hanced by being place
Arthur Evans.

On the morrow of t
another were installed
Greece, in all the isles
and penetrated by the
The introduction of
tion. No copper-using
is now generally thou
brought into Crete by
beginning of the third
the south and from
Mediterranean race in
Libya and Egypt, whe
from the neolithic p
Cyclades. Recent ex
uncovered examples
Cyclades and of Cret
The new arrivals ca
inhabitants lived apa
lated, and began to u
now should be calle
during the Early Mir
their time, expanded
and established com
It was to the pow
owed its unity, and f
originality. That gre
enough to Mesopot
protected from then
To what can be a
was rich by compar
dry islands. The out
the needs of her o
From the wood of
a supply of copper
north of the island
shipping.
Her situation to
position to derive
touch with the islar

c

not only f
generally.
The Firs
synthesis c
It was twe
that the fir
give a chro
Minos as i
Middle and
in it we ca
together to
on six acre
It was fo
the very re
great scho
archaeolog
supremely
his vigorou
father, and
dedication
taxation w
and a glory
In 1928 t
that it had
to the third
was the cr
Knossos on
and include
metal inlay
In the sp
time. His p
a bust at th
the learned
he was mac
The last
whole work
it had to a
eighty-four.
knew that
readers.
1940 brou
Europe that

Portrait in the National Portrait Gallery by Francis Dodd, R.A., 1935

Fig. 4. Sir Arthur Evans

the other direction, she maintained commercial relations with Syria, and thus with the Egyptian civilisation, then at the height of its vigour.

Moreover, as she did not lie on the main lines of migration, she was able to develop her culture unhampered by the shock of intrusions from overseas.

In the early period of Minoan civilisation, there do not appear to be any indications of centralised unification. There are no signs of a capital. It was the eastern part of the island which developed first, including the rich plain of Mirabello open to the north and east. It was later on that there was an advance in the Messara plain open to the south.

Thanks to the great activity of an amalgam of exceptionally endowed races, Crete developed a civilisation all its own, a civilisation which has eclipsed all other prehistoric civilisations in the Aegean by the wealth of its remains; so much so that we must regard Crete as the fountain-head of Aegean civilisation as it was for so long its political and social focus. In Crete has been found the most varied and continuous evidence of this civilisation from the Neolithic Era to the twilight of the classical civilisation. The general standard of Aegean culture at its zenith yields to none that was contemporary with it, and to few that came after it.

The art developed during the Bronze Age in Crete may be considered not only as the forerunner of Greek classical art, but as an art complete in its own right. Its evolution may be divided into three phases: a phase of abstract art, a phase of naturalism, and a phase of conventionalism which correspond roughly with a period of isolation during the Neolithic and Early Minoan epochs; a period of exchange with neighbouring continental countries and islands (particularly with Milo) during the Middle Minoan and LM I periods; and a period of Aegean uniformity during the LM II and the LM III periods when its art merges into that known as Mycenaean.

The Cretans scattered the products of their artistic genius all over the Aegean, but whatever style was in vogue during its long history, it seemed as if in the principal centres of production, and at Knossos in particular, there reigned a discipline to which the artists had to conform, a discipline that imposed its ideas more and more strongly with the passage of time.

By degrees, however, the virile Minoan sap became exhausted. The strange stylised art that emanated from Crete spread first to the mainland of Greece and then to the potteries of eastern Greece such as Rhodes. With increasing distance, the strength of Cretan inspiration became weaker until finally it was overwhelmed by the Dorian invasion.

As one looks at the masterpieces uncovered by the spade of the archaeologist, it is with difficulty that we realise that we know virtually nothing of the people who created them. Their frescoes appear like the illustrations to a story of which we have lost the text. The Minoans have left not a single word to enlighten us about their philosophy of life, or their religion. What motives impelled the pilgrims to carry their simple offerings in those beautiful containers up their steep and rugged mountains to those almost inaccessible caves? Of these they have left us no written word.

The superiority of Cretan vases to those of all their contemporaries showed itself in a vigorous export trade. Cretan wares were shipped to Egypt, to Milo, to Thera, to Cyprus and to Troy. They went to Asia Minor, to Phoenicia and to all important sites of the Greek mainland. They have been found in Sicily and upon the mainland of Italy as far north as the top of the Adriatic.

Besides the normal clay vases and vessels, the Minoans used pottery for purposes where we usually employ glass, wood and metal. Boxes and coffins, gutters and drain-pipes were all made of terracotta; censers, lamps and loom-weights were of clay. Before the use of coins or writing in the form of inscriptions came into general use, pottery forms the most continuous and the most trustworthy material for the dating of sites, the movement of peoples and their commercial intercourse.

Ceramic art in Crete reached a specially high standard in fabric, form and decoration during the Bronze Age, and the products of that age compare favourably with any potter's work in the world. The designs that embellish these vessels display an aesthetic taste of such subtlety and vigour as to provide later artists with patterns of infinite variety.

Of all the available means for the study and reconstruction of pre-historic Greek culture, pottery takes first place. Of all things it is the most indestructible. The small sherd has great resisting powers, earth cannot destroy it nor can it rust away. It was not carried off nor melted down for the value of its material, which was the fate of most products of the Minoan metallurgists.

In the two thousand years covered by the Bronze Age culture, the Minoans changed both shapes and designs of their clay vessels so frequently, that by careful observation of the stratification of many Minoan sites, these changes can be placed in chronological sequence. With practice, the Cretan excavator is able to date a vase with considerable accuracy, either by its decoration, or, if it is unpainted, by its shape; although this last criterion is a less certain test.

Of all the civilisations of the ancient world the Cretan was the most artistic and the most original, with remarkable faculties for radiating a potent influence throughout the Aegean. Unlike Egyptian art to which it owed much, Cretan art was not limited by traditional restraint, but developed freely in accordance with the varying inspirations of its creators. Cretan art displayed a strikingly innate aesthetic sense, with the most diverse tendencies, uniting a vivid taste for reality with a bold decorative imagination which was almost modern in its abstract style.

No sooner had its creators invented one style than they sought for another, and the old style was entirely superseded by the new. In the joy of creation there seemed no limit to the fantastic versatility of their inventive ingenuity. Reinach wrote: 'That marvellous Minoan civilisation brought to light by the excavations in Crete, was not just one of those splendid meteors which vanish without leaving a trace. From it the sacred spark fell upon the Hellenic hearth. In spite of many transformations, Greece reaped its heritage; and the further science advances, the more it realises that Ionian Greece bears to Minoan Greece the same relationship as the Italian Renaissance bore to the Greco-Roman civilisation.'

The Aegean culture was a maritime one, and its preservation was rendered possible only by the sea. By the sea it lived, and when stronger races coming from the north, and bringing with them weapons of iron, dispossessed the Cretans of their control of the sea, their power collapsed and with it their great civilisation.

About 2000 BC power in Crete became concentrated in the hands of a few royal families with their palaces at Phaestos, Mallia and Knossos, where the king ruled also as representative of the deity – a goddess of nature. Round the king grew up an aristocratic class. Crete was divided up into small realms.

About 1700 BC at the end of MM II, a severe earthquake destroyed the palaces of Knossos, Phaestos and Mallia, while the settlements at Pseira, Mochlos, Gournia and Palaikastro were similarly laid low. There is a complete break between MM II and MM III.

A short time afterwards the palaces emerged from their ruins more magnificent than before, and to these belong the ruins that we see today at Knossos, Phaestos and Mallia.

The monarch received the tribute of his feudatories at the palace of Knossos, from whence radiated his maritime communications with Egypt and other parts of the Aegean. Thus by about 1600 BC we find Crete stronger than ever before. It was a period of great prosperity and productivity.

After the disaster in Crete, the mainland itself became saturated with Cretan culture although retaining its own individuality. This may have been due to a conquest of the mainland by the Cretans or to an influx of refugees from Crete. This extension of Cretan influence to the mainland started the Mycenaean civilisation. Meanwhile the Achaeans had settled in Greece. For two centuries or more this process continued, the

Mycenaean-Achaean civilisation on the mainland becoming stronger and the Cretan weaker.

About 1400 BC at the end of LM II, a terrible catastrophe caused the total ruin and desertion of the palaces and settlements, from one end of the island to the other. The catastrophe appears to have been so complete, that it seems to have been due to a series of earthquakes, or possibly a tremendous tidal wave which it has been suggested was caused by an explosion of the volcano of Santorin (Thera) which split that island into two, and covered its prehistoric remains which belong to that period with a deposit of pumice.

Phaestos alone seems to have partially escaped the destruction judging by the large amount of pottery discovered in store there. Here we can see a whole series of store rooms, staircases and corridors belonging to different phases of the earlier buildings.

Thenceforth Crete ceased to be the centre of Aegean culture. Her inheritance passed to the mainland, which under the leadership of Mycenae, established a great dominion such as that which Homer depicts under the leadership of Agamemnon. Then arose the great fortresses of Tiryns and Mycenae. Then were built the proudest of the beehive tombs, then the Aegean products of the mainland style reached the furthest corners of the Mediterranean world, from Macedonia to Egypt, from Sicily to Palestine.

Two centuries pass and we reach the beginning of the twelfth century, traditional date of the Trojan War, when Egypt was vexed by the Peoples of the Sea.

Another hundred years to about 1100 BC when the final catastrophe took place. Mycenae and Tiryns went up in flames. Iron took the place of bronze, and Aegean art as a living thing ceased on the Greek mainland and in the islands.

The great disaster was due to an incursion of northern tribes possessed of superior iron weapons – those tribes which later Greek tradition and Homer knew as the Dorians.

Tiryns and Mycenae fell, and their splendid palaces were sacked and burned. Argos became the city which the Dorians made great, and though new settlements grew up within the ancient walls of the old fortresses, these strongholds were never great and populous again. Did Knossos share the same fate at this time? Of this we are not really sure. At any rate Crete seems to have sunk back into the position of a little world just sufficient for itself, and incapable of holding any longer the dominating position which its geographical situation had enabled it to take more than a thousand years before. Its palaces were forgotten and buried, and nearly three thousand years as yet unborn would pass before their ruins were uncovered again. The old civilisation of the Bronze Age was crushed and the Iron Age took its place in Greece and in the islands. When once more, two centuries later, we see it faintly illuminated by a light that pierces the darkness which fell upon it, we find the Aegean area dominated by Hellenes. It is a light announcing the prelude to a new dawn.

EARLY MINOAN I 3000–2500 BC

The Neolithic Era did not end suddenly, but Cretan ceramics developed gradually over a century through a sub-Neolithic into the Early Minoan I stage, when the advent of metal to Crete, about 3000 BC, marked the beginning of the Minoan or Bronze Age – although at first the metal was copper, not yet alloyed with tin. The early Minoan culture is believed to have been introduced into Crete about this time by immigration from Anatolia or Syria.

The main centres of civilisation in Crete at this period were in the eastern part of the island where excavations have produced evidence of contact with Egypt and Asia Minor.

The EM I period was in the nature of a transition from the Neolithic to the full Bronze Age of EM II. Its pottery was inferior to the true Neolithic, but the range of shapes was enlarged, and the commonest forms include large open bowls, small jugs, miniature cups, ladles and rectangular trays.

Ear handles or lugs for suspension were common, sometimes pierced with vertical and sometimes with horizontal holes. The pottery was still hand-made with coils or wads of clay. It begins to show a reddish core, due perhaps to increasing skill in the use of the potter's oven.

The main difference between the pottery of EM I and that of the preceding age is that the burnishing of the whole surface of the vase died out, its place being sometimes taken by a slip. In this case, when the vase was made, it was allowed to dry, and was then immersed in a bath of liquid clay of finer quality. By this process the surface of the vase was rendered smooth even when it was made of coarse clay. Unable or unwilling to produce the burnished surface of the old ware, the early Minoan potters devised this first lustrous black slip on which they painted the old patterns in a tenacious white, evidently with the intention of imitating the old white-filled incised lines.

The abandonment of the lengthy process of burnishing and its replacement by coating the vessel with a good stable medium so as to produce a lustrous effect when fired, is understandable. A handsome, bright, and almost metallic finish could be obtained more easily than by the old-

a. Footed pyxis
Aghia Triada

c. Jug, Aghios Onouphrios style
Crete

b. Spouted pot
Pyrgos

e. Bulbous pedestalled vase
Pyrgos

d. Squat globular pyxis
Gournia

f. Mug
Partira

Fig. 5. Early Minoan I vessels

fashioned method of burnishing by hand. It was no doubt the invention of a progressive Cretan potter, and once adopted, the idea spread quickly. Thenceforward, the burnishing was only used for special purposes. Sometimes black bands were painted on the buff clay surface. Thus for the first time the Greek technique of gloss painting on pottery was practised, an invention of the earliest years of the Bronze Age, which continued to flourish right through the Minoan, Mycenaean and Classical eras till late Roman times, a method of decoration in which all the triumphs of the Greek vase painters of the fifth and fourth centuries BC were executed. The invention of this dark gloss paint, though technically undeveloped at this early stage, was thus of the highest importance for the whole history of Greek vase painting. We shall have some more to say on this subject at the end of this section.

At Pyrgos on the north coast, half-way between Herakleion and Mallia, a large rock shelter was excavated by Stephanos Xanthoudides, curator of the Herakleion Museum in the early years of this century, which had been used as an ossuary in Early Minoan I and later times. It contained an abundant deposit of pottery, including not only incised pyxides, but also beaked jugs with simple rectilinear designs in a reddish-brown lustrous paint (Fig. 5). At Pyrgos there is an advance in shapes in the tall, stemmed chalices (Fig. 6), some shaped like an hour-glass with a burnished decoration developing from certain pedestal vases of the neolithic time and perhaps representing grained wood. These have a grey surface and are sometimes decorated with incised patterns. The painted ware from Pyrgos also includes a remarkable variety of beaked jugs on which the decoration is entirely dark-on-light.

The pottery of EM I varies in different parts of Crete. The shapes of pottery in the north of the island, and especially those from Pyrgos, seem to owe an affinity to the Cyclades which lie due north of Crete. Although the population of the Cyclades was probably of similar origin to that of Crete, their pottery developed along somewhat independent lines, with the result that Cretan pottery received another cultural impulse but modified by its passage through the Cyclades.

Besides these chalices and beaked jugs, the pottery of northern Crete includes simple forms of hemispherical bowls and cylindrical cups, flat plates, ladles and little globular pots with tie-on lids which had persisted with but slight variation from neolithic times. Suspension pots were also made with a high neck to imitate gourds and with pierced suspension handles. These have a grey surface and are often decorated with incised patterns.

In southern Crete, the EM I pottery is also mainly grey, but the shapes are an advance on those found in the north and centre of the island.

a. Chalice
Pyrgos

b. Suspension pot
Eileithyia

c. Chalice
Pyrgos

d. Chalice
Pyrgos

Fig. 6. Early Minoan I vessels continued

Suspension pots are common, but with a short collar, and not the long bottle-neck of the north. Good examples of this come from Aghia Triada near Phaestos. Some of these are placed on a tall base, and one from Aghios Onouphrios is fitted with a small cap.

In southern Crete incised decoration mostly takes the form of dots all over the pot, or diagonal lines in bands round the body, and sometimes concentric semi-circles resting on a line encircling the body on a background of dots.

Perhaps the best example of painted pottery from southern Crete is the well-known beaked jug from Aghios Onouphrios with its yellowish background decorated with thin reddish horizontal, vertical, and diagonal stripes (Fig. 5c). Its round bottom is a clear indication of its period which marks the difference between the jugs of EM I and EM II.

Generally speaking, the decorative elements of EM I pottery consist of simple linear patterns: straight and zig-zag lines, hatchings, hatched triangles and lozenges, 'butterfly' patterns, squares and semi-circles (Fig. 7). This kind of decoration was inherited from the preceding neolithic stage.

The decoration of Cretan pottery during EM I, whether light-on-dark or dark-on-light, was exclusively linear, generally in very simple combinations. It was only at the end of this period that curvilinear decoration played a part of any importance. Excavations show that the civilisation of this period had moved from the centre of Crete to the eastern end of the island, and whereas during the Neolithic Era the majority of sites are an hour or more from the coast, the principal settlements of EM I seem to have been chosen for their proximity to the sea. Exceptions to this were either sacred or burial caves, or areas where the population had already expanded and settled in fertile areas such as the plains of Messara and Lassithi.

Even at this remote period, conditions were by no means primitive. Some of the people lived surrounded by artistic objects in solidly built houses, and they had communications with the outside world.

The most important remains of the Early Minoan period, therefore, have come to light in eastern Crete in the small towns of Gournia, Vasiliki, Palaikastro, Zakro and in the neighbouring islands of Pseira and Mochlos. At these sites an abundant supply of EM I pottery has been discovered. Round-bottomed beaked jugs, carefully painted in a semi-lustrous reddish-brown paint come from Gournia. Suspension pots with short conical necks come from Palaikastro with bands of herringbone, chevrons or cross-hatching decoration running round the body of the vase.

It is evident that Anatolia exercised an important influence on the

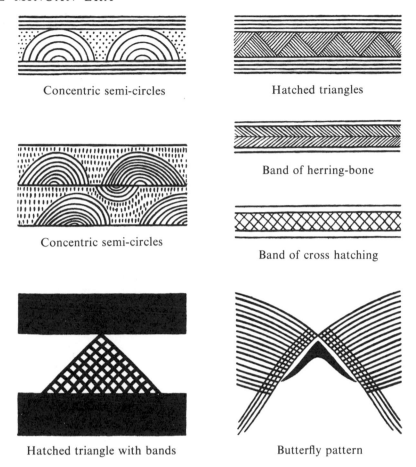

Concentric semi-circles

Hatched triangles

Concentric semi-circles

Band of herring-bone

Band of cross hatching

Hatched triangle with bands

Butterfly pattern

Fig. 7. Patterns on Early Minoan I pottery

pottery of eastern Crete. This is shown by the similarity of the beaked jugs in both areas, but more especially by the fact that in both the Anatolian jugs and those of EM I, the lower end of the handle is thrust through the wall and projects on the inside.

The similarity of the products of Anatolia and those of eastern Crete is probably to be accounted for by a wave of immigrants from south-western Asia Minor about this time.

Little pottery of Neolithic tradition has been found in eastern Crete. Exceptions are vessels found in a rock shelter near Palaikastro where ladles and hemi-spherical cups of coarse red clay sometimes covered with a reddish wash without decoration have been found.

In northern Crete the old Neolithic traditional style continued in use. At Knossos most of the EM levels were swept away by later palace buildings but the commonest shapes seem to be open or pedestal bowls, ladles and handleless cups.

DECORATIVE GLOSS PAINT

The technique by which the masterpieces of Greek vase painting in the classical period were executed was practised as far back as Minoan Crete, but its invention was not Cretan. Painted pottery had been made in prehistoric Mesopotamia and Egypt long before it appeared in Aegean lands.

Pre-Sumerian ware bears decoration fired on pale clay in a dark medium of ferruginous earth fused with an alkaline flux, and one variety of Egyptian pre-dynastic pottery has dull white pigment fired on a dark ferruginous ground. Both processes were applied in early Minoan pottery. At the close of the Middle Minoan period when Cretan arts were transplanted to the Greek mainland, the Mycenaean fabric of Minoan inspiration displaced the inferior and largely hand-made Helladic and Cycladic wares which distinguish the earlier cultures.

By the end of the Mycenaean period, the pottery of the whole Aegean area including its decoration, was uniform, except on the northern and eastern borders, where Danubian and Anatolian influences seem to have prevailed.

The pottery of Greece, both of the Bronze and Iron Ages, is distinguished from all other pottery of the same period by its type of painted decoration.

In the classical period the painter's art was so far separated from the potter's, that the two were nearly always the work of two men, and there can be little doubt that the best Minoan ware was also the joint product of two craftsmen.

Though the Geometric painters of the Iron Age do not seem to have adopted a single element of design from their predecessors of the Late Minoan and Mycenaean periods, the technique of potter and painter passed without alteration across the apparent gap in culture that separated the Aegean ages of Bronze and Iron.

The chemical composition of clay varies according to the finely divided mineral matter present in it. This usually consists of hydrated silicates of aluminium, iron and alkalies. There are a great number of clay deposits in Greece, the best known of which in antiquity were in Athens, Corinth, and Chalkis in Euboea. There are also many in the islands. Most of these are sedimentary clays in which the composition as revealed by spectrographic analysis differs little between one site and another. The differences in colour, which range from bright red, through brown to light beige, have a fairly large iron content in the form of oxide of iron (Fe_2O_3). Apart from iron, the principal elements are silica, aluminium and calcium. A dozen others are also present but in extremely small quantities, all under one per cent. Among these are magnesium, titanium, potassium and manganese. But these trace elements make no difference to the gloss which is so distinctive of Greek ceramics. There are also a certain number of deposits of pure or residual white clay. This material, which does not possess the plasticity of sedimentary clay, was not used for the manufacture of vases.

When it left the earth, Greek clay was heavily adulterated with impurities and needed prolonged refining. This consisted of several washings and decantings, after which it was left for some time in order to 'ferment' under the action of bacteria, which gave it greater plastic qualities. Finally it was kneaded in order to give it homogeneity and to get rid of air bubbles.

To a large extent, the ancient Greeks used their iron-bearing clays to achieve their polychrome vases. Since both fabric and paint were made from the same clay, the two had similar coefficients of expansion and the paint adhered firmly.

In the decoration of Greek pots, there are two questions which have puzzled experts until recently, and even now the answer to the second one is not really satisfactorily settled. Firstly, what was the technique used to obtain the faint sheen on the undecorated surface of the pottery? Secondly, what was the composition of the black glossy pigment like highly polished shoe-blacking with which the designs were painted in the Black-Figure Pottery, or which formed the background in the Red-Figure style of classical times?

Although this black gloss reached its highest perfection in the classical period, there was in fact no substantial difference between it and the earliest Minoan, Cycladic or Mycenaean 'glosses'. It was the degree of skilled control and finish which varied. In both periods the material used was the same. This gloss paint was no discovery of the classical period in Greece. It was used two thousand years earlier in Crete as we mentioned above. But the technique ceased to be used at the end of the Hellenistic period, and no record of the process employed has been found. Take the sheen on the undecorated surface of the pot first. It has been suggested that this was produced by polishing the pot before applying the decoration, but as no marks of a polishing tool have been found, this is unlikely.

Research and experiments were carried out by Dr Theodore Schumann in the 1940's at Heisterholz near Minden in Germany on the assumption that whatever process was used by the ancient potters, it must have been a simple one. His final conclusion was that the smooth, shiny surface was produced by covering the vase before firing with a thin wash of very fine impalpable clay powder to which potash in the form of wood-ash had been added. This potash acted as a peptic, much in the same way as digestive juices act on food in the stomach, and so disintegrated the fine clay particles still further. As this alone would not prevent even these minute particles from drifting together and giving a matt surface like an egg-shell, a protective colloid or fixative (Greek *kolla*, glue) was added to stabilise them, and this colloid could be either urine or sour wine.

It has been suggested that this fine clay may have had in its composition a mineral such as illite, the particles of which are flat, and if the clay was applied in a thin coat, the particles tended to lie flat and reflect the light.

Another theory is that substances composed of exceedingly small particles melt at a lower temperature than larger lumps of exactly similar matter, so that at dull red heat when the parent clay is barely adequately baked, the minute particles extracted from it are already fused and form a glossy and usually watertight coating of infinitesimal thickness. But this coating remains unalterably clay and is not glass and therefore not glaze.

How is this very fine impalpable clay obtained? If you take a lump of clay and leave it to stand in a bucket of water, it will separate up into three layers, the heavy which sinks to the bottom, the medium which comes half-way up, and the very fine at the top. But it is necessary to put some potash, say wood-ash, into the water to act as a deflocculant, otherwise even the minute particles would clump together and sink to the bottom. After a fortnight or so, this top layer can be removed into another vessel, when part of the water is evaporated, and a creamy, slimy substance of no palpable structure remains. This is the material from which the Greek gloss was made. It is applied to the unfired ware and is known as a 'colloidal slip'. The process of obtaining this finely levigated clay is known as peptisation.

Its colours vary as clay colours vary – from white through gold and yellow reds to coral, Venetian, and blood-red, and in fact a whole range of reds unavailable to the glass-maker.

Now take the second question. What was the composition of the black shiny pigment that played so important a part in the decoration of Greek pottery in classical times and the dark red or brown one in which the patterns of Minoan and Mycenaean times were executed? This was evidently a thicker pigment than the one just described, as can be seen from the lines which stand up in slight relief from the background.

The conclusion has been reached that this thicker pigment was in fact of the same mixture as that used to cover the pot before firing, but thickened by evaporation. After evaporation, one got a dark brown paste which could be applied with a brush, and which after baking produced a dark glossy pattern whether the background had been previously treated with the thinner paint or not.

When painted on, it would have been of the same colour as the preliminary wash, but deeper in tone owing to its greater concentration, or else perhaps mixed with some fugitive colour to assist the artist, but which disappeared in the heat of the kiln. Much thought has been given and much discussion aroused regarding the implement used to apply this thicker pigment for the decorative patterns. It has even been suggested by an American writer that the vase decorator used a sort of tooth-paste tube made of leather from which he squeezed the pigment.

It does not seem that there need be any mystery about the matter. A visit to the Ikaros pottery factory in Rhodes will show scores of men and women at work with brushes shaped like a peg-top coming to a very fine point, so that they have plenty of reserve capacity to hold the pigment. These are used for designs of comparatively short lines. For those needing longer lines, the brush used is shaped something like a person's index finger and about the same thickness and length. This can also be brought to a fine point and has an even larger reserve capacity for the pigment. The hairs are set in a quill ferrule fitted to the end of a short wooden handle. The hair used is camel-hair taken from the ear of a camel, of which there are still large numbers in Asia Minor, separated from Rhodes by only a few miles of sea.

The camel is one of the oldest of domestic animals, and although there is little or no record of it in Egypt before Roman times, camels are mentioned in the Book of Genesis as featuring among the herds of Abraham, who is estimated to have lived about 1450 BC. Camels are also known to have existed in Mesopotamia and Syria about 2000 BC. If brushes for stiffer paint were required, bristles from hogs would have been readily available in antiquity, as they are today. We can reasonably assume, therefore, that the Minoans and Mycenaeans of the Bronze Age, as well as vase painters of the classical period, used camel-hair or hog's hair brushes for the decoration of their pottery without seeking for any other implement. The subject of brushes is dealt with in detail in the *Encyclopaedia Britannica*.

Unlike the modern 'biscuit', it is probable that the Greek vases were baked only once, but that this baking consisted of several stages. As they had no instrument by which to measure temperature, the potters had to guess the temperature of the kiln from the incandescent colour of the furnace, and by the help of trial sherds which they could withdraw during the baking. The general principle was the alternation of 'oxidising' and 'reducing' phases. In the oxidising phase, air was freely admitted to the oven, and formed carbon dioxide (CO_2) in combination with the fuel.

D

If, however, the supply of oxygen was reduced to a minimum by checking the supply of air, carbon monoxide (CO) would be produced, and a reducing atmosphere created in the kiln.

After painting, the pots were placed in the kiln and baked in a clear oxydising atmosphere at a temperature of 800°–900°C, when the whole surface of the pot with its high content of ferric oxide of iron (FeO_3) became red, including those parts painted with the thicker pigment, although this became darker and glossier. This process is called oxydation.

The pots were then subjected to a reducing atmosphere by checking the air supply and so producing carbon monoxide. This carbon monoxide, extracting oxygen from the ferric oxide in the clay, transformed the red ferric oxide into black ferrous oxide (FeO) and the whole pot turned black. During this reducing process, damp fuel, such as green wood, was introduced into the kiln to hasten the process of reduction. This action, though producing smoke, was not responsible for transforming the pot from red to black.

Finally, air was reintroduced (the smoke disappeared) and the oxygen in the air, penetrating the thin wash, turned the clay of the pot red again, while those parts which had been covered with the thicker pigment resisted the penetration of oxygen and remained black. At this point the fire was raked out before the oxygen in the air had time to penetrate the thicker pigment of the black painted parts and turn them red again.

It was this simple process, arrived at empirically, that the Greeks probably used in the decoration of their pottery, a process which remained until so recently a mystery to the archaeologist. If the kiln had been allowed to cool without opening the vents, a completely black vase would have been produced in the *Bucchero nero* style.

In the case of white vases, they were covered with a white slip of residual clay without iron, and therefore insensible to oxydation.

EARLY MINOAN II 2500–2200 BC

Early Minoan II was the climax of the Early Bronze Age in the Aegean. The use of metal had become general, but of copper with only a low proportion of tin to which the Cretans had no direct access.

Their pottery was the product of a people much more advanced than the original settlers. They were in a phase of civilisation during which, while stone was still used for many of the needs of daily life, men had learnt how to smelt copper, and hammer it into tools and weapons.

The metal was still rare and costly, but its introduction meant that all sorts of things could be done which were impossible when only stone tools were known. It meant a great step forward in civilisation.

a. Spouted goblet
Sphoungaras

b. Angular shaped jug
Aghia Photia

c. Bowl
Mochlos

d. Goblet
Aghia Triada

e. Jug
Knossos

Fig. 8. Early Minoan II vessels

The simple ways of the Neolithic Era had been left far behind, and Crete had become a civilised and highly artistic country. She was not yet the equal of Egypt and Babylon in culture, nor was she to reach that standard of civilisation for another hundred years at least, but already Crete gave promise of what she was to become. The ware was very hard and fine, and the pots so well rounded that they would appear to have been made on the potter's wheel. This was not the case, for the tournette or slow wheel, probably a Persian invention, in which the revolving wheel was supported on a pivot, had not yet reached Crete.

The eastern end of Crete was still culturally ahead of the other parts, but the south was making a rapid advance in population.

The first EM II pottery was more or less uniform throughout the island and of a monochrome grey ware, directly descended from the style of EM I. A good example is the spouted pedestalled vase from Mochlos made of fine fabric and of distinguished shape (Fig. 10c). Other monochrome vessels are of rough red or buff clay, more finely levigated and covered with a thick slip which took a good polish. The goblets of the period usually have a low base (Fig. 8d). Cups with high swung handles have also been found at Knossos, Vasiliki, Gournia and Trapeza, open bowls are common, and the jugs have a flat bottom with spouts higher than in EM I, but not of the exaggerated type from Vasiliki in the latter part of EM II.

By this time it seems to be apparent that a common civilisation extended all over the populated areas, and the differences between one district and another were no more than could be expected when communications by land were so difficult.

In southern Crete, particularly in the Messara, circular tombs which first appear in EM I are dotted all over the plain. In eastern Crete, finds centre round the ports of Palaikastro, Mochlos, Pseira, Gournia and Zakro, with the inland site of Vasiliki not far from the sea.

The most notable products of EM II are the sophisticated and even fantastic forms which are characteristic of this period. One in particular is the jug with a loop handle and a long, weird, trough-shaped spout, 'schnabelkanne' (snout can) in German, 'tea-pot' in English and 'théière' in French (Figs. 10a and d). It is usually characterised by an 'eye' on either side of the spout which gives it the impression of a bird with a long beak, almost like a toucan. From this Cretan original it seems to have become a speciality in the island of Thera (Santorin). It may have been copied from Egyptian metal prototypes.

Recent excavations in the Trapeza cave shelter near Karphi, about six miles south of Mallia, have extended our knowledge of the burial customs and pottery of the Early Minoan period. The cave contained two classes

Fig. 9. Patterns on Early Minoan II pottery

of pottery, one a smoked grey ware and the other a buff surface with simple rectangular lines in grey paint. The grey ware includes chalices similar to those of EM I discovered at Pyrgos, pyxides with high necks to take cylindrical lids, conical cups with one handle, two-handled beakers, carinated jars with cylindrical necks and ovoid jars.

The decoration of EM II began with rectilinear figures in red-black ferruginous paint in vertical, horizontal and slanting hatchings drawn on a natural clay ground (Fig. 9).

Later in the period, although there was no great advance in the style of patterns, there was a considerable improvement in the quality of the painted decoration. The surface of the vessel was more carefully prepared, and the rather dull red or brown varnish stands out more effectively.

Lattice work and hatched triangles were a favourite form of decoration, especially on small spouted pots; and on jugs two hatched triangles were often joined at the apex to form a sort of 'butterfly' pattern.

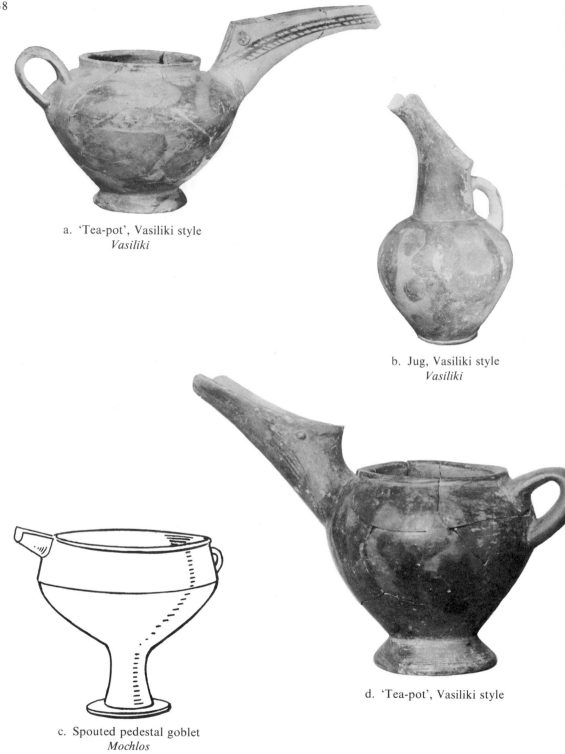

a. 'Tea-pot', Vasiliki style
Vasiliki

b. Jug, Vasiliki style
Vasiliki

c. Spouted pedestal goblet
Mochlos

d. 'Tea-pot', Vasiliki style

Fig. 10. Early Minoan II vessels continued

Such cups as have any decoration are generally limited to a narrow band of colour just below the rim.

Dishes and bowls also have a band round the rim or, as in the case of a few of these vessels from Knossos, they have a broad band of lattice work right across the inside.

A particularly fine bowl from Mochlos (Fig. 8c) has an elaborate and successful decoration; the slip is more than usually thick which accounts for the paint standing out so well. The design consists of concentric segments of circles, hatched 'butterfly' motifs and a Maltese cross in the centre.

Another style produced in EM II is known as Vasiliki ware from the village near Gournia where the best examples were found (Fig. 10). The mottling was at first probably accidental, but later on was deliberately cultivated to produce an ornamental effect of varying tones of brown or red, orange or black which fade into one another with great delicacy. The vase was then polished.

Vasiliki was evidently a ceramic centre of great activity, and the clay and finish of the pottery was so well made there that it was at first thought that the potter's wheel had already been introduced. It is almost certain, however, that the quick wheel did not make its appearance for another four hundred years, although it is possible that the tournette or slow wheel was employed.

Although used on ordinary shapes as well, the Vasiliki style of decoration is particularly associated with the fantastic long-beaked 'tea-pots' referred to above.

Sir Arthur Evans has seen in the exaggerated spouts of Vasiliki a reflection of early Egyptian copper vessels, where the prominent spout connects with the interior by a very small hole, a feature which is also found in the Cretan 'tea-pots'.

Certainly the influence of metal jugs is often shown by angular shapes accompanied by imitation rivets (Fig. 8b), and since a number of other Vasiliki ware shapes have these indications of a metal original, it seems likely that Sir Arthur Evans was correct in his opinion.

In some cases where dots run down the side of a vessel it may indicate the stitches of a leather prototype.

The individuality of the Vasiliki style, however, lies in its mottled surface. This was achieved by uneven firing when the fuel in the oven was actually allowed to touch the pot at intervals so as to give a yellow centre surrounded by an irregular dark ring, while the background remained brown or red. This Vasiliki ware is a highly specialised form of 'Urfirnis' ware with a possibly Danubian origin. It too was covered with a lustrous wash, and it seems possible that a few settlers from the north rather than from the east landed near Vasiliki and so introduced it into Crete. Innumerable variations of decorative pattern have been found, for the method employed rendered formal design impossible.

Before the end of EM II vases of this style were distributed to other parts of Crete where local imitations were made, sometimes by the same method as at Vasiliki, and sometimes with the mottling copied in paint as in the Messara and at Trapeza. Towards the end of the period, the lustrous, mottled surface was sometimes used as background for a design in white.

Although not ceramics, one should not lose sight of the wonderful stone vases whose manufacture began and culminated in EM II. They are carved in green, black and grey steatite, marble, alabaster and limestone – all of which are to be found in Crete. The colouring of many of these vases is brilliant, and the veins in the marble are used with great skill to produce beautiful effects. Although a number of these stone vases were inspired by Egyptian originals, the art was to become Cretan and their shapes were often direct translations into stone from clay originals of the period. In no succeeding period did the art of stone cutting reach so high a level of excellence as it did at the small sites of eastern Crete in EM II.

EARLY MINOAN III 2200–1900 BC

This short period was marked by the rise of Knossos and Phaestos in central Crete while the sites in the east end of the island began to decline. While in some ways EM III can be considered as a transitional stage between the Early and Middle Bronze Ages in Crete, yet it has features of its own discovered in the east and south of the island, while in the north and centre it is seen to be the end of the archaic Early Minoan period.

Mottled pottery of the Vasiliki style and the dark-on-light style of decoration still survived, but the principal difference between the pottery of EM III and that of the preceding periods was the substitution of a light-on-dark for a dark-on-light decoration. This took the form of designs in matt white paint on a black or dark brown slip. This change also took place about the same time on the mainland of Greece.

What was the reason for the reversal? During the latter part of EM II the mottled Vasiliki style had become the fashion and had practically driven out the dark-on-light geometric decoration. The mottling was a matter of chance, and almost impossible to regulate, but as undecorated monochrome ware never appealed to the Minoans, some form of decoration was essential to them.

They tried incision and punctuation on the mottled ware, but this form of decoration was not very effective, and as the dark varnish paint of EM II would not show up against the dark mottled background, the designs were drawn in matt white. It was then realised that the mottled background did not add greatly to the effect, and very soon the white designs were drawn on a lustrous black background. The best examples of the new white on black decoration have been found at sites in the eastern end of Crete. In fact, no type of design which appears in any other part of the island is unrepresented in eastern Crete.

The strange long-spouted 'tea-pot' still persisted for a short time, but the exaggerated length of the spout became shorter. Fig. 11d shows a handsome example of one of these. It is complete except for the greater part of the spout, the exact length of which is, therefore, uncertain. The ground is a thin, dull, brownish black. The white of the design has almost disappeared, but the pattern is clear and consists of a number of C's reversed and linked, so making a very dignified composition.

Although more characteristic of the Middle Minoan period, the hole-mouthed beaked jar made its appearance before the end of EM III (Fig. 22). It is a more or less globular jar with a strong horizontal spout, sometimes bridged. As a rule it has two vertical or horizontal handles, one on either side, with occasionally a single handle like that of a basket with one end attached to the rim over the spout. A rivet was made at the bottom of the spout showing its metallic origin.

The hole-mouthed jar was of Cretan origin, and became very common in the Middle Minoan period. This type of jar spread from Crete all over the Aegean, but it was freely modified to suit local taste.

Shapes also typical of the period are the cups. The most common shape is the rounded tea-cup usually without a handle, but occasionally it has small horizontal handles up to four in number.

Another cup shape is the straight-sided mug which is the prototype of the Vapheio cup shape that became so popular in the MM II and LM I periods. Many of the cups of this period are of very fine fabric and almost come within the category of 'eggshell' ware.

It was in EM III that 'Larnax' and pot burials came into favour (Fig. 11e). The clay coffin or 'Larnax' made its first appearance in EM III and in the MM period its use became general.

From LM I to LM III it looks very like a bath. In fact, pottery baths were often used as Larnakes, and this may account for the stories of the great ones of the Mycenaean period having been murdered in their baths, as for instance, Agamemnon by Clytemnestra.

Another shape typical of EM III is the conical dish sometimes with and sometimes without a spout (Fig. 12a).

a. 'Tea-pot'
Vasiliki

b. Jug
Mochlos

d. 'Tea-pot'
Kamares

c. Cup
Pseira

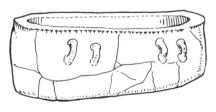

e. Larnax
Pachyammos

Fig. 11. Early Minoan III vessels

a. Spouted conical dish
Gournia

b. Spouted squat bowl (also MM I A)
Porti

c. 'Tea-pot'
Knossos

d. Flask with large handle
Palaikastro

e. Jug with 'breasts'
Kalathiana

f. Cup
Mochlos

Fig. 12. Early Minoan III vessels continued

The decorative motifs of EM III which are nearly all in matt white paint on a dark background consist partly of the old geometric patterns and partly of a new series of motifs (Fig. 13). Among the former are triangles, lozenges and segments of circles. These are merely elaborations of those of EM II. The commonest rectilinear pattern is a zig-zag

Fig. 13. Patterns on Early Minoan III pottery

between lines, running round the body of the vase with the triangles so made being left alternately plain and hatched.

Most of the motifs of this type are confined by bordering lines which sometimes run up at a slant or hang down in loops. Designs are as a rule horizontal and not vertical as in MM I.

One rather surprising motif is the St Andrew's Cross between panels of vertical lines which bears a remarkable resemblance to the 'butterfly' motif (derived from the 'double axe' motif) of the Mycenaean I period five hundred years later.

Among the new series of motifs is the spiral which also appeared on the mainland and in the Cyclades at this time. Much discussion has taken place as to possible sources from which the spiral motif may have been derived. Nature provides any number of them: a coiled rope, shells, seeds, a curled leaf or a wave breaking upon the beach.

Neither the spiral nor any curved line had been used by the Cretan neolithic potter, as such lines do not lend themselves to the motion of the incising tool on the surface of a vase. Straight lines and zig-zags were easy, but when the brush superseded the incising tool, a curved line was easier to make than an angular one and so the spiral became a practical possibility as a decorative motif.

Nearly every variation of the spiral appears in Crete during this period: spirals with solid centres, simple forms of connected spirals joined by one or more lines or a thickened tangent line, or even an elaborate design taken from contemporary seal stones. A further modification of this motif is a row of horizontal S's which probably owe their existence to the ease with which they can be made by a turn of the brush.

Close contact between Crete and the Cyclades during E M III is shown by the number of figurines and incised pyxides, vessels of island marble, and the great increase of obsidian blades which have been discovered in Crete during this period, a period which corresponds to Early Cycladic III, and during which the spiral made its appearance in the Cyclades.

A common form of decoration in EM III are bands of ornament round the upper part of the vase. Within these bands the basic motif is the zig-zag, inherited, no doubt, from earlier incised decoration. The arcs or semi-circles are translations of the zig-zag into curvilinear design, so that this period is marked by a transition from rectilinear to curvilinear ornament, caused by the increasing use of the brush.

Among these early curvilinear experiments appear some which bear a slight resemblance to natural objects. Where, for instance, the artist wished to insert an ornament into an angle, he first drew a chevron in the corner, and then bent the ends round and the result was what in later

Fig. 14. Conventionalised leaf

times would be called a conventionalised leaf. Thus we see that such designs are not necessarily derived from natural objects, but that in his early experiments to find a pleasing decorative shape, the artist hit by chance upon a motif that resembled a natural object. The idea pleased him and in this case, recognising its resemblance to a leaf, he pursued the idea and so began designs really inspired by nature.

It is the circles of this period with their hatched segments, squares and crosses, which are the forerunners of the rosettes which became such a feature of later Minoan, Mycenaean and Geometric pottery.

EM III also saw the first appearance of animals. The idea began by an adaptation of the old 'double axe' motif which suggested the body of an

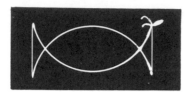
Fig. 15. Animal motif

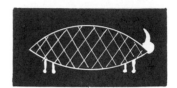
Fig. 16. Animal motif

animal to which the head of a goat was added. In the same way a head or legs could be added to a hatched oval. Thus we see another example of naturalistic forms evolving out of chance resemblances in geometric motifs.

MIDDLE MINOAN I 1900–1800 BC

It was at the beginning of the second millennium that new peoples made their appearance at the north of the Eastern Mediterranean – peoples of Indo-European tongue. Their place of origin is obscure. Whether they came from northern India, from Persia or from Siberia is still unknown.

That they had some sort of common origin in the third millennium appears certain from linguistic similarities as well as from the 'corded' pottery which they made, a term given on account of the ornamentation obtained by pressing rope into the soft clay – a form of decoration used today by native tribes in Africa who still produce hand-made pottery under neolithic conditions.

The dispersion of these Indo-European peoples occurred during the course of the European Bronze Age towards the latter end of the third millennium. At the end of their common existence, and before their dispersion, the Indo-Europeans were a pastoral people, and as such semi-nomadic, but who practised agriculture.

They left the Neolithic Era and learned the use of copper. They had domesticated the horse which, like the ox, they harnessed to waggons at a time when the horse was unknown in Mesopotamia, Egypt and Crete, and so gave themselves a mobility that enabled them to move from their native plains in all directions to the extremities of Europe and Asia.

At the time when the Indo-European peoples appear in history about 1900 BC, their dispersion had already occurred, and it would seem that their principal groupings which would soon be called upon to play so important a part had already been formed.

The slow progress of these tribes along the shores of the Aegean, and the sharp reactions which it caused in Greece, did not at first affect the islands. The invaders used the impetus of their drive against the mainland before embarking upon the sea, and although their influence was already felt in the Cyclades by the middle of the second millennium, it was not yet felt in the southern part of the Aegean Sea.

Thus, although surrounded by revolutions and battles, the southern Archipelago enjoyed a relative tranquillity for several centuries to come. This temporary calm was of great advantage to Crete. Her civilisation was in full course of expansion, and as master of the seas, her ships were able to sail unhindered from one side of the Mediterranean to the other. A noteworthy advance in Cretan civilisation was made at the advent of the Middle Minoan period.

The Early Minoan period was characterised by simple village communities and communal tombs. The Crete of the Middle Minoan period was marked by the foundation of cities, the construction of palaces at Knossos, Phaestos and Mallia, a naval supremacy, an expanding trade with Egypt and Asia Minor and a strong central government. Cretan civilisation reached its first climax during this period. It was distinguished by brilliance, dignity and a remarkable progress in all the arts.

For reasons as yet unknown, the centre of power in MM I was transferred from eastern Crete to the north and centre of the island; and the first of the great palaces appeared, a process that seems already to have started in EM III.

The foundation of the old Palace of Knossos took place at the very beginning of MM I and the Palace of Mallia belongs to the same period. Phaestos would seem to have been founded during the latter part of MM I.

These three palaces, somewhat destroyed by later construction, have all, in spite of individual differences, certain characteristics in common. No precaution seems to have been taken against the possibility of attack. The walls have no defensive value, and the doors are wide open to the outside. The small rooms, arranged haphazard in quarters, are grouped around an interior courtyard. Their store-rooms contain huge jars or pithoi set in lines along the walls, or else on little stuccoed pavements to contain the liquid and solid foods of the palace.

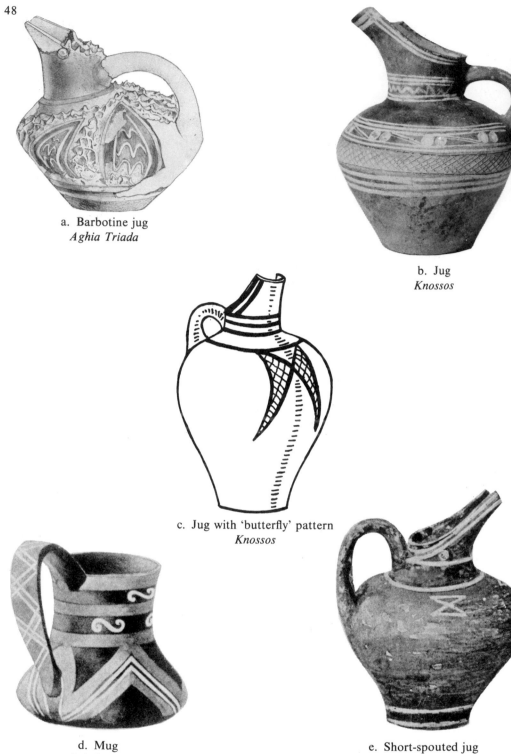

a. Barbotine jug
Aghia Triada

b. Jug
Knossos

c. Jug with 'butterfly' pattern
Knossos

d. Mug
Palaikastro

e. Short-spouted jug
Mochlos

Fig. 17. Middle Minoan I A jugs

Tablets form the palace archives, and upon them are inscribed with a
point on the soft clay pictographic signs of familiar objects which appear
to indicate some sort of inventory of the royal possessions in a code of
which we do not yet possess the key.

Her fleet enabled Crete to make a wide distribution of her products.
Minoan pottery has been found in the most diverse and widely separate
localities. Thera and above all Milo bought large quantities of it, and
their local wares were largely influenced by Cretan models.

Cretan pottery is found at Delos and in Argolis, and although not
much of it has been discovered in northern Greece, many examples
found their way to Cyprus, the coast of Phoenicia and the valley of the
Nile. The density of this trade clearly attests the wealth of Crete with its
expanding civilisation, a civilisation both peasant and princely, rustic
and luxurious.

Carving and engraving were executed in the greatest variety of forms
and materials. Seals in particular were engraved with pictoglyphic signs
on jasper, agate and chalcedony. The wonderful skill which the artist
displayed make these little stones real masterpieces of delicacy. Their
designs were frequently borrowed by the vase-painter for the decoration
of his vases.

It was also in the early part of MM I that communication along the
great route across the island from Phaestos in the south to Knossos in
the north was improved.

The potter's wheel was not known in the first Early Minoan period.
Although it is possible that the slow wheel or tournette was employed
as early as EM II for making Vasiliki ware, it was certainly in use at the
beginning of MM I, and was probably introduced from somewhere in the
East. By the end of the period it had established itself for the making of
finer and smaller vases, and gradually replaced the laborious but often
brilliantly successful craftsmanship of the earlier artisans.

Many of the vases of the period show parallel striations where they
were cut off the wheel by means of string. Much, however, was still done
by hand as can be seen by the pinching in by fingers of the stems of
cups.

It was just before the introduction of the quick wheel about 1900 BC
that the potter's craft was at its best. The clay was worked to egg-shell
fineness – waved rims and fluted bodies were copied from delicate metal
cups.

A new type of building dating from MM I and MM II in the form of
a sanctuary built on a mountain peak has been found on Mt. Juktas south
of Knossos and on Mt. Profetis Elias above Mallia as well as at other
places. The origin of their sanctity has been lost in the mists of time, but

E

a. Storage jar
Gournia

b. Spouted jar
Vasiliki

c. Beaker
Palaikastro

d. Small pithos
Vorou

e. Two-handled vase
Mochlos

Fig. 18. Middle Minoan I A vessels continued

votive offerings and figurines have been found in these places dating from these periods.

In dealing with the Middle Minoan I period, it is convenient to divide it into two phases, MM I A and MM I B, and in discussing the ceramics of these two phases, to take the pottery of northern Crete, southern Crete and eastern Crete separately.

Although pottery typical of MM I A has been found at Mallia, the action of the soil has destroyed most of the paint. The best examples of this early date come from Knossos, where an almost complete range of vessels of the period has been found.

MMIA (NORTHERN CRETE). Typical vases of MM I A from Knossos are the common short-spouted jug in buff clay with the hatched 'butterfly'

Fig. 19. Patterns on Middle Minoan I A pottery from Knossos

pattern on the front (Figs. 17c and 19). This pattern was particularly popular in EM II.

Jugs of MM I A are usually more graceful than in EM III and have narrower spouts. An excellent example from Knossos has a background merging from red to black and a decoration of orange circles with a white cross in the centre.

Imitation rivets on the spouts still appear on some of the coarser vessels. Some of these have three handles.

A magnificent polychrome beaked jug of this phase found at Knossos (Colour Plate IVa) which, to judge by the deep red employed, must belong to the very beginning of MM I A. It is painted round the shoulder with a series of double axes outlined in red, bordered with white, and filled with white dots on a dull brown ground.

The most typical vessels of the period are the small jugs with a short cut-away neck, usually decorated with a broad slash of paint shaped like a leaf drawn diagonally across each shoulder with two white lines to mark the centre of the leaf. White bands are painted round the neck and body above and below the diagonal slash.

The spouted jar is also found in large numbers. Some of these have trough spouts or bridge spouts (Fig. 22) and some round spouts (Fig.18). They provide a great variety of decoration from simple white lines to elaborate patterns.

Even commoner are the handleless cups with or without pedestal, and decorated below the rim with a band of red or black paint on a buff or brown ground or of white on a black ground. Although virtually absent from the eastern part of Crete, they are extremely abundant in MM I deposits at Knossos.

Another cup of inverted conical form has a pleasant decoration of three red blades with a central rib of white.

Tumblers also occur sometimes in the finest egg-shell ware. These are often mottled in the Vasiliki style and occasionally decorated with circles surrounded by dots.

Open bowls were often elaborately painted inside. One fine example has a red-brown background with a big central ring of orange-red surrounded by two white lines. Round the lines are five white lozenges with white dots and orange lines inside.

The pithos is the best known type of storage jar (Fig. 18), but during this period it has thin walls and seldom stands more than three feet in height.

At this time the dead were often buried in jars, and a great number of such early burial jars have been found in Crete. They are sometimes decorated with a 'trickle' ornament obtained by dropping the paint on to them from a sponge and allowing it to trickle down the side of the jar. On others the decoration takes the form of dots linked together in a network. A vessel which begins to be common in the MM I period is the 'chytra', a clay tripod cooking pot or cauldron, often with a small trough spout. It is hardly found on the mainland of Greece before the sixteenth century BC when the type was probably adopted from Crete.

It was in MM I A that appear the beginnings of 'Barbotine' decoration (Fig. 17a). This is principally distinguished by a fantastic ornamentation of barnacles or knobs on the surface of the vase, and in a lesser degree by diagonal ridges. (The dictionary translates 'Barbotine' as 'worm-cast'.) At first it was usually applied to cups and bowls only, but later on it was applied to jugs and other types of vessel. When applied to vases of the Kamares style, the barbotine decoration consists either of small raised points or of irregular ridges made apparently by dabbing the tacky surface of the still wet clay with the tip of the finger and so producing small cells surrounded by ridges. These roughened surfaces were gaudily painted with the usual Kamares colours. As a rule, barbotine raised decoration does not cover the whole vase but is used in conjunction with flat parts on which a pattern is carried out in white and red paint.

In MM I B it began to be used in conjunction with painting which when used in moderation was a reasonable idea. In the south of Crete much of it has been found at Aghia Triada, where during MM I B it became the prevailing form of decoration. The painting then consisted mostly of bands of plain colour and an occasional spiral. This type of decoration in the examples from Arghia Triada was applied to a large number of comparatively squat jugs with horizontal spouts and usually three handles. Some of these jugs, however, are monochrome and the coating of knobs is varied by an occasional plain flat disc.

Barbotine decoration continued until the end of the period when the quick wheel was introduced which meant the end of this fanciful form of ceramic ornament. In MM III, however, there was a recrudescence of it at Knossos, and a number of vases of that period have been found decorated with applied sprays of barley and moulded reliefs of crabs, shells and barnacles.

MM I A (SOUTHERN CRETE). In the Messara Plain, pottery of the MM I A style comes from the strata immediately below the store-rooms of the first palace. Most typical are the squat bowls with a short spout, while others have been found at Aghia Triada, Porti and other neighbouring sites, but not in any great quantity.

MM I A (EASTERN CRETE). In the east of Crete, the pottery of EM III seems to continue right through the MM I A phase and no pottery similar to that found at Knossos has been found in eastern Crete.

MM I B (NORTHERN CRETE). For MM I B a good selection of vases has been found at Knossos, of which the most typical shape of the period is a low cup with straight or slightly concave sides. It has a ribbon handle and is ornamented with polychrome decoration in crimson bordered with white.

Fig. 20. Patterns on Middle Minoan I B pottery from Knossos and the Kamares Cave

The fabric is generally finer than that in the previous phase, and some of the cups are as thin as any of the eggshell ware of MM II. The shapes become more sophisticated and flaring rim more common for cups.

MM I B (SOUTHERN CRETE). In the south of the island, some graceful vessels with pleasant decoration have been found in the shape of conical tumblers, carinated cups and open bowls with simple patterns inside. Fig. 21e shows a cup of the period with a linear pattern consisting of

a. Spouted jar
Vasiliki

b. Small cup with concave sides
Aghia Photia

c. Squat bridge-spouted Kamares jar

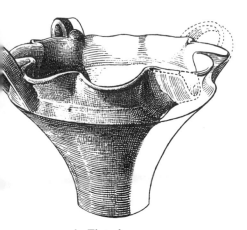

d. Fluted vase
Pseira

e. Cup with concave sides
Kamares

Fig. 21. Middle Minoan I B vessels

panels crossed by diagonal lines and a cruciform motif of white picked out with red. This cup shows very markedly by its simple angles the traces of metal technique observed in MM pottery.

The vases from the Kamares cave on the southern slopes of Mount Ida fall into a category of their own. For the most part they belong to MM II but some are dated to MM I. A large proportion of them are open spouted jars of a more squat type than has been found elsewhere. Fig. 22d is an example of one of these. It has a fine black ground, and the pattern consists of four large quatrefoils with alternate red and yellow triangular leaves edged with white.

The most extreme example is of a shape somewhat similar but so much flattened that it seems quite different (Fig. 21c). It is the MM prototype of a form comparatively common in LM times. There is a small boss at the back decorated with white spots. This boss, the spout and the two handles, divide the field into four parts, each occupied by a strange design about which some uncertainty seems to exist, but recognised by some as a murex shell. It must be admitted that it is not a very striking likeness. It is drawn in white and the corrugations of the shell are rendered by rows of small raised lumps.

The vacant spaces are filled by rosettes with a red centre surrounded by a white circle and a ring of white dots, while the raised lip is decorated with a running S pattern.

Four spouted jars from the Kamares cave dating from the MM I period are so beautiful that they each merit a few special words of description. Colour Plate IIa is most interesting as being a very early example of the use of the octopus on Minoan pottery. At the end of the tentacles, which are only six in number, are orange discs with a crimson blob in the centre and surrounded by white dots. Orange plumes run back from the lowest pair. The whole animal is surrounded by a double series of white loops. The whole design, which is painted on a black lustre ground, exhibits a remarkable piece of conventionalisation.

Colour Plate IIb shows a trough-spouted jar with a pattern which consists of a lattice-work in white with the triangles filled in with dots arranged in four vertical bands on an orange and red ground. The red consists of a line round the mouth and two parallel lines on each side of the bands of lattice work.

Colour Plate IIc is a splendid specimen of this class of vessel. It is evident that the original finder set great store on it from the number of holes which he drilled in it to rivet the fragments together. The vertical bands of ornament, which are cut short by horizontal bands above the base, consist of two broad stripes of white with bars between them, and are themselves decorated with red stripes. The spaces below the spout

a.

b.

c.

d.

Plate II. Middle Minoan I & II spouted jars from Kamares cave

a. Two-handled vase
Vasiliki

b. Fluted vase
Gournia

c. Spouted jar
Palaikastro

d. Spouted Kamares jar

e. Spouted Kamares jar

Fig. 22. Middle Minoan I B vessels continued

58

a. Kantharos
Palaikastro

b. Beaked jug
Palaikastro

c. Fruit stand
Kamares

d. Beaked jug
Palaikastro

Fig. 23. Middle Minoan I 'Kamares style' vessels

and handles are filled with the drawing of a fish in white outlined in red.

Fig. 22e is a trough-spouted, two-handled jar with a somewhat globular body. The decoration consists of four vertical bands, and a red line round the mouth. Each band contains three festoons of red and white lines, and their vertical borders are diversified with the white cable pattern so often found on EM III pottery.

Although Kamares ware is mostly associated with the next period (MM II) because it was then that it reached its highest achievements, a large proportion of it belongs to MM I B with strikingly ornamental designs, as we have seen. An example of exceptional design is a 'Fruit Stand', a shape well known in MM, but which in this case (see Fig. 23c) is decorated with a remarkable pattern. The ground colour is a pale brownish slip, and on this is a rough network of red, against the sides of which are blotches of an ochreish yellow. The ground is dabbed over with touches of black. The red network and the blotches of yellow are edged with a line of white. This curious pattern is an imitation of one of the natural stone breccias out of which the Minoans delighted to cut vases and dishes. The outside, and as much of the foot as remains, are decorated with slanting lines of white and dark brown.

At Porti in the Messara to the east of Phaestos clay lamps have been found. Some consist of an open flat-bottomed bowl with a cut in the side for a wick and a stick handle.

Another type has a projecting spout for the wick and a loop handle, while a third type has a short thick pedestal.

MM I B (EASTERN CRETE). Although it is not easy to make an exact distinction in assigning pottery from eastern Crete to MM I A or MM I B there is no doubt that a considerable variety of graceful shapes with beautiful designs belong to MM I B. One group in particular found at Palaikastro, Pseira and Gournia consists largely of two-handled cups derived from a metallic origin and which testify to the considerable skill in silver and copper work at that time. Some of these two-handled cups are fluted (Fig. 22b), and their metal prototypes probably originated in the second city of Troy. Other shapes of the same period include cups with wavy rims, a concave basket shape with two handles at the rim, spouted jugs, mugs, amphorae and pithoi. The vase decoration is so varied during MM I that a few special words on the subject seem called for.

Generally speaking, the chief change in technique from EM III to MM I is the use of colours such as red, crimson and orange to enhance the white designs. But there is also a marked difference in the decoration of the two periods. The patterns of the earlier period were applied in

Fig. 24. Patterns on Middle Minoan I pottery from East Crete

horizontal zones, each of which as a rule contained a single decorative motif repeated sufficiently often to encircle the vase, whereas the designs of MM I are arranged with greater variety and freedom.

In the infrequent cases where decoration is still arranged in bands, the designs are more elaborate in character, an elaboration which forms the most distinctive difference between the ornamentation of MM I and EM III.

During MM I A, the creamy white of EM III was replaced by a more flaky, chalky white, the Indian red becomes orange and the black background of EM III now varies from lavender grey to purplish brown. Among motifs of this phase are circles surrounded by dots, roundels joined by diagonal lines, lozenges, hatched 'butterfly wings' and other designs shown in Fig. 19. A selection of the principal motifs during MM I B is given in Fig. 20.

The decorative patterns on the cups of northern Crete are purely geometrical at first, and consist of vertical and horizontal bands, loops and St Andrew's crosses.

More natural forms of motif begin to appear, however, in the shape of plant forms which, although stiff, are recognisable as being intended for vegetable motifs.

Fig. 25. Tailed and running spirals

During this phase, the decoration tends to become 'closer', and more of the vase to become covered with it. Certain of the motifs such as the tailed spiral and the running spiral have an affinity with those of the preceding period and become typical of eastern Crete from MM I B onwards. Finally we see an increase in realism in the designs of MM I B in the shape of fishes, flowers and leaves.

MIDDLE MINOAN II 1800–1700 BC

The brilliant development of Crete during the second millennium was not without repercussions all over the Aegean Sea. The expanding power of the Cretan princes allowed them to extend their influence among the other islands. This influence, which enabled Cretan mercantile shipping to sail throughout the Archipelago with a freedom previously unknown, resulted in greatly expanded trade.

At the same time, the wealth and display of the Cretan civilisation must have attracted the inhabitants of the Cyclades to see the wonderful cities of the great island, their palaces, their ceremonies and their religious rites.

Before that it would seem that the wide stretch of ocean lying between Crete and the southernmost of the Cyclades alarmed the early seamen, accustomed as they were to purely coastal navigation within sight of land. Only the bravest sailors had ventured to make the trip, and then only for the transport of essential goods, and particularly obsidian, that most useful of minerals, to be found in large quantities at Milo. Its use was recognised so early that Melian obsidian has been found in Crete even in neolithic deposits.

It was under the conditions prevailing at the beginning of the second millennium that the first palaces of Knossos, Mallia and Phaestos were built. It was at the same time that the ceramic style of Middle Minoan developed, and when painted pottery became one of the most flourishing and original luxury industries of Crete – an industry which soon achieved a vigorous export trade.

Thus an increasing quantity of Cretan vases dating from the Middle Minoan period onwards has been found, not only in the islands, but all over the Peloponnese in the south, as far as Thessaly in the north, in Cyprus to the east, and in Italy to the west. Much Middle Minoan Cretan pottery has also been found in deposits of the XIIth Dynasty in Egypt. To explain this, we should remember that excavations at Knossos have shown that olive oil was one of the most important products of Crete. Middle Minoan deposits have yielded olive presses and olive oil separators, seals have been found bearing an olive branch with olives, and vessels have even been found containing olives preserved in them for eating. The purple dye derived from the murex shell was exported by the Cretans of the Bronze Age to the valley of the Nile with wool, copper and pottery.

As mentioned before, the tournette or slow wheel, a revolving disc supported on a pivot, reached Crete during EM III.

It was the introduction of the quick wheel during MM I that made possible the great strides in the output of ceramics in MM II.

It was this quick wheel in which a fly-wheel is moved by the feet of the potter that gave him both hands free for shaping his vase. It was not a Cretan invention as it already occurs in Troy a good deal earlier. It is reasonably certain that it was introduced from Egypt or the Near East when Crete had already reached an advanced degree of civilisation, and when her potters were already highly skilled in making vases by hand. Its introduction was of decisive importance in the history of Greek pottery.

a. Pithos
Phaestos

b. Jug
Knossos

c. Beaked vase
Phaestos

d. Pithos, Kamares style
Phaestos

e. 'Fruit-stand'
Palaikastro

f. Amphora
Phaestos

g. Bridge-spouted jar
Phaestos

h. Vase, Kamares style
Phaestos

Fig. 26. Middle Minoan II vessels

It is, however, possible that the slow wheel continued to be used in Crete side by side with the quick wheel, and that the latter somehow went out of use after the collapse of Greek culture at the end of the Bronze Age and was not reintroduced until some time later. The quick wheel meant that egg-shell vases could be made more easily and so became more common, and put a final end to Barbotine ware.

It is the wonderfully shaped and beautifully decorated Kamares style ware (Figs. 26 and 27) that gives the MM II period its greatest distinction, and which differentiates Minoan art so completely from that of other civilisations.

As for its place of manufacture, Professor Marinatos (*Crete and Mycenae*, p. 125), in his description of Knossos says, 'The workshops can still be picked out in which the royal potters of the Old Palace made the superb egg-shell vases and other Kamares pottery.'

Although many examples come from the older palaces of Knossos and Phaestos which were destroyed about 1700 BC, this pottery takes its name from a cavern on the southern slopes of Mount Ida near the village of Kamares not far from Phaestos where it was first discovered.

It was in the early nineties of the last century that Dr Hadjidakis secured a number of vases and a few figurines from a shepherd who had found them in the cave, but it was not until 1913 that its full excavation was carried out by a party from the British Archaeological School at Athens conducted by Professor R. M. Dawkins, then Director of the School.

Until then the cave had rarely been visited, for even in the height of summer it was often much choked with snow, and access to it was very difficult. It lies in a remote spot some 5,500 feet above sea level with a splendid view over the mountains, valleys, plains and coasts of southern Crete. No more magnificent situation for a sacred cave could be imagined.

The cave consists of an outer and an inner cave. Professor Dawkins's party were rewarded by finding an immense quantity of pottery all in the outer cave lying in the crevices between broken masses of rock. The cave itself had not changed, so they concluded, since Minoan times, when the offerings were placed among, and in some cases in crevices underneath the rocks in the cave. No pottery was found in the inner cave. It was, save for a few later sherds, all Middle Minoan. It was scattered in all directions and greatly broken, but enough was collected and mended to enable water-colour drawings to be made of a series of beautiful vases, which were as fine as anything of their class till then found in Crete (Fig. 27 and Colour Plate II).

Besides many coloured jars and cups, the party found a great mass of unpainted ware, big jars, and what seem to have been tie-on covers.

a. Mug
Phaestos

b. Three-handled jug
(MM II–III) *Knossos*

c. Cup
Palaikastro

d. Storage jar
Phaestos

e. Amphora
Phaestos

f. Spouted pithos
Phaestos

g. Fluted vase (MM I B/II)
Gournia

h. Storage jar
Phaestos

Fig. 27. Middle Minoan II vessels continued

Judging by vegetable remains, it seems that corn of some kind was amongst the offerings they once contained.

Since much the greater part of the pottery found was Middle Minoan II, it appears that the vogue of the cave as a sanctuary lasted only for a comparatively short period.

The Kamares cave is only one of many cave-sanctuaries among the mountains of Crete to which worshippers came from far and wide to make offerings of votive objects to the deities; but none have revealed more beautiful objects than the pottery found in the cavern of Kamares.

The fertility of its hybrid shapes, the richness of its colours, the harmony of its designs, make it one of the most attractive styles of pottery in the world. The remarkable ingenuity, the incredible fantasy and the imaginative versatility of its ornamental themes have supplied an infinite variety of patterns to inspire the decorative artists of all subsequent periods. Its chief colours are white, orange, crimson, red and yellow, painted matt on a lustrous black or dark brown background. Cups, beaked jugs, beaked bowls and amphorae with handles at the mouth were especially common.

Although much of the decoration derived its inspiration from nature, the designs are not naturalistic but very much stylised (Fig. 28). The colouring itself bears no relation to nature, and the combination of vegetable and geometric motifs are of purely decorative quality. The painters of Kamares ware showed great skill in arranging these motifs in harmonious designs which cover the whole surface of the vase without giving the impression of overloading.

Many of the Kamares vases, whose name is synonymous with the MM II period, are real masterpieces, and the grace of their designs is emphasised by a splendid and varied colour scheme standing out against a dark background. In its artistic style, in the good taste of its polychrome decoration, it represents the best of the ceramics produced in that remote period. The decoration generally covers the whole of the vessel and is not divided into bands separating the neck and the foot from the principal decorative zones as in so many other styles.

There is no doubt about the high degree of technical ability shown by the potters who formed its graceful and harmonious shapes, nor of the innate artistry of the painters who created the striking and original designs with which Kamares vases are decorated. In the splendour of their colouring, the balance of their geometrical designs, their natural exuberance, they reach the summit of ornamental style. Such perfection of technique implies a civilisation far removed from primitive art.

Though Kamares ware photographs well in black and white owing to its strong contrasts in tone, it can only be fully appreciated in colour. It

Fig. 28. Patterns on Middle Minoan II pottery

is interesting to note, however, that when the party led by Professor Dawkins carried out excavation of the Kamares cave in 1913, they found that the white and red paint on the vases was in a very bad condition and that the only possible way of making a picture of these vases so that one could appreciate the designs, was to make a water-colour drawing, restoring the red and white in those places where there were indications, however slight, that they originally existed, and where parts of the vase were missing, they were restored in the drawing.

The larger and more solid examples of Kamares ware include poly-chrome decoration of palm trees, garlands, spirals and sun-rays, but strangely enough there is an almost though not entire absence of natural-istic marine motifs. These do not make their general appearance till the LM I period when naturalism takes the place of the elaborate MM patterns.

A number of vases do, however, have conventional patterns inspired by marine and vegetable subjects which give them a special charm.

Egg-shell ware, as we saw, was already made in MM I A, but during MM II it reached an even higher standard of excellence.

Although not many metal vessels of MM II have been discovered, it is fairly certain that metal work exercised a considerable influence on the pottery of the period. The egg-shell cups with their flat handles and rivet-like knobs are certainly derived from prototypes in gold and silver. The variety of Kamares pottery is endless.

Though MM I deposits contain the earliest examples of Kamares ware, its most brilliant phase was MM II, but with the development of the naturalistic style of LM I, the Kamares style disappeared. The riot of colour and weirdness of design had reached their zenith and then died down. They were characteristic of the fantastic side of Cretan genius, but neither the polychrome nor the Barbotine style of decoration found favour in the next era.

Provincial sites acquired examples of Kamares pottery from the centres of manufacture, but it was only the richer ones that could afford it, and these imports are found sometimes in a little deposit by themselves as if they were specially precious.

Offerings of the best of it were made to the sacred caves of Kamares, Dikte and Trapeza. Recent Italian excavations of fine MM II pottery from Phaestos show that the potters there were little if at all inferior to those who supplied the Kamares ware to Knossos.

The most impressive vessels discovered at Knossos and Phaestos belong-ing to MM II are the large pithoi found in the royal store-rooms (Fig. 26a). A typical one found at Phaestos is a great globular vessel fitted with rows of handles to facilitate transport, and ornamented with knobs and ropes as well as a trickle ornament imitating the stains caused by an overflow of some liquid content.

Other storage jars have a high rounded shoulder, a tapering body and a short flared neck. The handles, when horizontal, are placed somewhat low down at about the widest point of the jar (Fig. 27d); when vertical, they meet the lip of the vase and so produce an oval-shaped mouth (Fig. 26f). Several of the most splendid of these storage jars come from Phaestos and so date from the period of the early palace.

One in particular decorated in the grand manner is exceptionally effective. It is a tall jar of globular conical shape with narrow neck and two rather low horizontal handles (Fig. 27d). The decoration consists of four linked scrolls. The outer angle where the connecting tangent leaves each scroll is painted red, and from it project spiky leaves. A diagonal line runs across the centre of the pattern from left to right to join the top and bottom scrolls. In the spaces left on either side of it are objects that look like falling leaves in red and white. The whole pattern is enclosed in a circle which might be taken from the outline of a seal-stone, and it seems feasible that the vase-painter adopted and enlarged the design taken from a seal-stone to decorate this impressive vessel.

Another large jar of ovoid shape with pinched-in mouth from Phaestos has broad vertical divisions of alternate buff and brown separated by white lines (Fig. 27e). In the buff divisions is a design in brown rather like the trunk of a palm tree with a white centre. On the brown divisions is a vertical running spiral pattern in white with scarlet flowers floating about in the field.

The commonest form of vase from the Kamares cave is the small two-handled spouted jar, a characteristic Cretan form. In its early form it has a pair of vertical handles and at right angles to these a spout, generally open above but which in later examples have a clay bridge.

A beautiful example is shown in Colour Plate IId. Below the handles are two white bands encircling the body. Above them is an orange band with a row of crimson discs. Above this again is a row of white crocus plants with anthers shown in red growing in rocky ground. Round the lip is a row of white scallops. The whole design is drawn quite freely, but without any loss of decorative effect. We may be sure that the naturalistic design of this pot was borrowed from some other art, and we have good reason to believe that this art was fresco-painting.

Another splendid example of the Kamares ware of this period is a black bridge-spouted jar found at Knossos decorated on the front and back with an elaborate design in white and orange (Colour Plate IIIa). In the centre is a circular design of five-tailed stars that rather remind one of a Catherine wheel. Surrounding this are four orange-coloured carrots which in turn are surrounded with more stars in circles, and groups of three leaves. Below the handles at the side is a fleur-de-lys. It makes a complicated but beautiful pattern that combines conventionalised natural as well as abstract motifs. It is the highest achievement in this direction.

These bridge-spouted two-handled jars decorated in the Kamares style are particularly characteristic of MM I B and of MM II. One from the Kamares cave has a striking floral design rather like a large daisy or the chrysanthemum on the Japanese flag. It is almost identical with one found at Abydos in Egypt in which there were found cartouches of Sesostris III (1878–1841 BC) and Amenenhet (1842–1797 BC). Another example is decorated with a remarkable design to look like conglomerate.

Yet another shape characteristic of MM II is the fruit stand, consisting of a shallow bowl standing upon a tall stem (Fig. 26e). These fruit-stands are decorated with elaborate designs that embody the most varied selection of motifs forming a close pattern covering the whole surface of the vase. One found at Phaestos has radiating petals in the bowl and formal bands of petals and lozenges on the stem.

Among the smaller vessels of MM II are the cups. A typical shape of the period is the pedestalled cup usually with a band of white paint on the dark background below the rim. They are very like those of MM I A but the body of the cup is more rounded and slopes gradually down to the pedestal.

Another type of cup, more appropriately called a mug, is comparatively straight-sided but widening towards the top (Fig. 27a). It has a small strap handle, the top of which is level with the rim of the cup. These small strap handles are indicative of MM II. The mug has a background of dark gloss with an almost metallic lustre over which is painted a design in white rather more creamy than in MM I and more fugitive than in EM III.

Besides the shapes described above are others which are derived from metal originals. One of these is similar to the gold Vapheio cups and the shape continues for a long time. Other particularly beautiful ones have real fluting or are painted to imitate it (Fig. 27g).

Also in imitation of metal is the embossing to be found on some vessels of this period. A good example is a spouted mug from Phaestos with cockle-shells in relief on the outside round the lower part of the body with corresponding marks of fingers on the inside which show where the clay was pressed into a mould.

A form of decoration which started in MM I but which became popular in MM II are the bands of paint or the outlining of bands so as to imitate veined marble, and another form of decoration that imitates stone is

Fig. 29. Patterns on Middle Minoan II pottery continued

obtained by white dots like the flecks on liparite (Fig. 27b) – a form of decoration probably inspired by IVth Dynasty Egyptian originals.

Generally speaking, the designs of MM II may be said to be of two kinds: 'abstract-geometric' such as circles, crosses, spirals, swastikas and zig-zags, and 'conventionalised-naturalistic' such as leaves, palm-trees, radiating petals and crocuses (Fig. 29).

Towards the end of MM II, polychromy tended to die out, especially in the smaller jugs and cups which were decorated with spiky foliate bands like the trunks of palm trees (Fig. 28), a decorative motif that is contemporary with the pointed tips of petals of the great sunbursts that mark this phase (Colour Plate IIIc).

Some examples of representation of flowers and plants herald the approach of a naturalistic impulse which was to develop so powerfully during the course of the next two centuries.

The Middle Minoan II period ended in a disaster about 1700 BC, a disaster which affected the whole island, for its destructive effects are evident not only in the eastern end of the island at Palaikastro, but also in the north at Knossos and Mallia, in the south at Phaestos, and at Tylissos, most westerly of the Minoan settlements. The three palaces of Knossos, Mallia and Phaestos were laid in ruins.

An earthquake seems the more probable cause of the disaster, for a number of deposits at Knossos and Phaestos were covered in, leaving them unmixed with the remains of later periods. At Pseira, Mallia, Mochlos, Gournia and Palaikastro, a similar disaster seems to have occurred at the same time. At all these sites the succeeding MM III period seems to have begun immediately, but at Vasiliki the shock may have wiped out the population, for it was not reoccupied.

It is only on the assumption of some catastrophe such as a severe earthquake that we can account for the complete break which occurs between MM II and MM III. That it was not a disaster brought about by enemy invasion seems clear from the absence of burning which would no doubt have occurred if the island had been sacked, and also from the continuity with which MM III follows on after MM II.

One would also suppose that if the destruction had been caused by an armed raid, the palaces would have been fortified when they were reconstructed as a precaution against similar attacks in the future. This, however, does not seem to have been done.

MIDDLE MINOAN III 1700–1580 BC

MM II closed with the disaster which affected all the Minoan settlements and destroyed the palaces. Whatever the cause of this catastrophe, the

Colour Plate IIIb opposite
Photo: Hannibal, Greece

a. Bridge-spouted jar
Knossos

b. Beaked jug
Phaestos

c. Beaked jug
Phaestos

d. Stemmed krater
Phaestos

Plate III. Middle Minoan II 'Kamares style' vessels

palaces were rebuilt more magnificently than before, representing an even more magnificent way of life.

MM III marked the beginning of a new era in Crete. It marked the rise of the great palaces whose ruins we see today. Although the plans were considerably altered in detail later, the layout of the foundations is substantially the same today as it was three thousand six hundred years ago.

These great buildings presuppose a centralisation of wealth and the achievement of position by regal families of whose path to power we have no knowledge. They were symbols of the country, part palace and part administrative centre. In their complex group of buildings, they housed princes, courtiers and officials; clerks, artisans and storekeepers to serve the offices, granaries, store-rooms and workshops. Their elaborate interiors and their fresco-covered walls demonstrated the artistic vigour of the country and the genius of its craftsmen. Self-sufficiency was the keynote of Cretan life. It was a close-knit and highly-developed society, free from want, and with an economy based on overseas trade, agriculture and crafts, many of which depended upon the patronage created by the court and whatever strange deities were worshipped.

The Cretans lived in a robust age, confident in their maritime shield. Not only did the island recover quickly from the disaster, but the population increased appreciably during the century and a half of MM III. The centre of power remained at Knossos, although Phaestos must have wielded considerable influence, judging by the size of the palace. It is probable that the small palace of Aghia Triada was built early in MM III.

Closer contacts with Egypt and Anatolia stimulated the natural inventiveness of the Minoans to produce a culture both derivative and original.

In ceramic art we seem to see the operation of a more restrained taste which reduced the wild exuberance of the preceding period to a greater orderliness of idea. By the end of MM III the forms of the vases had become less grotesque, and pottery became more sober in form and decoration.

Another advance was in the potter's kiln where a higher temperature became possible. But this technical change was attended by the disadvantage that the heat burned the colours, so that orange, carmine and vermilion were no longer a possibility.

MM III consequently showed some deterioration in ceramic style. It must have received a set-back owing to the earthquake at the end of MM II, and possibly more attention was being given to the making of vessels of bronze. The continuity of various decorative motifs indicates that there was no complete break between MM II and MM III, but no longer was the lustrous black paint used, and red paint hardly at all. Colours were reduced to black and white with touches of red and yellow, but they lost much of their brilliancy, and shapes became less graceful.

But the beginning of Middle Minoan III also marked the unseen beginnings of a new era elsewhere than in Crete – beginnings that were to grow in size and strength until three hundred years later they caused the destruction of Crete.

It was in the years following the earthquake of 1700 BC that the first Cretans landed on the Greek mainland and settled in Argolis. They were the emigrants who first imported Cretan culture to the Peloponnese and, mixing with the mainlanders, created that civilisation which two hundred years later we know as Mycenaean.

The huge pithoi or casks (Fig. 31a) standing well over six feet high and with a circumference of some fifteen feet are a fascinating product of MM III. At Knossos gigantic examples have been found and can still be seen there in their original positions. They are of similar shape but somewhat more elongated than the conventional wooden barrel and have rows of handles round the body to help in moving them. Their principal decoration is an elaborate rope pattern imitating the rope cradle in which they must originally have been transported. This rope pattern helps to distinguish the pithoi of MM III from those of earlier periods. According to the old technique which goes very far back, the ropework ornament had been pressed into relief by the thumbs. In place of this, some flat instrument, probably of wood or bone, was now used, by which a succession of overlapping tongues of clay were produced.

Fig. 30. Rope pattern motif on pithoi

Many of these pithoi are also decorated with knobs in relief strongly reminiscent of metal work, and on some are impressed discs or circles.

These enormous vessels with their bulging bodies and wide mouths were used for the storage of large quantities of wine, grain, oil, honey, figs and the like. They were sometimes sunk in the ground as cellars. A corridor some eighty yards long running north and south along the west side of the palace of Knossos gives access to more than twenty storerooms which still contain their stocks of huge great pithoi. When full these casks were closed with a circular stone or a cover of clay. Sufficiently capacious to hold a man, the famous 'tub' of Diogenes was of this shape. These great vessels were made in sections, sometimes on a framework of

b. Jar, trickle pattern
Knossos

a. Pithos, rope pattern
Knossos

c. Beaked jug
Mochlos

d. Storage jar
Pseira

e. Jug
Knossos

Fig. 31. Middle Minoan III vessels

ozier or wood. The sections were joined to each other by a tongue and groove, and the junction was concealed by a band of clay which was the one moulded into the rope pattern.

It is possible that a tournette or slow wheel was used for making these huge containers, for although the pithos may claim a great antiquity among Greek vases, similar pithoi are made this way today in the village of Thrapsanos about twenty miles to the south-eastward of Knossos just as they must have been made three thousand six hundred years ago (Fig. 32). Today, as in antiquity, they are used for the storage of food and drink, but today and perhaps also in antiquity, they are used to form chimneys of cottages, and perhaps most strangely of all, as containers for the trousseaux of brides. The inside of the pithos is first lined with sheets and then the girl's dresses, bedspreads, aprons and other linen articles are carefully folded as they are made, and stored till the day of their transfer to her new home.

Other and smaller storage jars have two horizontal handles, slightly below the rim of the vase, and some four.

Others have vertical handles joining the shoulder to the lip of the jar and so form an oval-mouthed amphora (Fig. 33d), a shape peculiar to Crete where it dates from MM II onward and becomes common in MM III. Some jars of the period are so narrow for their length that they are almost tubular (Fig. 31b).

Another large vessel characteristic of this period is a tall storage jar of truncated piriform shape curving slightly outwards towards the top which presents the peculiarity of a false or atrophied spout or even a mere knob just below the rim (Fig. 33), thus showing evidence that they were originally derived from handled jugs with spouts for pouring.

Two fine examples of these from Knossos have a striking decoration on an almost lustreless purple-tinted slip: one (Fig. 33a) has a cruciform pattern of four axe-like spokes radiating from a central ring with sprays between each limb like blades of grass which also appear beneath the handles, the other (Fig. 33b) is decorated with white lilies on a black ground. This latter is a purely naturalistic design and marks the acme of realism in Cretan vase painting. Its date would be rather later than 1600 BC.

One of the best-known vessels discovered at Phaestos of this period is a fine amphora over eighteen inches high (Fig. 33c). On its lustrous black background are painted three palm trees in dull white with outlines in red. It shows the intrusion of naturalistic motifs into a period characterised almost entirely by conventional ones. It is interesting to note that the palm tree still grows wild in Crete.

Lastly among the larger containers are the burial jars. One of the most

Fig. 32. Making pithoi today

a. Storage jar
Knossos

b. Storage jar
Knossos

c. Amphora
Knossos

d. Amphora
Pseira

e. Flask
Zakro

f. Storage jar
Knossos

Fig. 33. Middle Minoan III vessels continued

a. Burial jar
Mochlos

b. Burial jar
Pachyammos

c. Suspension pot
Knossos

d. Beaked jug
Knossos

e. Cup
Mochlos

Fig. 34. Middle Minoan III vessels continued

beautifully decorated vessels of this type comes from Mochlos (Fig. 34a). It is a very fine example of MM III monochrome light-on-dark style. Just below the neck is the chain pattern of horizontal S's which is of very early origin, and can be traced back to the Early Minoan period. Between the handles are pairs of incised double-axes picked out with a border of white dots which have almost entirely disappeared. On the body of the vase are two rows of linked spirals extended into an ogival shape. The general design is a favourite one in this and the succeeding period.

From Pachyammos near Gournia comes another fine burial jar with a design of dolphins and sea-foam (Fig. 34b), while yet a third has a decorative motif in the form of a six-rayed star surrounded by a circular arched border (Fig. 33f). This border is an enlargement of a rosette pattern in which the dark petals are traversed by white rays.

Among the most typical vessels of the period are the cups, but with larger handles and more spreading rims than in MM II. Two of these come from Zakro with a tendril pattern.

A differently shaped cup from Mochlos (Fig. 34e), although simply and formally decorated, is one of the most graceful and charming among the cups of this period. It has a high swung handle, a vertical rim and a swelling body coming sharply in to the base. It is decorated with a form of meander pattern which is unusual in Minoan art, but it is interesting as it shows that something like the meander ornament of classical Greece was already known and used a thousand years earlier by Minoan artists. This is an additional piece of evidence that much of what is admired in classical Greek art was derived from this earlier Aegean culture. Both in form and design it is one of the most graceful examples of the potter's art yielded by the cemetery of Mochlos.

A number of interesting vessels come from eastern Crete with some new patterns. One of these is known as the 'ball and racquet' design which consists of three loops leaving a central disc at a tangent. In view

Fig. 35. 'Ball and racquet' or 'propeller' motif

of its sense of rotation, a more appropriate name would seem to be 'propeller' or 'Catherine wheel'. A few vases decorated in Barbotine style and dating from this period have been found at Knossos.

A curious form of vessel also found at Knossos is a round vase with a flat base and a ring at the top for suspension (Fig. 34c). The only opening is a large round hole at the side surrounded by an outward curving or flaring lip. At first it was thought that they might have been lanterns to shelter small clay lamps, but all the lamps discovered were too broad to pass through the opening, nor has any trace of smoke been found in them. Sir Arthur Evans suggests that they may have been hung up for swallows to nest in. A somewhat similar form with a knob on top called a 'salt kit' was used in the Midlands in England to keep salt in.

Another vessel, also of somewhat similar shape, is shown in Fig. 22 of a pamphlet *Pots and Pans of Classical Athens*, published by the American School of Classical Studies at Athens.

Fig. 36. Patterns on Middle Minoan III pottery

G

The pamphlet calls it an 'Amis' and describes it as a convenience, while local opinion seems to be that it was carried round by an attendant at a festival to enable guests to relieve nature. As the Minoan civilisation seems to have been little less socially sophisticated during MM III than the classical about a thousand years later, is it possible that the vessel in question may be a Minoan 'Amis'?

Generally speaking, vases of MM III may often be recognised by their dull purple slip and powdery white paint. They differ, therefore, from the ware of the preceding period in the loss of the fine lustrous black ground, and the decline of polychrome decoration. From LM I vases on the other hand, they are distinguished by the frequent use of white for the main design instead of for minor details of the decoration.

Since we are making a survey of Minoan pottery, we should not perhaps forget to mention a branch of ceramics not generally referred to in works dealing with this subject. The new Cretan palaces of MM III incorporated remarkably fine systems of fresh water supply, of sewage and drainage for their domestic quarters.

Great lengths of clay piping were laid to deal with these amenities, made up of pipes about twenty-seven inches long. These earthenware pipes are tapered so as to fit into one another where they are cemented and have collars to prevent them jambing.

The end of MM III was marked by another catastrophic earthquake involving the destruction by fire of a large part of the west wing of the Palace of Knossos, probably once again associated with an explosion of the volcano of the island of Santorin (Thera). It seems that the other Cretan sites were not seriously affected.

LATE MINOAN I 1580–1450 BC

The earthquake at the end of MM III seems to have acted as a spur to the Minoans, and by the early years of LM I Crete found herself in the middle of the greatest and most flourishing era of the Greek Bronze Age.

It was the era covered by the MM III, LM I and LM II periods from 1700 BC to 1400 BC – the three hundred years succeeding the disaster which caused such destruction in Crete about 1700 BC.

In the Late Minoan period we are confronted with a vast mass of material. Although this period is called Late, one must not associate any idea of decadence in power or in art with its first two stages. It was in them that we see a second and even greater climax of Minoan civilisation, the one we particularly associate with the name of King Minos.

These stages represent the full development of the Aegean Bronze Age, when the influence of Knossos was paramount in that area and along the shores of Greece. In spite of fundamental differences between the Minoan and Mycenaean civilisations, there were many features which were remarkably similar in both, and it is evident that the arts of the Mycenaean world were both derived and largely influenced by those of Crete.

In LM I it seems that in spite of this powerful influence, both Crete and Mycenaean Greece were separate and independent states, each maintaining its own contacts with Egypt, Syria and Anatolia.

The wealth of Crete may be assumed from the superbly decorated ceramics of the period which have been excavated, while that of the Greek mainland is evident from the rich contents of the shaft graves of Mycenae, uncovered by Schliemann, and which date from this period. It is only with the last stage that the Minoan decline becomes apparent.

In 1918 separate systems were proposed by archaeologists for the civilisations of Crete (Minoan), the mainland of Greece (Helladic) and for the Aegean Islands (Cycladic). These three systems in their last phases are almost parallel, since from the beginning of the Late Bronze Age in about 1580 BC the material culture of the whole Aegean area was more or less uniform.

Crete entered upon an even more prosperous period than she had known in the preceding century. Although it was a peaceful period, the roads were well guarded as is apparent from the number of sites which may have been small forts or posting stages along the course of the main road between Knossos and Phaestos, and on to the unexcavated port of Komo. It was the highway of Minoan civilisation, though perhaps it would be more in keeping with the peaceful character of the Minoan civilisation and the convivial Cretan habits that these buildings were taverns rather than forts.

By LM I Crete had become a strong power governed from Knossos, with her influence extending to the mainland of Greece. It is a period that represents the height of prosperity for the smaller towns of Crete.

During this period, which coincided with Mycenaean I (or Late Helladic I), Cretan artistic ideas spread over the whole Aegean area, largely supplanting earlier local traditions. The Achaeans, intrusive Greek-speaking tribes from the north, who were already settled in Mycenae and the other citadels of the mainland, had learnt painting and the other arts of civilisation from the Minoans, and so started the Mycenaean civilisation.

Ceramically speaking, LM I is divided into two phases: LM I A and LM I B. Broadly speaking the vessels of LM I A are decorated with vegetable motifs, those of LM I B with marine subjects. In the pages that follow, vessels are described in order of shape, and therefore belong, with some exceptions, to LM I A or LM I B according to the class of decoration. The separation between the two phases takes place about 1510 BC.

The pottery of LM I strikes an entirely new note of naturalism in its painting. While the Kamares potters took their inspirations from the natural world but conventionalised them, their successors used nature in a fresh spirit. In LM I A the designs are full of grace and exuberance. Grasses, ivy, crocuses and lilies were shown in a more natural style. Reeds and flowers and stems with long pointed leaves adorn their vases. With a true instinct for beauty they chose as their favourite flowers the iris and the lily, the wild gladiolus and the crocus, all natives of the Mediterranean basin.

The precision in vase decoration which the newly aroused interest in natural objects required, was obtained by an improved technique. The fine black gloss which had formerly been used for the ground colour was now used for the designs themselves, and a subtler polychrome was discovered by using the natural tones which clay and gloss acquired in firing. The clay of the background varies from pale yellow to warm brown, and the black gloss of the designs shades with the oxydation of the iron in it through olive green and brown to red, while the whole surface shines with a soft lustre. These processes, as in fact the whole manner of ceramic decoration, were a Minoan invention, and of all Minoan inventions, they are the most evident in the artistic heritage of classical Greece.

It is worth noting that a revolution in their use, the change from Black Figure to Red Figure design, occurred in Attica about 500 BC, ten years or so before the Battle of Marathon, and was occasioned by a similar demand for greater clarity in drawing natural objects. In Crete the change came at the parting of the Middle and Late Minoan periods, about eleven hundred years earlier.

The vase decorator of LM I B was specially concerned with the life of the sea and all the wild things that are in it. These he reproduced with astonishing fidelity, and his designs had an enduring influence upon ceramic tradition. His choice is to be explained not only by the intrinsic beauty of his subjects but also by the local conditions in which they were produced.

The sea was the highway of the settlements which fringed the coasts of prehistoric Crete. The members of the ruling class derived their wealth from overseas commerce, while then as now the sea provided much of the food of the poor. The inhabitant of the Cretan shore or the islands of the Archipelago may not necessarily have been a sailor, but he must always have had an interest in fishing, and a familiarity with the sea and

a. Peg-top filler
Phaestos

b. Ritual sprinkler
Palaikastro

c. Stirrup jar
Gournia

d. Lentoid flask
Palaikastro

e. Cretan squat alabastron
(*Found Egypt*)

Fig. 37. Late Minoan I 'Marine Style' vessels

its fruits. The flesh of the octopus was a delicacy, while the triton sup-plied him with food and its shell with a trumpet. At ports where fisher-men and sailors, divers for sponges and purple-shells called and departed, it was natural for an imaginative and creative race to acquire a sense of the magic and mystery of the sea, and a curiosity about the life in its depths, which found expression in the ceramic pictures which enlivened its vases. It was, therefore, marine plants and animals and shells which formed the principal subjects of interest to the vase painter of this period.

It is indeed an open question whether the shells painted upon the Minoan vases are murex or triton (Figs. 37b and 38b). The artist seems to combine the spiky surface of the one with the elongated shape of the other. One thing is clear, however, and that is that the Cretans had antici-pated the Phoenicians in the manufacture of purple dye. Banks of pounded murex have been discovered along the coasts of Crete and its off-shore islands associated with Middle Minoan vases. When we remember that these coasts are still visited each summer by fleets of caïques from the centres of sponge fishing, we may hazard a guess that sponges as well as purple dye were among the wares exported from Crete to her markets in the east.

It was the octopus and the nautilus that exercised a special attraction for the vase painter of the period. The octopus, that prince of marine monstrosities with the flexible shape that will fit any surface; the octopus with his spiral coils that made such perfect material for the Minoan artist, and which he could adapt to an endless series of designs for an endless variety of vessels; the octopus which lives in the side of the rocks and stretches out his long black arms, and can make night come when he wills.

The nautilus, which has a boat of her own carved out of an opal and steered with a silken sail; the cuttlefish with waving tentacles swimming among shells and starfish; the dolphins and the sea-snails and the gardens of the sea where the filigree forms of coral wave, and anemones grow on the rocks. All these adorned the surface of his vase which the potter fashioned at his fancy.

It was a style unique in the long history of Greek vase painting at a time when there was a taste for natural objects. Some of the vase painters of the period were great artists.

Many lovers of Minoan pottery consider that it was at its best during LM I as showing a purity of artistic spirit that is not always found in the great palace vases of the next period. The polychrome abstract and con-ventionalised patterns of MM II, or the severely simple motifs of MM III, were succeeded by the flying fish, the argonaut, the octopus and the worn limestone rocks of the Cretan coast fretted by the waves into fantastic forms with bunches of seaweed streaming out from them (Figs. 37 and 38). It was a pleasing fancy to have the cold liquid in the jars surrounded by this display of marine life.

The greatest triumph of LM I vase painting is the wonderful octopus on the globular stirrup-jar from Gournia now in the Archaeological Museum at Herakleion (Fig. 37c). It stares at us with fierce, glaring eyes. The monster's sucker-covered arms writhe all over the surface of the vase, with one of them gripping its neck.

The spaces that are left are filled with bits of coral and seaweed. Looking at it one may imagine the vase as a stone which the polyp is grasping tightly with its tentacles in the depths of a rocky pool. The design, which is a favourite theme of this period, is eminently suited to the curved surface of the pot; and its decorative character is emphasised by simplification of both drawing and colour.

The shapes of the vessels, although simple, show a wonderful sense of form, and amongst the types introduced into this period is the filler vase – sometimes called the funnel vase and sometimes the conical rhyton (Fig. 38).

The filler vase was perhaps a vessel used for filling larger pots with liquid. In its simplest form it is an inverted cone open at the top where it has a small handle. These long conical fillers seem to have been first introduced into Crete from the East. Examples from Gournia are decorated with bands of running spirals (Fig. 38a), or of connected rosettes with their thick outer circles and solid central discs so characteristic of LM I.

Large quantities of LM I pottery now in the Archaeological Museum at Herakleion come from the little Minoan town of Gournia near the eastern end of Crete.

Some of the vases are painted in the fashion prevalent at the end of MM III, namely with white designs on a dark ground, but more numerous are those painted in the beautiful fully developed technique of LM I with a dark glossy paint on the light ground of the clay. A combination of the two techniques of light-on-dark and dark-on-light is characteristic of this period.

I trust the reader will not regard it as a piece of selfish nostalgia for a glorious cloudless morning in 1961 when I stood among the grey stone ruins of Gournia covered with brilliant yellow poppies, if I give a short account of their discovery exactly sixty years earlier.

It was in the spring of 1901 that Miss Harriet Boyd Hawes, with her friend Miss Wheeler, paid her second visit to Crete under the aegis of the American Exploration Society of Philadelphia. She was so inspired with enthusiasm by the results of the British and Italian excavations at Knossos

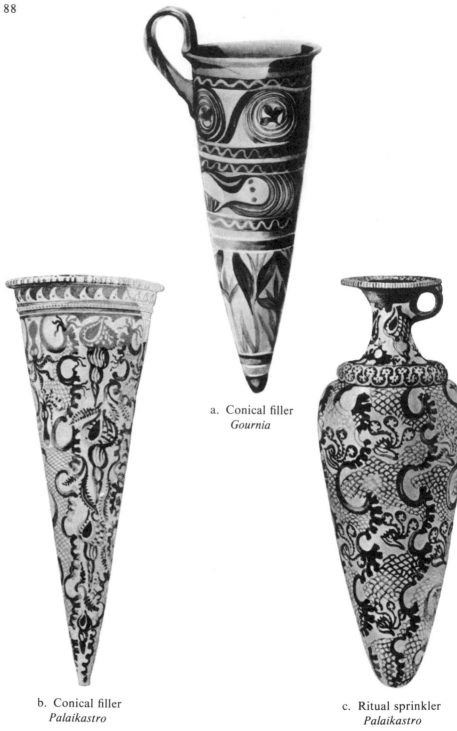

a. Conical filler
Gournia

b. Conical filler
Palaikastro

c. Ritual sprinkler
Palaikastro

Fig. 38. Late Minoan I conical fillers and ritual sprinkler

and Phaestos, that she longed to discover a Bronze Age site and to excavate it herself. After consulting Sir Arthur Evans she selected the narrow part of the island at Hierapetra, which she felt sure would have been used as a thoroughfare by the Minoans, and decided to explore it carefully. The two ladies rode up and down looking for a likely spot. At last a peasant heard of their search, and sent word through the local schoolmaster that at a place called Gournia he could show them a hill not far from the sea overlooking the steep slopes of the gulf of Mirabello. Here, he said, there were bits of pottery and old walls. In May 1901 they met the peasant at a roadside inn, and after walking for nearly a mile they came across the tops of some ancient walls nearly hidden by thick vegetation.

They wasted no time, and it was arranged that on the very next day thirty men should make trial excavations on the site. To their delight it soon became evident from the great quantity of finds that they had lighted upon a prehistoric settlement which had been lost for some three thousand years. Within three days they had unearthed the foundations of a small town with paved streets, and discovered a great quantity of pottery decorated with octopus, ivy-leaves, double-axes and other unmistakable Minoan designs.

They had discovered a Bronze Age settlement of the best period of Cretan civilisation. For the three excavations of 1902, 1903 and 1904, they increased the number of their men to a hundred, with ten girls to wash the potsherds. The result was the uncovering of one of the most interesting and fruitful of the smaller sites in Crete.

It always seems as if the name rhyton should not be applied to these funnel and filler vases so long as the same term is applied to a totally different class of vessel which appears in an infinite variety of fanciful shapes, principally in the form of animals' heads. Conical fillers all end in a hole at the bottom, and no satisfactory explanation of their use has yet been offered; but from the prominence given to them in wall paintings at Knossos and Thebes, where metal conical vessels are borne in processions, and in view of their rich decoration, it seems probable that they played a part in important functions of a religious or ceremonial character. (See special note on Conical Wine Filters, page 287.)

Another vessel, related perhaps to the conical filler, has a small mouth with projecting lip and a shoulder ring separating the neck from the ovoid- or pear-shaped body (Figs. 38 and 39). It has hitherto been called a rhyton or pear-shaped filler and much speculation has been aroused as to its purpose, although it was apparent that it must have served in religious ceremonies.

There would seem little doubt, however, that it was a ritual sprinkler.

At the present moment, hundreds of vessels of similar size and somewhat similar shape are made in Rhodes and other islands of the Dodecannese (Fig. 39e). These are filled with a mixture of water and perfume made locally in the villages for ritual sprinklings at baptisms, weddings and funerals and for sprinkling the bier of Christ during the sacred procession on the evening of Good Friday. Many examples made of glass, about a hundred years old, are to be found in the antique shops of Rhodes and Crete.

The vessel is known as a *kani* or *kanaki*, which means a ritual sprinkler. Just as in the similar vessel of about 1500 BC it has a small hole at the lower end and a somewhat larger one at the top which can be corked or plugged. There would seem little doubt that the Minoans also used this vessel for ritual sprinkling on religious occasions like those of the Orthodox Church today. In a similar way the Roman Catholic Church uses a vessel called an Aspersory or Aspergillum for sprinkling the people with holy water before High Mass. It is so called from the words in verse 7 of Psalm li, *Asperges me, Domine, hyssopo* (Purge me with hyssop).

For this reason, it is suggested that the words rhyton or filler be abandoned to designate this type of vessel, and that the word ritual sprinkler, aspersory or kanaki, all of which have the same meaning, be used instead.

Two delightful examples of this type of sprinkler from Palaikastro show great skill in decorative composition (Figs. 37b and 39b). The wide space on the shoulders is filled with a design of rock-work and seaweed enclosing a large star, while the tapering murex shells are well adapted to the narrowing field lower down. There is some difference of opinion as to whether or not the star is meant to represent a starfish. On the one hand it is treated much more conventionally than other forms of marine life on this vase, and it may be that the star is meant to have some religious significance symbolical of the light above. Whether meant symbolically or naturalistically, it certainly has a great aesthetic value in the design.

One of similar form is clothed with a fantastic web of rocks where conch shells lie in crevices under waving weeds, and little cuttlefish lurk in pools. Another bears a rhythmical design of argonauts sailing among jagged rocks (Fig. 38c). It is a curious fact that these sprinklers, which certainly served in religious ceremonies, seldom occur singly but in hoards, and in point of design there is a tendency for them to go in pairs.

These three sprinklers from Palaikastro belong to a set of seventeen which were found standing side by side on the floor of a room. As ritual vessels, they serve as an example of the love of nature revealed in the religious art of Crete. The Minoan religion was a worship of nature. Its sanctuaries were in mountain solitudes, gorges and caves where devotion must have led to an intimate understanding of the life and beauty in the works of nature.

Two more beautiful examples of this class of sprinkler must be mentioned, both from Pseira on the Gulf of Mirabello, also in the eastern part of Crete. The decoration of one consists of dolphins swimming up and down the vase in a pattern of dotted scales or the meshes of a net (Fig. 39a). The other shows strong influences of the LM II Palace Style (Fig. 39c). The motif is evidently that of a date palm, and although not yet in the stiff architectural style of the full Palace period, the design is already close to those of the great jars of Knossos with their lotus and papyrus.

This oviform or pear-shaped sprinkler seems not to have made its appearance till the end of LM I when it attained so great a popularity as almost to exclude the conical straight-sided filler, although the conical shape survived into LM III after the bottle shape had disappeared with the end of LM II. Whether ovoid sprinkler or conical filler, both forms seem to be derived from a metal original, and we can imagine that they were made in bronze or gold for use in the royal palaces as we see just such a filler borne by the well-known cup-bearer in the fresco at Knossos. Sprinklers were also made in a number of other graceful and interesting shapes. Globular ones (Fig. 39d) from Gournia and Zakro are directly derived from the ostrich egg, while a 'Peg-top' sprinkler, from Pseira, is decorated with running spirals (Fig. 39f).

The classical term 'rhyton' belongs, strictly speaking, to a late class of vases terminating in animals' heads for use as drinking horns at banquets. Owing to the analogy in form due to a hole at the animal's mouth, the word has been applied to this Minoan class of libation vessel used for religious purposes. Although a large number were made in clay, by far the most famous is the celebrated steatite bull's head rhyton (Fig. 40b). It has been largely but very skilfully restored, and is a most remarkable object. The horns which seem originally to have been made of wood were fixed in position by square attachments secured by a locking pin. The ears were also fixed into sockets. In the neck behind the horns is a fairly large hole for pouring in the liquid, and in the mouth is a smaller one for allowing it to escape slowly. The eyes are of red crystal, one of which is original and the other a copy. Long hairs which are engraved about the face of the animal show that it was of a shaggy breed.

The religious symbolism of animal head rhytons is confirmed by the appearance also during the LM period of lions' or lionesses' and dogs' head rhytons among Minoan and Mycenaean remains as these animals are also associated with the cult of Minoan divinities.

a. Ritual sprinkler
Pseira

b. Ritual sprinkler
Palaikastro

c. Ritual sprinkler
Pseira

d. Egg-shaped sprinkler
Zakro

e. Modern sprinkler
Rhodes

f. Peg-top sprinkler
Pseira

Fig. 39. Late Minoan I and modern ritual sprinklers

a. Waisted strainer
Mochlos

b. Bull's head rhyton, of steatite
Knossos

c. Double jug
Gournia

d. 'Shopping bag'
Pseira

Fig. 40. Late Minoan I vessels

Animal heads, evidently representing rhytons, are shown among the vessels borne as offerings by the Kefti chieftains in processions represented on Egyptian tombs. Among the Cypro-Mycenaean rhytons found at Enkomi in Cyprus is a glazed ware example in the form of a ram's head. Rhytons of typical Minoan class in the form of a dove with a large opening on the back and a smaller one in front of the head have also come to light among Hittite remains in northern Syria.

The largest vessel of LM I, as it was in the preceding period, is still the great pithos, of which the palaces of Knossos and Phaestos provide innumerable examples (Fig. 41). Many of them are very similar to those of MM III except that the rope pattern has degenerated into wavy bands with slightly curved incisions, and into ordinary bands surrounding the vessel.

A special pithos, peculiar to this period, is known as the medallion pithos (Fig. 41d). A number of these have been found in the Palace of Knossos. They are enormous vessels, rather more elongated and less bulged than the pithoi of MM III.

A fine example over six feet high has four rows of handles. Between each row are three clay bands decorated with small incised circles, and between each handle are two circular rope grommets surrounding a boss and so forming the medallion, of which there are no less than thirty-two and from which this pithos takes its name. These medallion pithoi of LM I seem to have continued in use up till the end of LM II.

A particularly beautiful example of a large pithos is at Mallia (Fig. 41e). It is decorated with incised clay bands, a wavy rope pattern, a vegetable motif, and large running spirals, all moulded in relief. It is perhaps the most decorative of all Minoan pithoi so far discovered.

Another remarkable shape (Fig. 37c) which derives from Crete, and where it first appears in the latter part of LM I, is a closed pot with a false neck flanked by two handles, and a short tubular spout to one side. It originated in the two-handled jar with pinched-in mouth which had become common in the MM III period. It is known as the stirrup or false-necked jar. It has been found in immense numbers not only in Crete but all over the mainland, and persists right through the later Minoan and Mycenaean periods. It exhibits many variations of size, shape and decoration, but by studying decoration as well as shape it is possible to date it, and so provide valuable chronological evidence for the levels at which it is found. A notable feature of some of the earliest stirrup jars is that they have three instead of two small handles attached to the false neck. The peculiar form of the stirrup jar with stopped up neck where the mouth should be, while the spout itself sticks out lower down, is easily explained.

a. Cylindrical jar
Gournia

b. Barrel jar
Gournia

c. Barrel jar
Mochlos

d. Medallion pithos
Knossos

e. Pithos
Mallia

Fig. 41. Late Minoan I jars and pithoi

The potters of MM III had closed their wine or oil jars in the usual way with clay over a stopper. Since this stopping was a trouble to remove, they left it in place and adopted the easier method of boring another hole in the jar to one side into which they inserted a tube. Then some potters imitated this arrangement in a new jar, and produced a pot with its original mouth permanently stopped up and a tubular spout at the side. The new shape, which was original and striking, became popular, and the stirrup jar then became one of the commonest forms of Bronze Age pottery.

As mentioned above, the globular one from Gournia decorated with the octopus (Fig. 37c) is the most striking example so far excavated, but a great many other graceful and beautiful examples have also been found.

Other forms of vessels characteristic of LM I were the great variety of jugs with beaked and bridged spouts of which a bridge-spouted jug from Pseira decorated with argonauts and rock-work forms an excellent example (Fig. 42a). The shape of this vase betrays a metal prototype by the clay 'rivet' which fastens the handle to the body.

One cannot leave the subject of jugs without mentioning two beautiful examples from Gournia and one from Palaikastro. The first is a large trough-mouthed jug of metallic tradition which shows itself in a clay pellet imitating the rivet where the handle joins the rim, a prominent neck ring, a deep groove in the foot and a pair of small horns on each side of the rim (Fig. 42b).

The jug itself is of smooth medium-pink clay with a decoration in many intermediate shades of blue and purple. The important accessories are picked out in white. The main decoration consists of a broad band on the upper part of the jug with a design of five large conventionalised ivy leaves in which the lobes are white rosettes filled with dots. The rest of the jug is covered with bands of spirals and dots, some in dark-on-light, others in light-on-dark.

The other jug from Gournia is entirely different in both shape and scheme of decoration (Fig. 42c). A bridged spout projects from a wide rim that converges sharply to a small foot. Opposite the spout is a ring handle, now unfortunately broken. The jug itself is of fine pink clay with decorations in red or shading from bluish to black. The base is covered with a solid wave, the curve of which is repeated in a band just above it. The principal design in a free field combines a double-axe and sacral knot (secular and religious emblems) that occurs three times interspersed with circles of dots. Light bands cover the outside of the spout and a forked ornament is painted below the handle. The neck and shoulder are ornamented with bands of drop ornaments separated by a row of dots.

a. Bridge-spouted jug
Pseira

b. Trough-mouthed jug
Gournia

c. Bridge-spouted jug
Gournia

d. Jug
Phaestos

e. Bridge-spouted jug
Palaikastro

Fig. 42. Late Minoan I jugs

Although less than five inches high, it is an exquisite little jug both in shape and decoration, and the whole design is strongly influenced by metal art work.

The jug from Palaikastro has a long bridged spout, a cylindrical neck and is of characteristically Cretan shape (Fig. 42e). The main decoration consists of a large sweeping design in gracefully curved bands and lines, the 'ogival canopy' pattern of Sir Arthur Evans in a broad zone, with above and below a conventional motif suggestive perhaps of the waves of the sea. The characteristic bordering rows of small dots add to the decorative effect. On the neck is a series of simple connected spirals, and the top of the rim is, again, marked by dots, while the gracefully curved handle bears a succession of slanting lines. All this is painted in black paint on a grey ground. The design is a conventionalised representation of seaweed growing from rocks. An almost identical jug was found by Professor Blegen at the temple of Hera near Argos, but painted in red.

Finally, perhaps the best known of all Minoan jugs is the one from Phaestos covered with an overall pattern of grasses (Fig. 42d). It has a steeply rising beaked trough spout and wide shoulders tapering steeply to a narrow base.

Among the larger vessels are some splendid oviform and pithoid jars with two tiers of four handles, forerunners of the famous 'Palace Style' jars of LM II (Fig. 43).

Fig. 43a shows a fine burial jar from Mochlos of the LM I style, and belongs to the early part of that period. The ripple design which covers the base seldom appears in the LM I stage and is more characteristic of MM III. Round the middle of the jar is a curious design in white on a black band that incorporates a number of spirals and perhaps thistle leaves, but the design is unique. It uses a good deal of red, especially in a band just below the handles which shows that the polychrome tradition of the Middle Minoan period still continued in the early part of LM I. The shape is also unusual in this period but has a most graceful curve.

A superb jar from Pseira is ornamented with facing bulls' heads carrying double-axes between the animals' horns and below the handles (Frontispiece). This large jar is one of the finest examples of LM I that has been found in Crete. The use of white paint for the details, and the chalky red band on the rim prove that it belongs to the last stages of the period. The design of bulls' heads and double-axes is conventionally treated, for such a combination does not lend itself easily to naturalistic treatment. It is the olive sprays on either side of the axes that bear witness to the love of naturalism which characterises the artist of this period.

a. Burial jar
Mochlos

b. Jar
Pseira

c. Burial jar
Pseira

d. Jar
Pseira

Fig. 43. Late Minoan I jars

The lower zones of the jar are decorated with splendid examples of the various types of spirals and highly conventionalised ivy-leaves with which the LM I potters loved to adorn their vases, and which one meets over and over again during this period.

From the lavish use of the double-axe motif it is probable that this jar had some ritual or royal purpose. It was the Cretan symbol of sovereignty. It appears upon the top and sides of the rim, between the horns of the bulls' heads, under the handles, on the base, and even the handles themselves take their shape from this imperial symbol. The large axes on the shoulder bear on their blades the same designs in white paint that occur so often on seal-stones and in scenes of ritual worship, and which presumably represent the manner in which the axes were decorated, perhaps by silver inlay or by coloured silk ribbons wound round them. Round the rim is a row of small holes through which a needle could be passed to sew a cloth covering over the top of the jar. Alternatively could it be that the holes were not for a cloth, but for stretching a skin, and that the vessel was used as some sort of a drum? Is it possible that by rubbing the fingers over this skin, a noise akin to the roar of a bull could have been produced? Such vessels have been found in France and are known as *Tambours à Friction*. The splendid results obtained by the slip are well shown here where the coarse clay is covered by a heavy coat of finer clay, so well polished that there is no sign of the rough clay beneath.

The bulls' heads are painted in a dark gloss with trappings of white which rather contradicts the idea that the bull most acceptable to the gods was white, but in this case a white head on a light buff background would not have provided sufficient contrast. This vase represents the highest level of technical achievement in the ceramic art of LM I in which the qualities of paint, gloss paint and slip are unsurpassed by either earlier or later wares in the Minoan era.

Another jar (Fig. 43d), also from Pseira, of rather different design, and with two tiers of six handles each, is covered with a design of linked spirals. It must have been designed for ornamental rather than practical use as its small base would make it very top heavy if filled with any liquid. The moulded rim, on which some chalky white had been employed, seems like an imitation of a round well-head deeply worn by the grooves of a bucket rope. The body is of coarse clay covered with the usual polished buff slip which, except for a zone near the base, is covered with a network of connected spirals in dark gloss paint, picked out with white dots. The lower zone, separated from the rest by dark bands, is decorated with a row of large loose spirals. The whole jar looks as if it might well derive from a metal original with a spiral metal net in relief with the white dots inlaid in silver.

Another jar of precisely similar design, except that it has a plain rim and is slightly taller, keeps this one company in the Herakleion Museum.

Two other large jars, although one is from Gournia and the other from Pseira, have a remarkable family resemblance (Fig. 43c). Both have projecting rims, ornamented with vertical lines. Both have four vertical handles on the shoulder ornamented with zebra stripes. Both have a band of 'ball and racquet' (two-lobed whorls) design round the greatest width of the jar, although in the case of the Gournia jar, this motif alternates with a double-axe. In both cases the lower part of the jar is ornamented with tufts of grass or leaves. Both have projecting bases. There are a number of minor differences in the ornamental designs of the two vessels; but it is evident that the vase designs of both were either by the same person or inspired by a common source.

These large jars are, of course, much smaller than the great pithoi, but the name pithoid jar may be conveniently applied to them. In the case of the large pithoi, the handles would have been used for actual ropes to assist in moving them. In the case of the pithoid jars, the handles are merely ornamental and serve no utilitarian purpose.

Among so many graceful shapes it is difficult to select one more graceful than another, but certainly the oenochoe or ewer must rank high among the remarkable Minoan vessels which first came off the potter's bench in LM I. It must certainly owe its origin to a metal prototype, for the potter still preserved in clay the rivet that joined the top of the handle to the wide-spread lip.

There are two exceptionally beautiful specimens representative of this class of vessel. One was found at Palaikastro in 1904 (Fig. 44b), and was the finest vase unearthed that year. It probably dates from about 1480 BC. The clay of the vase is pinkish covered with a warm buff paint with the decoration in reddish brown. This consists of a branch rolled into a great leafy spiral ending in a flower. The vessel itself is most gracefully shaped, swelling upwards from a narrow base, and crowned by a wide-brimmed lip.

The other (Fig. 44a), although somewhat uneven, is of a still more graceful shape. It is one of the best known of all Cretan vases and is called the Marseilles Ewer as it is in the Marseilles Museum. No certain details of its discovery are known, though it is believed to have been found in Egypt.

It is quite small, being just under ten inches high. The principal motifs of the design are a number of nautili swimming among rock and seaweed, and painted, like the Palaikastro ewer, in dark brown on a buff ground. Both these ewers may well have come from the same workshop.

Another ewer from Palaikastro (Fig. 44c), also of LM I but of a rather

a. The Marseilles Ewer

b. Ewer
Palaikastro

d. Libation vessel with
figure of eight shield
Knossos

c. Ewer
Palaikastro

e. Tall alabastron
Aghia Triada

f. Squat alabastron

Fig. 44. Late Minoan I vessels continued

less graceful outline than the other two, is interesting as showing how more formal elements were invading the field of vase decoration. The decoration consists of an imaginary plant bearing conventionalised papyrus flowers which rest their fan-shaped heads upon the wide shoulders of the jug. The large rosettes which complete the design are the painter's idea of what his flowers would look like if viewed full-face. It is a design which belongs to the end of LM I and tends towards the grandiose 'Palace Style' of LM II which led in due course to the Mycenaean formalism of LM III.

A particularly interesting shape characteristic of this period is represented by the polychrome libation vessels found at Isopata, just north of Knossos, shaped like graceful buckets with two high figure-of-eight handles (Fig. 44d). The finest of all (not illustrated here) bears a spiraliform design in blue with black outlines on a Venetian red ground, and horizontal bands with the same colouring. Round the vase just below the rim is a series of red discs – a tradition from the Middle Minoan period. From a painting upon a sarcophagus we learn that these buckets were used for libations in front of sacred double-axes at Minoan shrines. Unfortunately, the colours are comparatively fugitive, which only goes to confirm that these vessels were for religious use, as the powdery Egyptian blue would not have stood the wear and tear of daily handling.

Two other vessels slightly smaller but of similar form were also discovered in the same tomb with the same spiraliform decoration, but in the case of these two, one has a figure-of-eight shield (Fig. 44d) and the other a crested boar's tusk helmet with ear-pieces superimposed over the spiral decoration.

In a neighbouring tomb at Isopata was found another vessel of the same class with double-coiled handles. In this case, however, it had a dome-shaped cover, in the top of which is a round hole. It also was probably used for holding libations. Like the others, it was originally, in all probability, covered with a design in fugitive Egyptian blue and Venetian red, but in this case they are entirely obliterated. A number of these picturesque vases have also been found at Aghia Triada and Phaestos.

A vessel of undoubted Cretan origin, found in Egypt and of Egyptian make which has been found in Crete, is the tall alabastron (Fig. 44e). The earlier specimens are of alabaster and the later ones of clay with a decoration which is clearly an imitation of the veining of the original alabaster alabastra.

Another notable and curious shape that made its first appearance during this period is the squat alabastron with its designs of conventionalised rocks (Fig. 44f). Such alabastra were no doubt made to contain

Fig. 45. Patterns on Late Minoan I A pottery

some sort of unguent or oil for anointing the body, and these LM I prototypes were much copied, with variations, during the Mycenaean II period
on the mainland of Greece. Squat alabastra may in fact be a mainland
invention as they also occur in Mycenaean I contexts and are more
plentiful than in Crete.

A vessel which appears to be peculiar to LM I alone and without successors in later periods, is a bulbous-shaped vessel on a pedestal (Fig. 40a),
examples of which have been found at Mochlos and Gournia. In describing the one from Mochlos, R. B. Seager calls it a 'waisted strainer',
for the base is pierced with small holes to form a sort of strainer. The
decoration, he says, shows LM I at its best and displays a technique new
in that period. The colouring and decorative scheme are certainly attractive, for the upper global part has little white four-petalled flowers painted

Fig. 46. Patterns on Late Minoan I B pottery

on a pinkish ground that shades to pale orange. A band of feather-like ornaments runs round the middle. The base is painted with conventionalised lilies, a design not uncommon in LM I.

Among other noteworthy shapes of LM I are the double-vase (Fig. 40c), which consists of two small jug-shaped receptacles joined at the rims by an arching handle and again at the widest point of the body. The right-hand receptacle has a wide mouth, the left-hand one is a spouted jug with a diaphragm across its neck pierced with fifteen holes so as to form a strainer. A tubular connection joins the two recipients.

A beautiful example has been found at Gournia made of bright pink clay. The decoration of both receptacles is identical. Across the greatest width is the principal design, a mollusc or nautilus occurring several times on each jug; shells and tentacles are outlined with dots. In the background are small flower-like objects. On the neck and upper part of the jugs are bands of varied brush work; while below the principal decorated zone are six horizontal bands with zig-zags in the two upper spaces between the bands. The rim and handles are of solid colour.

A number of very beautifully decorated cylindrical jars (Fig. 41), some almost purely cylindrical, some barrel shaped and some in the form of a flower pot, have been unearthed at Gournia. Of the former, a good example has a flat projecting rim, a spout and five handles just below the rim (Fig. 41a). A thick wave pattern above and below a narrow central band encircling the jar forms the principal decoration, while a fish scale pattern is painted below the spout. The whole decorative pattern is extremely simple but impressive.

Of the barrel-shaped jars, a good specimen has a low collar, the top of which is ornamented with a number of radiating white lines (Fig. 40c). Although broken, it has just below the rim three vertical and two horizontal handles. The jar itself is of coarse pink clay with a pale yellow slip of low lustre. The decoration of the top half consists of four large waves and two small ones. The small waves are plain while the large ones are ornamented with a double arch over a rough spiral motif. The lower part of the jar is ornamented with white dots on dark bands and dark dots on a light band. The whole decoration is carried out in black-red paint.

A large flower-pot shaped jar (Fig. 47d) has no spout, but a flat rim ornamented with radiating white lines. Below it is a narrow rope moulding. Below this moulding are vertical and horizontal handles ornamented with white stripes. The top part of the jar is ornamented with lilies and crocuses, white dots and ascending 'plant-spirals'. Dark waves outlined in white divide this zone into panels. The lower half of the vase is ornamented with a series of three bands. Between the top two are dots, surrounded by circles, and above the lower bands is a row of running spirals.

Another splendid barrel jar (Fig. 41b) from Mochlos of somewhat different form, which has a spout and a lid, is of its kind perhaps the best example that has come to light. It belongs to the most advanced stage of LM I decorative art in its beautiful range of colours. The principal decorative motif appears to derive from the date-palm with its irregular trunk although the design is very much conventionalised. Round the base are three bands of dark lustre paint on which is painted a ripple design in white, a continuation of the MM III ripple wave tradition. Both the red and the white paints on the vase are extraordinarily well preserved, and except near the base where the action of the salt has caused the surface to flake away, the jar is in a wonderful state of preservation.

Of the cups, some are small and handleless and unpainted. Some have handles of the 'Vapheio' shape and a spiral decoration.

Others are lower and more rounded, and generally adorned with sprays of leaves, sprays which are often painted in matt red (Fig. 47b). Others again are goblet shaped with a single high-swung handle (Fig. 47a).

A round box which might be called a pyxis (Fig. 47c), with raised rim, two horizontal handles and three spiral legs is an unusual and attractive form of jar. It has a domed lid with handle which is decorated with black circles, while the decoration of the box itself is in black-brown paint in bands, spirals and a degraded fern spray. The handles have stripes on them.

Two unusual vase shapes of LM I remain to be mentioned, one is known as the lentoid flask (Fig. 37d). The best-known example was found at Palaikastro in Crete and has an octopus design strongly reminiscent of the famous globular stirrup jar from Gournia. The other is a bag-shaped vase decorated with double-axes found at Pseira (Fig. 40d). It is not particularly graceful but presumably takes its inspiration from a leather shopping bag, if such things were used in 1500 BC.

Before going on to deal with the Late Minoan II period, mention must be made of the most important archaeological event in Crete for half a century. This is the discovery of a fourth Minoan palace at the eastern tip of the island by Professor Nicholas Platon at Kato Zakro. Kato Zakro lies in a bay with a safe anchorage facing east, a favourable position for overseas trade in antiquity.

In 1901 excavation by the British School of Archaeology in Athens under the direction of Dr Hogarth uncovered some outlying houses there, but since that time little further work had been done on the site.

In 1961, Professor Platon reopened excavations in the hope of finding a palace. His efforts were soon rewarded by the discovery of large sections of buildings including a long corridor with store-rooms leading out of it like the 'Corridor of the Bays' in the Palace of Knossos. They were evidently part of a Minoan palace of imposing size. In the store-rooms were found a number of large storage pithoi of the LM I period similar to those at Knossos.

As excavations proceeded, it seemed evident that the buildings had been destroyed in some catastrophe, perhaps by earthquake associated with fire in the LM I B period, somewhere about 1500 BC.

a. Cup
Knossos

b. Cup
Gournia

c. Pyxis
Gournia

d. Flower pot
Gournia

e. Mug
Gournia

f. Stirrup jar
Gournia

Fig. 47. Late Minoan I vessels continued

For some reason, the palace does not seem to have been rebuilt after its destruction like the other three at Knossos, Phaestos and Mallia at the end of MM III. Moreover, unlike the others, it appears to have remained unplundered from that time onwards. The result is that spectacular discoveries of the highest importance have been made, many of which are displayed in a special room in the Archaeological Museum at Herakleion for the delight of visitors.

By the early part of 1964, about two thousand square yards had been uncovered, or an area estimated at about one-third of the whole building. Among the treasures brought to light are elephant tusks, bronze ingots and a cauldron, gold riveted swords, a bronze ceremonial double-axe, as well as graceful chalices of richly veined marble, basalt, obsidian, alabaster, porphyry and rock crystal.

Two specially noteworthy discoveries are of steatite, one a splendid bull's head rhyton like the one at Knossos but smaller, and the other an elongated oviform vessel exquisitely carved in low relief of a building rising from a rocky landscape. Some wild goats leap among the rocks and four others are seated on the roof over a doorway ornamented with running spirals. In the domain of ceramics, a vast treasure of some two thousand vessels had already been unearthed by the spring of 1964.

Apart from the great quantities of storage pithoi, mostly adorned with rope-work ornament, many splendid examples of vessels characteristic of the end of MM III and early LM I have come to light.

Among them are pithoid jars, beaked jugs, stirrup jars, cups and fruit stands, conical fillers, ritual sprinklers, many painted in the marine and floral styles characteristic of these periods. One specially graceful jug is decorated with argonauts. It so closely resembles the famous Marseilles Ewer that there seems little reason to doubt that both come from the same workshop.

Finally, a discovery of much interest lay in the archive room. It consisted of a dozen or so of Linear A tablets similar to those found at the Villa of Aghia Triada. The tablets, it is hoped, will make a useful contribution towards the decypherment of Linear A inscriptions.

All the indications are that the palace and its neighbouring houses flourished for only a short period during MM III and LM I when they were finally destroyed for ever.

LATE MINOAN II 1450–1400 BC

The fifteenth century BC saw the rise of an even more powerful dynasty at Mycenae. It was probably this dynasty which conquered Knossos just before the end of LM I and gradually extended Mycenaean sway over the rest of the island, although from the evidence of the rich burials in Crete as well as Mycenae, the general level of prosperity in Crete was even higher than before.

The animated naturalism of LM I did not last long. By the beginning of the next period, the decorative motifs, both floral and marine, were treated differently and stylised; and the last vestige of Kamares pottery disappeared. The eager imitation of nature vanished, and conventionalism triumphed. Lilies and palm trees stiffened; the octopus and the nautilus became formal designs rather than live animals, and a new form of decoration more architectural in style came into favour, with some return to the older taste for spirals and waves. The new style was peculiar to Knossos. It was the pottery of the empire.

It is known as the 'Palace Style' (Fig. 48) and harmonises well with the grandeur of the royal palaces reconstructed after their destruction by earthquake at the end of MM III. This form of decoration which characterises the vases of LM II is often very splendid to look at, and the conventionalised variations designed by the artists of this period fully harmonise with the interior decoration of the apartments themselves.

The keynote of this Palace Style is pomp and splendour, and its stately style reflects the magnificence of the last dynasty of the Cretan kings. Before AD 1900, the boldest could never have imagined that in this island of the Mediterranean, a race of men had developed a civilisation so rich in the satisfaction of the senses and for the mind, a thousand years before the age of Pericles. The Palace of Knossos was a town in itself. It stood four stories high on the east side, and covered a floor space of some five acres. Companies of skilled craftsmen and artists worked within the palace walls.

Vessels became larger than in LM I, and form was more carefully studied. A favourite shape was the pithoid or piriform jar, usually with three vertical ribbed handles and with high shoulders curving gracefully down to a narrow moulded foot. It is worth giving a thought to try and find the most appropriate name for these vessels, for when we think of Minoan ceramics, it is perhaps these stately vessels which come first to our mind. Sir Arthur Evans referred to them as 'amphoras', between inverted commas. Later writers have left out the commas and refer to them as amphoras. But the amphora is a two-handled vessel or jar which can be carried from both sides, therefore with or without commas it is not a really good name, more especially as it is applied in Minoan, Mycenaean, Classical, Roman and even modern times to vessels which are of a type bearing little resemblance to the great three-handled jars so characteristic of Late Minoan and Mycenaean times. Some writers call them piriform jars, but piriform means pear-shaped. Some, it is true,

b. 'Palace Style' jar
Knossos

a. Trough-spouted jug
Knossos

c. Three-handled beaked jug
Knossos

e
Knossos

d
Knossos

f
Knossos

Fig. 48. Late Minoan II 'Palace Style' jars and jugs

are pear-shaped, but others certainly are not. Moreover, the term seems rather pedantic except in special cases to define a particular shape.

Sir Arthur Evans gave the name pithoid jars to those vessels of the class when they had more than one row of handles, a feature characteristic of the pithos to assist in moving it by hand or with ropes, although in the case of the pithoid jar, the lower rows were only for ornamental purposes and were later abandoned. Furumark, however, applies the name pithoid jars to all vessels of this class, and for lack of a better word it would seem best to follow his example. Specimens have been found at Pseira, Palaikastro and Gournia, but they were probably brought from Knossos. They have a formal, stylised type of decoration, in some ways a reversion from the naturalism of LM I.

The Palace Style of vase enjoyed a wide popularity outside Crete, and examples of it were exported to all parts of the known world. The princes of Mycenae and of the other citadels of the Greek mainland were eager to obtain them for the decoration of their palaces in life and to furnish their graves in death. The style continued right up to the end of the LM II period when the Cretan palaces of Knossos, Phaestos and Mallia were ruthlessly destroyed about 1400 BC. With the destruction of the palaces, the Palace Style also disappeared.

A form of decoration inherited from LM I is the formalised octopus waving its tentacles in regular spirals symmetrically on either side of the animal instead of crossing in all directions as they did in the vases of LM I (Fig. 48b). It is characteristic of this grandiose phase of ceramic art that the animal should occupy nearly the whole field. Suckers gradually disappear and instead of the varied and interesting details of LM I, they are succeeded by a rather monotonous background of stippled sand.

Dolphins occur, but very formally treated. Little of the pot was left undecorated. There was an advance, both technical and decorative. This may have been partly due to some influence of Egyptian art, but mostly it was a manifestation of contemporary artistic fashion in vogue at the court of the kings of Knossos, for LM II pottery in Crete was practically confined to Knossos alone.

By far the most magnificent creations of the palatial ceramic style, however, were unquestionably the stately jars decorated with highly stylised plant groups, largely based on the conventionalised papyrus. It is this exotic plant with its long associations with the Nile valley, that the Cretan artist transferred to his own island and made the principal plant element for the decoration of the Palace Style vases.

Another source of many of the composite plant forms that are employed on these great vases belongs to the frutescent palm-tree motif

a

b

c

d

Fig. 49. Late Minoan II 'Palace Style' jars

which plays so large a part in the evolution of Minoan decorative art.

It was indeed a heterogeneous collection of elements woven together, that formed the grandiose plant compositions on these great Palace Style vases. The papyrus spray, and the sacred wand, the indigenous lily, the reed and the palm, all contributed in varying degrees according to the taste of the painter to their highly composite decoration. Sometimes one element predominates, sometimes another. It seems to have been some passing desire on the part of the rulers of Knossos to glorify their power that found expression in these grandiose ornamental jars, decorated in the brilliant Palace Style of LM II. On them, the utmost resources of the potter's craft were lavished, for they represent the highest achievement of the LM II period. Let us take a look at some of them.

The surface of the jar is divided into bands, with the principal decorative zones occupying the body, while neck and foot are covered with other zones of ornamental patterns such as white wavy lines on a dark ground.

A frequent decoration for the shoulder is a single or double band of drop pendants, while the main designs consist of a stylised octopus, a

Fig. 50. Band of drop pendants

great plant composition, or what Sir Arthur Evans calls an architectonic form of decoration. A taboo long prevailing in the art of vase decoration prevented the inclusion of human figures in the design of these vessels. The aim was not so much picturesque beauty as stateliness of effect by the use of a monumental style of decoration.

A jar shown in Fig. 48b is decorated with a polyp with ten carefully delineated tentacles and, therefore, probably belongs to the Haledon species rather than an octopus. Its arms are symmetrically arranged without overlapping, and the only other decorative elements in the field of this vase are sprays of seaweed falling from the handles, and a wisp of sea grass rising from below them.

The lower zones have a waved linear pattern. It will be seen in this example of the Palace Style series that in the case of cuttlefish decoration there is a progressive disappearance of natural motifs while the octopus arms are reduced to symmetrical sinuosities.

This fine jar was found in what Sir Arthur Evans calls the Tomb of the Double Axes at Knossos, and in the same grave were also found two particularly graceful jugs, one a fine spouted jug with the wavy linear striations as its principal decoration (Fig. 48a). In describing this vessel (*Archaeologia*, **65**), Evans points out that this motif is directly inspired by the same one on the walls of the Palace.

The other is a beaked jug (Fig. 48c). It has a globular body with three handles to the neck. Just below the neck is a band of crested spirals while the large and small rosettes on the main part of the body are exact reproductions of some of the commonest features in the fresco decoration of the LM I period.

The noble jar on Fig. 48d has a central plant motif which is interesting in that the papyrus blossom which is still close to its Egyptian prototype, and the lily which is characteristic of LM I, have become confused so as to form a combination of both, but it is the lily motif which flowers from the stems on either side of the central plant itself, where the filaments of the stamens are linked by double curving lines. The outer edge of the rim of this vase has what is sometimes known as the 'adder mark' in its earlier form with a dot as well as a wave.

The jar shown on Fig. 48f, presented to Sir Arthur Evans, and now in the Ashmolean Museum, has a design displaying another combination of some of the elements on the preceding example. It shows a remarkable restraint in its arrangement with each plant standing up separately.

The jar in Fig. 48e is a work of profound imagination and magnificent design. It illustrates perhaps better than any other found at Knossos the conscious love of display that characterises these fine vases of the mature Palace Style. It was most skilfully put together from a number of scattered pieces and the picture gives a complete restoration of the jar. It is lavishly decorated with a stately papyrus-lily design most splendidly conventionalised, and although the sprays use the same elements as in the previous example, they are thicker and more closely set together, so that a much richer effect is obtained. Both this jar and the previous one have shoulder zones of drop pendants with reduplicated edges, a close imitation of the rims of the bronzework bowls from a hoard discovered in the North-west Treasury building of the Palace. The flat upper rim of this jar is decorated with the 'adder mark' pattern.

Another jar (Fig. 49b) which shows a similar metal-work pattern round its shoulders is unique in style. In this case the stems of the floral motif which rise from the foot are merely fine threads. The two halves of the body, moreover, are separated in a curious manner by upright waving bands, somewhat suggestive of serpents descending from the handles.

To take another example, Fig. 49a shows a three-handled jar of which the upper part is fairly complete, but a considerable portion of the base is missing. The band of ornament that runs round the shoulder varies on the two sides, but in both cases the motifs are spiraliform designs, derived in all probability from metal work. The double lines of connected spirals in particular recall the decoration of a gold oenochoe from Mycenae. The other pattern somewhat resembles the papyrus motif.

The field below this shoulder zone is divided into three parts by foliate sprays descending vertically beneath the handles. The three spaces thus divided off show a uniform decoration of very crude conventional sprays, evidently done in haste by the painter, and which are of a distinctly decadent style by contrast with the rest of the vase.

Two beautiful jars (Colour Plate IVc and Fig. 49d) show a certain family similarity of execution. The wave design (Kymalion) sweeps round the neck and foot of both vases, and the plant designs, stiff and conventional though they are, are splendidly decorative.

Although all the wonderful charm of the octopods of LM I has gone, yet the wavy loop which is all that remains of their tentacles, forms a grand design. A curious return to the style of MM II is shown in the preference for rosettes. Not only do they occur as separate decorative entities, but they are introduced as a secondary enrichment of other motifs. Many of these typical LM II jars are very large. They are small pithoi.

Of great interest is another jar (Fig. 49b), also from the collection of splendid vases from the 'Royal Tomb' at Isopata just north of Knossos. It is almost twenty inches high and the middle part of its body is surrounded with details of an architectural character, although these 'triglyphs' are really composed of pairs of highly stylised papyrus heads placed sideways. On the shoulder just below the neck is a band of crested running spirals, and the wide zone just above the foot is decorated with a series of elongated arches.

One very common motif which appears on this vase is the double drop pendant pattern that surrounds it in a band at the level of the handles, and also falls in bands from beneath the handles to divide the body into three parts. It may be that the idea was taken over from a metal prototype. It is natural that the cheaper clay should imitate the more costly bronze or copper, but the popularity of this ornamentation is doubtless due to the ease with which it can be applied with a brush, especially in narrow bands where there was an edge to help the decorator to keep the pattern even. Nevertheless, the fact that it has already been found on vases of LM I combined with the ease of application make it possible that its use in ceramics is as old as it is on metal vases.

Two tall jars of the 'pithos' type are particularly worth noting. One (Fig. 51a) is about forty-seven inches high and is decorated with vegetable clumps in relief. These plants are intended for papyrus with its triple shoots just below the rim of the vase encased in overlapping sheaths, which in the natural plant only belong to the base of the stems. On either side of the spray are raised medallions, which might be meant to represent the sun and the moon. On one side of the vase the central knob of these circles is impressed with stellate flowers, and on the other side by flowers with rounded petals. The water is indicated by means of undulating lines between the stalks.

The other most interesting vase of a similar 'pithos' type has four handles near its upper border and four near its base (Fig. 51b). Four double-axes with long shafts are ranged between the upper handles and four with short handles are placed symmetrically between them. Rosettes appear in the field beneath the handles and in two cases are placed over the shaft of an axe for decorative purposes. Reeds rise from the ground. They are mostly of naturalistic form but have fringed leaves. The edges of the double-axes are reduplicated, a common feature when these weapons are represented in a rather heraldic manner. Transverse bands which never appear on the axes made for actual use seem, as mentioned before, to represent some sort of ribbon wound round the blade for ceremonial purposes, or possibly coloured bands round consecrated weapons.

In all pottery of the great Palace Style class of decoration, the design is usually in a brilliantly lustrous gloss varying from brown to black, while surface effects are locally varied through intentional differences in firing that to begin with would have been accidental.

The constant recurrence of the double-axe device in Minoan art is remarkable because it has no outstanding decorative value for the vase painter. It is the only weapon that ever appears on Knossian pottery – never swords, sheaths or daggers, and only rarely a figure-of-eight shield. Evidently the object had an interest of its own apart from any decorative value. The reason is no doubt to be sought in the realm of religious or heraldic symbolism.

The fact that arrows, swords and chariots were stored in the arsenals of the Palace of Knossos proves that the Minoans were familiar with hunting and warfare, but battle scenes are conspicuously absent in their art. A number of tombs dating from LM II came to light in 1950 and 1951 at Aghios Joannis near Knossos which, to judge by the number of bronze weapons found in them, were those of warriors.

These graves, although modest in style, were so richly provided with weapons that they presumably belonged to members of some military aristocracy who commanded the bands of light armed troops or foreign auxiliaries at the disposal of the Minoan sovereign. It is from the style of the vases also found with the weapons that the grave can be dated to LM II, and their occupants were, therefore, presumably laid to rest not long before the final destruction of the palace about 1400 BC.

a. Large jar with papyrus
   decoration in relief

b. Large jar with double ax

c. The 'Bird' jar

d. Jar with argonauts

f. Beaked jug with argonauts

e. Squat alabastron

Fig. 51. Late Minoan II vessels from Knossos

Nevertheless, warfare seems to have been less popular than the arts of peace. The chief Minoan divinity was an earth goddess whose worship can be traced back to the Stone Age, and her function was the production of life, not its destruction.

A strange feature is the large number of squat alabastra found in these tombs (Fig 51e), because few alabastra of the squat form assignable to so late a period as LM II have been found in Crete, although a good many have been recovered from the mainland. It is, therefore, probable that this style of vase was of mainland origin, and that the early examples found in Crete were imported from overseas. In two of these Knossian 'warrior-graves' they were the only clay vessels found. The designs on them belong to the rather special series of 'rock patterns' that appear on Mycenaean mainland alabastra.

As for the three-handled pithoid jars found in these graves, the surface of the vases had in several cases suffered severely from the action of the soil so that the designs were difficult to distinguish; or showed up in silhouette with the parts from which the paint of the design had disappeared standing out lighter than the background as in the case of the 'Bird' vase (Fig. 51c).

It is interesting to compare the photograph of the vase with the drawing of it made by Mr P. de Jong in *B.S.A.*, XLVII, Plate 56 where he has reconstructed the design in black against the light background as well as a development of this bird and flower design (*B.S.A.*, XLVII, pp. 266 and 272). This naturalistic scene of birds among flowers may have been copied from or inspired by some fresco.

A stately little Palace Style three-handled jar of the same find is decorated with conventionalised papyrus and 'sacral ivy' similar to those found on the great pithoid jars of the Palace itself.

One three-handled jar and one beaked jug (Figs. 51d and f) have been decorated with conventionalised argonauts, which are of interest since argonauts have not so far appeared as a decorative motif of the great Palace vases on which the principal marine animal is the octopus. On the other hand, the octopus does not appear on any of these vases from Aghios Joannis.

Some changes were made in the pithoi of LM II. They were no longer decorated with rope work. Raised bands encircle the body at intervals, with wavy bands between them. These are sometimes decorated with various kinds of incision, particularly the herring-bone.

The stirrup jar becomes less globular and more piriform (Fig. 53c), and for this vessel shown at Fig. 53d the decoration is mostly a uniform pattern of scales and wavy lines all over the body except for the neck and shoulder where the favourite ornaments are rosettes.

Fig. 52. Patterns on Late Minoan II pottery from Knossos

Some stirrup jars are still ornamented with an octopus but highly formalised.

An important vessel of this period is the drinking vessel generally known as the two-handled pedestalled goblet (Figs. 53e and f).

In dealing with drinking vessels of the Minoan and Mycenaean periods, we are faced with the difficulty that no real standardisation of nomenclature has been agreed for a fairly wide variety of forms. Wace reserves the term 'kylix' for the tall stemmed goblet with one or two handles of LM III, or Myc. III and which, except for the handles, corresponds in shape most closely to our wine glasses. It is a name which seems very reasonable. For this shape, Furumark who is so meticulous in his analysis of shapes, uses the word cup, a term which does not really convey the

Colour Plate IVc opposite
Photo: Hannibal, Greece

(4) a. Polychrome jug
MM I

b. Amphora
MM III

c. Palace style jar
LM II

Plate IV. Middle and Late Minoan vessels from Knossos

a. Cup
Knossos

b. One-handled goblet (Late LM I)
Phaestos

c. Stirrup jar
Knossos

d. Stirrup jar

e. Two-handled goblet
Knossos

f. Two-handled goblet
Knossos

Fig. 53. Late Minoan II stirrup jars and drinking vessels

wine-glass shape to English-speaking people. Not only this, but he uses it for the predecessor of Wace's 'kylix', which, as stated above, is generally known as the two-handled pedestalled goblet and which made its appearance in LM II. Nevertheless, the dictionary definition of the goblet is a drinking vessel without handles, while our word glass for a drinking vessel is inapplicable to one made of clay.

As a measure of clarification, it might seem worth trying to obtain an agreed standard nomenclature for the various forms of pre-classical drinking vessels through the recommendations of a committee, for they form a significant part of the ceramic finds of the Minoan and Mycenaean periods. Meantime we must do our best without.

The earliest pedestalled goblets date from the very beginning of Minoan ceramic art, and even go back to the Late Neolithic Era. An interesting specimen from Vasiliki of EM II date shows its metal derivation by imitation rivet heads.

It was not, however, till LM II that clay pedestalled goblets of the stage prior to the true stemmed type or kylix made their appearance with handles on either side of the bowl. The band type of handle shows again that they were derived from metal originals. Some of the early specimens had only one handle, while the lower part of the bowl narrows as it approaches the base but without forming a stem. A specimen from Phaestos illustrates this phase (Fig. 53b). In this case, the clay imitation of a rivet head at the junction of handle and rim clearly points to a metal prototype.

Experience seems to have shown that a second handle was a convenience, and by LM II the two-handled form was coming into vogue, when it was the usual, if not practically the only, form of drinking vessel in use at Knossos, and conforms to the types grouped by Furumark as Myc. II B. The stems of these goblets from the Palace were hollow and presumably reflect metal models. This hollow stem is not, however, found in such vessels from the mainland.

It was not till LM III that the solid high-stemmed kylix of 'champagne cup' form appeared. This really belongs to the Mycenaean repertoire and becomes so universal throughout the Greek world that it is found from Crete to northern Greece on the one side, and in Rhodes, the Aegean Islands and Cyprus on the other.

Generally speaking, the rest of the pottery of LM II does not differ greatly from that of LM I, but before leaving the ceramics of this period, a few words should be said at this stage about household objects and domestic utensils which were virtually common to the whole of the two periods (Fig. 54). A huge quantity has been unearthed, and as far as the excavations at Gournia are concerned, it may be said that for every decorated vase, a score of undecorated pots and kettles was unearthed. One is tempted to ignore these ordinary and somewhat unattractive vessels, but if we did so we should lose something important in our picture of the past, for these domestic utensils are rooted in reality.

Even without the presence of the choicer specimens, the wide variety of ordinary household vessels found at Gournia would prove that its inhabitants were far removed from barbarism. The potter moulded his clay into a remarkable variety of shapes to fill needs for which today we should perhaps use wood, glass or metal. From them we can discern a well-developed standard of living. The houses of Gournia were amply provided with large and small storage jars as well as with amphoras and jugs for the daily supply of food and drink.

Pithoi are among the commonest vessels found on prehistoric Aegean sites, and their modern counterparts may be seen in the houses and shops of Crete for the storage of oil and wine and food, more particularly in the remoter districts. At Gournia as at Knossos there are two principal types, the earlier being of greater girth in proportion to the height than the later.

Amphoras are also of two types – the earlier form, slender and a little stiff with elliptical mouths, and the Late Minoan or Mycenaean type with fuller body, more flowing lines and a round mouth.

Fire boxes are common to all Aegean sites. In their simplest form they seem to have been intended to keep a fire alight. With a handle they also served for heating and also possibly as an incense burner. Fire boxes were, however, made in quite a variety of different shapes. They usually have a dome on the top, while the lower part is pierced with a number of small holes and one large one. All Cretan Minoan sites yield them in varying forms, and the box part frequently shows signs of burning.

In this connection, a number of 'chafing dishes' or braziers have been discovered. Those found in tombs have sometimes contained bits of charcoal and resinous matter inside. In this case, they may have been used for ritual fumigation of the sepulchral chamber. They are shaped something like an inverted hat with a broad rim, one side of which, near the handle, is turned up to protect the hand from the heat of the glowing embers inside. These ritual vessels had their counterpart for domestic use.

Dippers and scoops were made in artistic shapes. Saucepans and other pots were numerous. Tripod kettles or cauldrons were made to stand directly over a fire, but other forms suggest such arrangements for cooking as can be seen in the cottages of modern Crete: a raised hearth built of stone or clay, coated with plaster, and with recesses for faggots between the ledges which support the pots, or a simple method of resting the pot on stones or earth.

Hand lamps with ring or loop handles are forerunners of the usual classical type of hand lamp. For large lamps, the development seems to have been from the simple bowl-lamp to a standing lamp with bowl for oil and a heavy rim or projecting lugs for lifting it.

Among less familiar vessels is the oil vat for washing olive oil. After washing the olives in hot water and pressing them, the product contains more water than oil. The oil rises to the surface and the water is drained away from the bottom. By the two handles in front over the spout, one can turn the vat. At the back is a handle by which one can tip it. This vessel may also have been used for pressing juice from grapes.

During the Late Minoan II period, the relationship between Knossos and the mainland of Greece was a close one. In the culture of the mainland can be seen much that was of Cretan origin and conversely there are certain elements in the culture of Knossos that were of mainland origin. It is not certain how much colonisation of the mainland had been achieved by the Minoans, nor yet how much political domination they exercised over Mycenaean territory.

What does seem clear, however, is that Minoan power ended in a sudden and overwhelming disaster about 1400 BC which gravely affected the whole of Crete. It was a universal catastrophe which overtook all the Cretan cities – Knossos, Mallia, Pseira, Gournia and Mochlos in the north; Palaikastro and Zakro in the east; Phaestos and Aghia Triada in the south; all show traces of violent destruction.

It seems more than possible that the great disaster was due to a combination of circumstances, both natural and human; earthquake and fires and flood followed by revolutions, and above all by an invasion in which the Mycenaeans, seizing the opportunity of the overwhelming Cretan disaster, deliberately sacked and destroyed all that remained of the shaken cities in the island.

The catastrophe came upon the Palace with great suddenness. The sculptors were interrupted at their task; the workshops of the potters were destroyed; craftsmen and artists were scattered or slain. Fire swept through the corridors of the huge Palace buildings, melting bronze, carbonising wood, beans and wheat, and preserving for posterity by accidental baking the otherwise perishable tablets, tablets upon which were inscribed the symbols of a tongue that would not be decyphered for another three thousand three hundred years.

At the court of Knossos there was certainly no warning of its approaching doom. The life of the capital continued right up to the very moment when with appalling suddenness the crash came. The surprise was complete. The people of the city had scarcely time to flee – none at all in which to save their property. That morning a sculptor sat down to work

a. Olive oil separator
   Gournia

b. Large tripod kettle with
   trough spout
   Gournia

c. Stew pan and cover
   Gournia

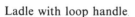

Ladle with loop handle

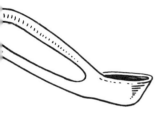

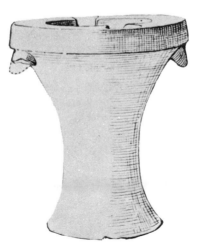

e. Large kettle with bridge spout
   Gournia

f. Chafing dish or brazier

g. Pricket candlestick
   Palaikastro

h. High standing lamp
   Gournia

i. Candlestick
   Knossos

Fig. 54. Late Minoan domestic utensils

on a stone vase, but the vase was left unfinished when the alarm called
the craftsmen to flee. Some rooms in the Palace were being redecorated.
The frescoes remain unfinished to this day.

The question whether Minoan civilisation was doomed, whether the
race was decadent, is not easy to answer. For a thousand years the people
of Crete had been developing their own peculiar civilisation. They had
displayed extraordinary activity as seamen, explorers and colonists, as
builders and artists. It was a remarkable achievement of creative energy
on the part of a small people. After 1400 BC, the Cretan people never
showed any signs of such talent again.

It would seem, and the conclusion is suggested by the suddenness of
its collapse, as though the Minoan empire was no longer the self-expres-
sion of an expanding people, but merely that most vulnerable of all
political organisms – a bureaucracy for whom the rest of the population
existed only to be taxed.

Command of the sea for some centuries may have led to a decay of
military qualities. Moreover the Cretans had learned from the Egyptians
to depend upon negro troops to form part of their military guard. The
sea-power of Crete ended suddenly in the loss of its fleet in an expedition
to Sicily. It was during its absence that Crete was invaded and Knossos
sacked. Crete was drained of its best fighting men. The Mycenaean invader had chosen his time well.

As a seat of the mighty, the Palace of Knossos ceased to exist. Its glory
and indeed that of Crete had departed for ever. It was the victory of the
Lion of Mycenae over the Bull of Minos.

AEGEAN BRONZE AGE SCRIPTS

The Cretans hold a distinct place in the history of civilisation by their
invention of the first method of writing that was ever practised in Europe
(Fig. 55).

Sir Arthur Evans recognised at least three different scripts: the earliest
was a pictographic hieroglyphic script in which the characters bore an
essential relationship to what they were intended to represent, which by
EM III (2200–1900 BC) is known to us mostly from inscriptions on seals,
and this system seems to have been used by the original inhabitants.
Since these pictograms are mostly carved on seals, the system might also
be called pictoglyphic.

The other two scripts he called Linear A and Linear B.

This pictoglyphic script gave place about 1800 BC (MM II) to a syllabic script, viz. one in which each sign denoted a syllable, such as ka,
ko, ku, mo, pi, sa, etc. This is the Linear A script. We might also call it

a. Pictoglyphic script (prism seal)

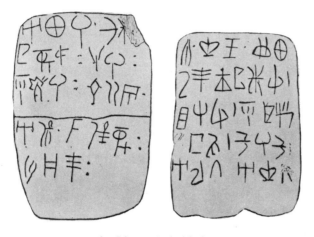

b. Linear A (tablet)

c. Linear B (tablet)

Fig. 55. Examples of Bronze Age scripts

the Minoan Linear script. Specimens known to us seem to consist of business documents or accounts or lists of commodities. They have been found all over Crete and are generally incised on clay tablets, but other examples are inscribed on stone or metal.

Linear A has not yet been deciphered and its language remains unknown, but opinion inclines to the view that it was not Indo-European and was, therefore, a non-Greek tongue.

A most interesting article in the magazine *Greece and Rome* for October 1964, 'Cretan Hieroglyphs: the end of a quest?' by S. Davis, however, summarises the author's illustrated arguments by pointing out that the pictures on the seals are not just symbols, but represent words or syllables. The earliest form of writing in Crete, he says, the pictographic script, has on elucidation proved beyond doubt that the language which the Minoans spoke was Hittite. This language, says the author, is the same as that of the Linear A inscriptions and is very closely related to the Hittite language, so that the Minoan language is entitled to be called Hittite. It belongs to one of the two main groups of Indo-European Anatolian languages, and the script, he says, is both syllabic and pictorial.

Since the Cretans took their system of writing with them, we find examples of it in other parts of the Aegean. Pottery excavated at Phylakopi in the island of Milo shows symbols in Linear A written not only on pots designed for export to Crete, but also on vessels which were made to remain in the island. Similar examples have been found in the island of Thera (Santorin).

About 1450 BC (LM II or Myc. II), namely about the time when the Mycenaeans may have occupied Knossos, Linear A was superseded by another script known as Linear B. This was during the final phase of the existence of the Cretan palaces and of the Palace Style of pottery. Although examples of Linear A have been found at a number of sites in Crete, those in Linear B have only come to light at Knossos.

In 1939 a Mycenaean palace, the Palace of Nestor, was discovered just before the outbreak of World War II at Pylos near the Bay of Navarino in the south-west Peloponnese, by the distinguished American archaeologist, Carl Blegen. One of the trial trenches exposed an archive room containing more than six hundred clay tablets and fragments of tablets inscribed in the Linear B script. They were the first to come to light upon the Greek mainland, although jars with painted Linear B characters had previously been discovered at Thebes, Orchomenos, Eleusis, Mycenae and Tiryns.

This Linear B script also remained obscure till it was brilliantly deciphered in 1952 by Michael Ventris and revealed itself to be an early form of Greek. Thus there seems no doubt that Greek was spoken in Crete in 1450 BC, or at all events, in that part of it under the control or influence of the Mycenaeans. While Linear A may be called the Minoan script, Linear B may be known as the Mycenaean.

The inscriptions on all these tablets, those from Knossos as well as those from Pylos, also consist of lists of stores: arms and armour, horses, chariots and other items of equipment. They owe their durability and preservation largely to the fires which destroyed the palaces, and so baked the clay on which they were inscribed. In 1951 copies of all the texts found at Pylos in 1939 were published by the American, E. L. Bennett, and so were made available to those interested in the problem of deciphering.

In 1952 Volume II of Evans's *Scripta Minoa* appeared after the author's death, containing an account of a large part of the Linear B material found by him fifty years earlier in the Palace of Minos at Knossos.

These new publications stimulated fresh efforts to solve the puzzle offered by Linear B, and the most sensational result came in 1952 when Michael Ventris published a cautious suggestion that it was an early form of Greek. It took courage to launch this theory, for it ran directly counter to one of Evans's most positive statements, namely that Linear B script was Minoan and not Greek, a view then generally accepted by most archaeologists and historians. But Ventris soon found further confirmation of his opinion by the application of tests of other samples of Linear B to a syllabic grid which he had worked out.

Another tablet was found at Pylos in 1952 and made known to Ventris in 1953. When the signs on it were put to the test with Ventris's syllabury, many of them emerged as Greek words, as well as Greek personal and place names that are unquestionably Hellenic. It had long been held that the first Greeks who established themselves on the Greek peninsula did so between 2000 and 1800 BC, while excavations in Greece had indicated there was no evidence of the arrival of a new race in the Late Bronze Age, so that the discovery of written Greek in the Linear B script on Mycenaean tablets helped to confirm these deductions.

Nevertheless, philologists are of opinion that the difference between Linear A and Linear B was not merely a chronological one, but that they represent two different languages and cultures, and that Linear A must be Minoan (and possibly Hittite), and Linear B Mycenaean (and Greek). Linear B script, it is thought, was an Achaean modification of Linear A to meet the needs of a different language. Thus it seems that the Mycenaeans were Greeks of an early stage in the history of that race, before, perhaps, the full evolution of the Hellenic language.

A problem which has given rise to much argument concerns both the

K

relative dating of the thousands of Linear B tablets from the Palace of Knossos in 1900, and the equally large numbers found in 1939 at the Palace of Nestor at Pylos also inscribed in Linear B. Sir Arthur Evans records that most of the tablets from Knossos were discovered in strata of LM II, namely some time between 1450 and 1400 BC, although he says that a considerable number came from deposits containing pottery of a later date in LM III, all of which owed their preservation to the conflagration that laid the LM II palace in ruins.

The Linear B tablets found in the Palace of Nestor at Pylos had also been baked in the great fire which was responsible for their survival, while the palace itself was entirely destroyed.

The mass of pottery found in the Palace of Nestor dates the ruin of the building to the end of Myc. III B, about 1200 BC, or some two hundred years or more after the destruction of the Palace at Knossos in about 1400 BC.

In 1952 and even more recently, another lot of Linear B tablets was found at Mycenae which came from a stratum also assigned by the excavators on ceramic evidence to about 1200 BC. When compared, the tablets from the mainland and those from Knossos are almost indistinguishable both in shape, in style of writing and in their purpose.

Such differences as there are, are no more than might be expected in writing done by different people. These striking resemblances have led some scholars to wonder whether the two groups of tablets are really two centuries apart in origin, or whether there has been some mistake in dating on one side or the other.

The evidence from Pylos and Mycenae on the mainland seems unshakable; that from Knossos seems open to some element of doubt, since Sir Arthur Evans himself reported finding some of the tablets in an LM III context although the majority were found in strata of LM II.

Professor Blegen feels that the striking similarity of the tablets from the two regions, Crete and the mainland, both of which reflect the same bureaucratic system of administration, seems to indicate that they are of approximately the same date and not separated by two centuries or more. (*The Mycenaean Age* by Carl Blegen, 1962.)

Moreover, he says that some objects recorded on the tablets from Knossos look as though they represented swords, arrowheads and pottery that have not so far been discovered, in strata earlier than LM III. He is led to wonder, therefore, if it is not possible that the continued occupation of the LM II palace into period LM III, which Evans himself observed and reported, might not have lasted considerably longer than has been thought, but even if this were so, it would hardly be enough to fill the gap of two centuries or more.

If Sir Arthur Evans's dating still holds good, and Knossos was destroyed in 1400 BC, it would seem as if the Knossian tablets prove that a Greek-speaking Mycenaean people were already established at Knossos by 1400 BC, and that the destruction of Knossos was the result of a battle between Greek and Greek and not between Greek and Minoan. If this was the case, and an invasion of Crete by Achaeans took place, who established a ruling dynasty at Knossos, the King Minos of legend may have been Achaean and not Minoan.

The absence of Linear B tablets and pottery of LM II in Crete except at Knossos is explainable by supposing that an Achaean dynasty ruled at Knossos since about 1450 BC during the LM II period, while Minoan princes still using LM I pottery were ruling in other parts of Crete. Even so, this does not explain the strong resemblance between the tablets of Crete and those of the mainland if their dates of origin were separated by two centuries. In view of these uncertainties, it is evident that the whole problem needs further study and investigation.

The Linear B script continued in use for the rest of the Achaean period of the Bronze Age when it seems to have been lost and forgotten in the confusion of emigrations resulting from the Dorian invasions that caused the end of the Mycenaean civilisation during the eleventh century BC, and it was not till about 900 BC that an alphabet derived from the Phoenicians was adopted and modified, till by the end of the fourth century BC, uniformity in the main was attained throughout Greece and it became the ancestor of all the alphabets of Europe.

LATE MINOAN III 1400–1100 BC

The disaster at the end of LM II had broken the spirit of the Minoans. Some sites were deserted, others were reoccupied but on a much smaller scale. With the destruction of the main centres and the palace, the former concentration of power ceased. Perhaps the ruling class was wiped out. The great age of Crete was ended. The old centre of illumination was darkened. Power in the Aegean was transferred to the mainland of Greece. The sack of Knossos was the prelude to the last period of the old Aegean civilisation – LM III in Crete, on the Greek mainland Mycenaean III.

This was a long period covering three centuries, the age of decline and fall of Minoan culture throughout the Aegean world. It was the last flickers of the Minoan civilisation after a thousand years of maritime power and artistic glory. Cretan culture, however, did not suddenly disappear even after the destruction of Knossos, but the decadence or disappearance of the Minoan dynasty and the general impoverishment of the island resulted in a loss of demand for luxury pottery.

The finest works of art have always been produced when a country is ruled by an autocracy or an oligarchic aristocracy. When wealth is no longer concentrated in the hands of a dominant class to set canons of taste and to exact a high standard from the artist, an artistic decline occurs. Great art needs a wealthy patron. With the loss of his patron, the inspiration of the artist and the skill of the craftsmen vanish and degeneration sets in. The dynamic force of Cretan civilisation had expended itself and come to rest in a static condition which we call the culture of LM III, a static culture that continued to exist till it collapsed under the onset of new dynamic forces three centuries later.

Crete itself continued to exist in provincial obscurity, deprived of the political and military powers it once exercised. Its commercial power was transferred to Mycenae and Pylos on the mainland of Greece, and to the eastern islands of the Aegean: Rhodes and her neighbours. The next two centuries saw a unified and prosperous civilisation with safe communications all over the eastern Mediterranean between Greece and the great powers of Egypt, Syria and Anatolia.

The Cretan potter of LM III confined himself to copying monotonously the same motifs. He lost the sense of creating a design to suit the shape of a vase, a sense which before had been so vigorously alive. The decoration of the period is basically a degenerate and stylised form of ornamentation in vogue during LM I (Fig. 56). The plants and marine animal life were progressively altered and formalised till they became hardly recognisable.

Characteristic shapes of the era were the new skyphos and kylix and the open-mouthed krater that succeeded the great three-handled pithoid jars of LM I and LM II. The pottery of LM III, the 'reoccupation period', included bowls, cups and other vessels with degenerate versions of the Palace Style decoration of LM II. Of the older forms, the most common survival was the false-necked stirrup jar made in every variety of shape and size.

This and the kylix are the most typical vase forms of LM III (and of Late Mycenaean) and are found all over the Aegean world during this period. A few new shapes made their appearance. The tall alabastron was made with a longer neck, and small varieties of jugs often have a round spout instead of a beak, and the handle set lower down.

Towards the end of LM III, the Vapheio shape of cup died out and was supplanted by one with swelling body that narrows down to a low foot.

A characteristic shape from eastern Crete was the spouted cup

b. Bowl (skyphos)
Palaikastro

a. Mug
Palaikastro

c. Kylix
Palaikastro

d. Tall-necked krater
Palaikastro

e. Stirrup jar
Crete

f. Tall alabastron
Phaestos

Fig. 56. Late Minoan III vessels

134

a. High-stemmed kylix
with high handles
Milatos, Crete

b. Pedastalled spouted cup
Milatos, Crete

d. Stirrup jar
Crete

c. Pithoid jar
Palaikastro

e. Pithoid jar
Palaikastro

f. Squat alabastron
Knossos

Fig. 57. Late Minoan III vessels continued

(Fig. 57b). Some are without handles and some have a single handle at
the side or opposite the spout. Circular pyxides (Fig. 58a) have been
found as well as conical filler vases. The pithoi of this period are
barrel-shaped but squat, and painted on the upper part of the body
(Fig. 58c and d). They have four handles set just below the rim, two of
which are horizontal and two vertical. They have low necks and flanged
lips.

In LM III burial in a clay larnax (sarcophagus) became the regular
method of interment, and with rare exceptions, burial in pithoi had died
out. The usual shape is like that of a bath and they were generally
covered with a plain pottery slab. There is little doubt that they were
made for domestic use as baths before being used as coffins. An example
of this shown on Fig. 59a and found at Gournia in eastern Crete, has a
flat outstanding rim and four horizontal handles. It is made of coarse
red-brown clay decorated in black paint. A plain band runs round the
base and on the outer edge of the rim. One long side and one end are
decorated with debased octopus, head, body, and three rows of arms.
The other end is filled with vertical spirals and vertical bands. The
second side contains the principal design which shows a bull (?) without
horns, a cow with large horns and a suckling calf. The cow's legs look
rather unsteady. The bull's body has cross-hatching inside a wide edging.
The internal decoration consists of a cross of triple wave lines on the
bottom, and splashes of paint looking rather like flying-fish on the sides.
There is a hole in the bottom of the larnax.

Compared with the preceding periods, a style of ornamentation prevailed which was less vivid and announced the loss of strength and inspiration which marked the end of the Bronze Age before the Dorian
invasion.

The stylisation of motifs which was so evident in LM II became even
more pronounced in LM III. It was symptomatic of a growing decadence,
so that eventually the naturalistic motifs are hardly to be recognised
under their conventional disguises. Octopus tentacles degenerate into a
series of loops, and the once graceful triton shells become transformed
into a sort of corkscrew. Some of the decoration is even limited to
nothing more than bands round the vase.

Many graves of LM III have been excavated at Knossos and other
sites with a very wide range of vase shapes in which stirrup jars become
more and more numerous.

With the end of LM III power had passed to the mainland of Greece.
There was no question of the intrusion of a new civilisation, but it was
no longer Crete that was the directing force; it was only a province of
Mycenae. On the site of Aghia Triada near Phaestos has been found a

a. Pyxis and lid
Palaikastro

b. Squat alabastron
Palaikastro

c. Barrel-shaped pithos
Palaikastro

d. Barrel-shaped pithos
Palaikastro

Fig. 58. Late Minoan III vessels continued

a. Bath larnax
Gournia

b. Chest larnax
Palaikastro

Fig. 59. Late Minoan III larnakes

Megaron of the Mycenaean style. The princes of Crete were no more than the shadows of their forebears, occupying a corner of the old palaces.

Characteristic features of LM III pottery are the use of a smooth chalky slip and a larger proportion of painted to unpainted vases.

The decorative style of LM II continued into LM III but with a lower standard of execution. Although motifs specially characteristic of the mainland Mycenaean style appear in Crete, they are not sufficiently numerous to indicate an invasion or even a settlement from overseas.

At the beginning of LM III a sort of transitional style bridges the frontier between the two periods. A good example is a squat alabastron from the Isopata tomb at Knossos (Fig. 57f). A row of drop pendants surrounds the neck, and between the handles are discs below which runs a row of horizontal S's – a simplified form of running spiral. The lower part of the alabastron is covered with a crowded assortment of varied motifs: degraded lilies, a conventionalised clump of papyrus, crosses, a one-handled jug and a bird. At first sight the design gives a general impression of richness, but closer examination shows that there is no guiding motif, and that the whole is a rather uncoordinated jumble. It illustrates the rapid deterioration of Minoan ceramic design after the destruction of the Palace of Knossos.

The patterns used at the beginning of LM III are on the whole a further stylisation of those used in LM I and LM II. A characteristic example of this is the very conventionalised flower which gradually degenerates till stamens are reduced to a row of dots. Then it becomes still

 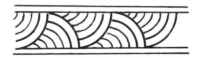 

Fig. 60. Degeneration of conventionalised flower

further simplified when used in the form of a chain when the side of one flower becomes the top of the next or becomes a motif of concentric semi-circles.

Both double-axe and the 'horns of consecration' seldom appear, but when they do they keep their normal form.

The octopus retains its popularity as a decorative subject, but it too becomes more conventionalised. The tentacles are reduced from eight to six, and although at first suckers are shown on them, they are very much prolonged, till on a jar found at Palaikastro, the two top tentacles are reduced to antennae, the middle pair become straggling lines, and the lowest pair form a loop round the bottom of the body (Fig. 57e).

The most noticeable change, however, from previous Minoan tradition lies in the introduction of bird motifs for vase decoration (Fig. 56f). It seems certain that the idea emanated from the mainland, where water-fowl had been a decorative motif since Middle Helladic times; but it was not until the early part of LM III that they made their first appearance in Crete. When they did appear it was in an already conventionalised form with no long tradition of evolution from a naturalistic original, which proves that they were an introduction from without. Sometimes fishes and water plants appear with them. Animals appear very seldom, and the two on the sarcophagus from Gournia are quite exceptional. Human figures as a decorative motif for pottery are virtually unknown in LM III.

Of the second phase of LM III pottery at Knossos, a number of stirrup jars have been found. On them the degeneration of the octopus has gone a step further. On one the head and eyes of the octopus are formed by two thick-centred spirals from which the tentacles emerge in two symmetrical series of loops round the body of the jar. On the other even the body of the creature has been omitted and only a single wavy line encircles the vessel.

Some interesting pottery, dating from the very end of LM III has been excavated from a tomb at Milatos, a few miles to the east of Mallia. It consists of two groups. In one group is a wide-mouthed narrow-footed krater decorated with a very conventionalised octopus with only two pairs of tentacles. Only the lower pair is connected to the animal's body, while the upper pair runs independently as a series of loops round the shoulder of the vase.

Another vase from this group is a long-stemmed kylix with high handles so characteristic of the Mycenaean era on the mainland (Fig. 57a). It is decorated with a curious 'triglyph' motif at intervals below the rim.

Fig. 61. Triglyph motif

Also in the same group is a low spouted cup on a pedestal (Fig. 57b) decorated with a series of concentric semi-circles, and two stirrup-jars, one with a rich and elaborate design on the shoulder in the 'close' style always associated with the very end of Mycenaean III C.

The second group from Milatos also contains a wide-mouthed two-handled krater decorated with a series of highly conventionalised triton-shells set vertically round the body and divided by rows of dots.

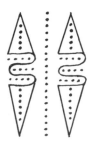

Fig. 62. Conventionalised triton shell motif

The other vases of the second group include a stirrup jar ornamented with bands round the jar, a high-stemmed kylix with a band of small circles surrounded by dots below the rim, and a deep dipper with a high swung handle. In all of these the degeneration not only of shape but also of ornamentation is very evident. With each group was a chest-larnax of a type that was no doubt copied from the wooden chests in the houses (Fig. 59b).

Belonging to the same date is a group of vases found in a store-room at Palaikastro. Among these vases is a necked krater divided up into panels, some of which are decorated with sprawling wavy lines making chevron patterns (Fig. 56d). In the angles are concentric semi-circles with small dashes outside representing degraded flowers. The other panels are filled with pairs of spirals between vertical lines or by a rough scale pattern with semi-circles filling the points of juncture.

Among the other LM III vessels from the store-room at Palaikastro is a large well-shaped pithoid jar (Fig. 57e) decorated with an octopus as stylised as that from Milatos, but with the animal playing a more important part.

Another pithoid jar has a well-moulded splayed foot (Fig. 57c). Wavy lines descend from the handles, and divide the pot into three panels. Two of these panels have treble lines running diagonally across them, every angle being filled with concentric semi-circles. The third panel has a great quatrefoil dividing it diagonally, the leaves of which are filled in solid. In the field are rosettes which also make their appearance on a mug with waterfowl (Fig. 56a).

The pottery of LM III can be said to fall into three stages. Firstly, the transitional style; secondly, the style of the early part of the period typified by the popularity of bird and octopus motifs; and finally the pottery of the latter part of the period characterised by a degeneration of the octopus, and by a greater coarseness in the clay of the larger vessels.

The Cretan pottery of the period is seen to be affected by the increasing popularity of the squat alabastron, the 'pilgrim flask' (Fig. 63d) and the

a. Spouted tankard
Knossos

b. Cup
Palaikastro

c. Calf's head rhyton
Ligortino near Phaestos

d. Pilgrim flask
Palaikastro

e. Ewer
Palaikastro

Fig. 63. Late Minoan III vessels continued

Fig. 64. Patterns on Late Minoan III pottery

'champagne cup' goblet which differed from its mainland contemporary by having a hollow stem.

It is not always easy to distinguish the Minoan work of LM III from the Mycenaean work of the same period, probably because the more skilled potters in Crete had emigrated to the mainland to satisfy the needs of new patrons, the Achaean princes of the Argolis.

In Crete itself, where by LM III the island seems to have been under the domination of the Achaeans, a style of pottery developed which was a mixture of Cretan motifs of the LM I and LM II periods with those of Mycenaean origin such as the waterfowl already typical of Mycenaean vases.

Although Crete still continued to produce vessels of its own native style, many indications bear witness to the new regime. The megaron made its appearance, domed tombs were used for the burial of the chiefs, the excavation of cemeteries has revealed swords like those of the acropolis of Mycenae; while Idomeneus, grandson of Minos, and leader of the Cretan contingent in the Trojan War, was a vassal of Agamemnon.

The fall of Crete to the Mycenaean forces had immediate consequences, Cretan artists and craftsmen were induced to offer their services at foreign courts. Some emigrated to Egypt, others to the Peloponnese. But some of the Cretan population expelled from their island reappear under another name. When the Jews, after departing from Egypt, settled in the land of Canaan, they encountered tribes of another race already established bearing the name of Philistines. Much speculation has been aroused as to the origin of these people, for according to Biblical tradition, they are a remnant of Kaphtor, the island of Crete, whence it is thought they may have been expelled at the time of the Mycenaean conquest, more especially as traces of worship, dress and ceramics upon the coast of Palestine seem to be associated with this tradition.

It was not long after the end of the Trojan War, which, for lack of any positive evidence, may be assumed to have occurred about 1250 BC, that the Mycenaean world, together with most of the Middle East, started to disintegrate. Many of the mainland palaces were sacked – it is not known exactly by whom – and there was a general decline in the standard of living. After about a century of precarious uncertainty, the final blow fell before the Dorian invaders and the Dark Ages followed.

Art may have lost its originality and letters forgotten, but swords increased in length as if to typify the greater part that strife was to play in the next stage of human history.

CHAPTER THREE

The Helladic Era

Helladic is the name given to the pre-Hellenic civilisation which occupied the mainland of Greece south of Thessaly during the third and second millennia BC. This definition gives us a northern limit running roughly from Volo on the east coast (which although in Thessaly includes Iolkos where parts of a Mycenaean palace have been uncovered) to the Gulf of Arta on the west. 'Thessalian' and 'Macedonian' as parallel designations are not yet clearly defined.

The term Helladic is applied to all three periods, Early, Middle and Late (and to nine phases), of this culture to correspond roughly with the Minoan periods of Crete. As we mention elsewhere, however (p. 165), many distinguished scholars are opposed to the use of the term Helladic being applied to that period which corresponds to Late Minoan, namely from 1580 to 1100 BC. For the reasons given, we also prefer not to use the expression Late Helladic for this period, but rather to use the expression Mycenaean.

The outstanding feature of the prehistoric mainland before the Mycenaean era was its subjection to a number of foreign influences as shown by its many varieties of pottery, and by their sudden and continued changes.

Thus Early Helladic has close connection with the Cyclades and Crete, while Middle Helladic was partly Anatolian and partly Cycladic with a later revival of Minoan influence.

Remains of the preceding neolithic cultures were gradually uncovered through the efforts of archaeologists in Phocis, Boeotia, Attica and the Peloponnese, and it became clear that this part of continental Greece had been closely populated during that remote epoch. Neolithic hand-made pottery in abundance and in a broad variety of shapes and styles, plain, incised and painted, has been unearthed.

EARLY HELLADIC (3000–1900 BC)

The Early Helladic period covers roughly the third millennium BC.

Though much has come from other sites, the Early Helladic period is best known from excavations in Argolis, Boeotia and Corinthia. Among the sites where Neolithic and Early Helladic remains have been found are Eutresis in Boeotia, seven miles south-west of Thebes. It is the scene of the Battle of Leuctra where the Thebans defeated the Spartans in 371 BC. It was excavated by the Americans in 1924–27 and again in 1959. The depth of deposit there was about twelve feet. Sites in the Peloponnese yielding Neolithic and Early Helladic remains are Corinth, Korakou and Zygouries, also excavated by the Americans; Asea (Arcadia) and Malthi (Messenia) excavated by the Swedes.

Another place which has yielded Early Helladic remains is at Cape Kolias, now known as Aghios Kosmas opposite the Elleniko airport of Athens. It was excavated by Mylonas (1930–31 and 1951) and was an Early Bronze Age site possibly of settlers from Milo trading in obsidian. Early examples of the 'Frying Pan' were unearthed there, but these strange vessels are more characteristic of Cycladic ware, particularly that of Syra, and so are described under the pottery of that island.

A pottery has been found in central Greece and the Peloponnese as well as in Crete, that belongs to both the late Neolithic Era and also to Early Helladic. It is generally covered with a black or reddish slip and is known by the German name of 'Urfirnis' (primitive glaze). It has almost no decoration but even so was developed to a high standard of excellence in EH II. Its thin walls are so hard as to be almost like porcelain. The elegance of shape of Urfirnis vessels is all the more remarkable when one realises that they were hand-turned without the aid of a potter's wheel. A beautiful jar of this style (see Fig. 65a), found at Orchomenos on Lake Copaïs, of EH II is covered with a dark gloss so that it almost gives the impression of metal. It is nearly of the shape classified by Furumark as 'depressed ovoid' with a flaring neck like the mouth of a trumpet. It has little ribbon handles at the widest diameter of the body just below the shoulders, which are linked to the base of the neck by incised lines.

In central Greece, a local style is known as Aghia Marina ware after a site in Phocis. It has white designs on a dark ground covered with Urfirnis gloss. This lustrous varnish was not a glaze like Egyptian faience. Though it was fused there was no glass in it, and lustrous gloss is a more correct term for it.

Much information on the Helladic Era has also been obtained from Iolkos at Volo, Lianokladhi near Lamia, Thebes in Boeotia, Eleusis and Athens in Attica, Corinth, Zygouries, Mycenae, Tiryns, Prosymna and others in the Peloponnese, but the most important site recently uncovered is Lerna not far from Nauplia, excavated under the direction of the American archaeologist, J. L. Caskey. It was here that Heracles killed the nine-headed Hydra as one of his twelve labours. The monster lived in the marsh nearby, and was so poisonous that its very breath was fatal.

L

At the lowest level of Lerna, neolithic remains were discovered and then those of EH II, but with apparently no contact between the people of the two phases in EH I. Lerna has provided a whole sequence of layers from Neolithic to Late Helladic. Here was discovered the 'House of Tiles', the most completely preserved building of the Early Helladic culture in Greece.

Caskey in describing his excavations at Lerna in 1952–58 says that the place was destroyed by fire in EH II by invaders who rebuilt it for themselves. This reconstruction lasted till the Middle Helladic period.

Pottery shapes characteristic of EH II found at Lerna are the baseless askos which we have described elsewhere under Myc. II and the sauceboat under Early Cycladic I. These two shapes have a wide distribution both in time and place.

A shape belonging to EH III and found at Lerna is a more or less spherical jar with high cylindrical neck and four tubular handles at its greatest circumference. The decoration consists mostly of triangular bands, with hatchings, zig-zags and chevrons painted in dark on a light clay ground. It is in the Argos museum.

By far the most remarkable vessel attributable to EH at Lerna, however, is a large globular jar in thinly glazed ware with three flaring trumpet-shaped mouths, the rims of which are joined together by a disc over the centre of the body (see Fig. 65b). The shoulder bears an intricate pattern of ridges with oblique slashings. Most of the bottom of the vessel was missing, but a fragment indicates that it had a moderately high pedestal spreading at the lower edge. It is sometimes known as a Tristomon.

Other EH shapes found at Lerna are jugs, broad open basins, big rounded jars with handles at the sides, small squat pyxides and big pithoi.

The double ringed ramparts of Lerna with their gates and towers, its unique palace, as well as the beautiful pottery found there and at so many other sites, give us a new view of the prosperity of the peoples inhabiting the mainland of Greece in the third millennium BC.

MIDDLE HELLADIC (1900–1580 BC)

There is plentiful evidence that somewhere about 1900 BC the mainland of Greece was invaded by new and destructive tribes.

It is possible that the people of the Early Helladic culture entered Greece from the south and moved gradually northwards. The distribution of its principal settlements supports the view that the new arrivals of the Middle Helladic culture invaded Greece from the north or possibly by sea from the north-east.

Whereas tools and weapons of copper made their appearance in the Early Helladic period, bronze replaced copper in the Middle Helladic period.

How the Early Helladic culture came to its end is not known, but with the arrival of the new tribes, the type of high varnish Urfirnis pottery hitherto produced on the mainland and characteristic of the Early Helladic period disappeared.

The invaders brought with them a new type of pottery, wheel-made, of a fine micaceous clay, and of shapes which seem to derive from a metallic origin. As this was first discovered in the province of Boeotia at Orchomenos, the new civilisation and its pottery were called 'Minyan' after the legendary inhabitants of that town.

Since this pottery and the other remains of the Middle Helladic period differ markedly from those of the Early Helladic period, we must assume that these differences mean a difference of race. This new race presumably in its turn overran and amalgamated with the survivors of the Early Helladic inhabitants. From this time onward there is no sign of any cultural break. The Middle Helladic period developed slowly into the Late Helladic, or as many people prefer to call it, the Mycenaean Era.

Technically Minyan is one of the best of prehistoric wares. Artistically its merits are humble. It is usually a slaty grey colour which sometimes varies from yellowish brown to almost black. The colour is usually the same right through. The surface is smooth and rather soapy to the touch. The clay is well baked and of a fair hardness.

The majority of pieces that have been found are goblets with a hollow stem, generally encircled with bands of raised rings and standing upon a spreading foot (Fig. 65c).

Another type is the kantharos (Fig. 65d) with two large ribbon loop-handles rising above the rim. One or two raised bands often run round the body of the vase. The shape especially points to origins in metal, for the spreading rim, the sharp angle at the shoulders and the broad handles, while natural and inevitable to the metal worker, would hardly occur spontaneously to the potter.

Besides this 'Grey Minyan', a yellow pottery has been discovered both in Boeotia and the Peloponnese known as 'Yellow Minyan'. The area over which Minyan pottery has been found on the Greek mainland shows that the people who made it were very widespread from the southern Peloponnese to the north of Boeotia. Virtually no Minyan ware has been found in Crete. For the excavator, Minyan ware has the merit of being of unmistakable appearance.

Another ware of the Middle Helladic period is known as Middle

a. EH 'Urfirnis' four-handled jar
Orchomenos

b. EH 'Tristomon'
Three-mouthed vessel
Lerna

c. MH grey Minyan goblet
Mycenae

d. MH Minyan kantharos

e. MH matt-painted pithos
Aegina

Fig. 65. Early and Middle Helladic pottery

Helladic Matt-painted pottery or sometimes as Aegina ware. The most striking examples are pithoi of a dull yellowish or greenish clay decorated with matt black or brown rectilinear or geometrical designs. A number of them are to be found in the Aegina museum (Fig. 65e). This fabric eventually fused with Yellow Minyan to form the basis of all Mycenaean pottery.

This Minyan, Middle Helladic culture, replacing that of an earlier race which had produced the Urfirnis pottery, is the first manifestation of a Greek civilisation in the land of Greece. It is believed that these Minyan tribes were in fact an invasion of Ionians who formed the first wave of Greek-speaking peoples to enter central Greece and the Peloponnese. Where they came from is not certain. We now tend to see Anatolian origins in more phases of Greek life than was the case thirty years ago. It is possible that opinion will swing back again when new Anatolian discoveries may appear as contemporary achievements without implying hereditary origin.

With the arrival of these invaders a radical change took place in social customs. Houses were built of a different shape, and burials were made in jars which were interred under the floors of houses or within the settled area of a site.

Shaft graves appear first in the Middle Helladic period. Their origin has not been settled. Some scholars feel that they are a development of the older cist graves. Others note the great differences of the shaft graves at Mycenae from previous burial customs: their great depth, the wooden roof, the rich collection of gifts, carved stelai, burial with armour and golden masks. If the builders were natives of the Middle Helladic culture, how did they become so rich and why did they depart so radically from tradition?

By the time Greece had settled down again after these incursions, one province had outstripped the others. This was Argolis in the Peloponnese, and its progress was largely due to the welcome it accorded to Cretan influence. With its numerous sheltered bays and harbours facing south-east, it made access easy for Minoan ships sailing along a route marked by the islands of the southern Cyclades. Ever since the eighteenth century BC Cretan seamen had been steering this course, leaving behind them in the Argive ports their polychrome pottery and the imprint of their seals. The Argive seamen learned to sail in the opposite direction, and it is possible that on one of their excursions about 1700 BC they may have returned with spoil and treasure and finely decorated vases as models for their own potters.

Although Argolis owed her early inspiration and the beginnings of her fortune to Crete, she still retained her own individuality which impressed with its own characteristics whatever was borrowed from Crete. It was not a mere reflection of Minoan civilisation.

In fact Crete was beginning to sink into a secondary position, the position of a provincial centre, while her inheritance was passing to the mainland of Greece under the leadership of Mycenae. Mycenae was a city standing some nine hundred feet above sea-level upon a hill twelve miles inland overlooking the fertile Argive plain.

It was surrounded by massive stone ramparts, provided with a good water supply, and therefore well placed to be a stronghold in a time of insecurity.

CHAPTER FOUR

The Mycenaean Era

1580–1100 BC

About 1600 BC the arrival of a new contingent of Greek tribes is indicated. They are the Achaeans, and their arrival strengthened the earlier Ionians. This marks the beginning of the age of greater expansion of the Mycenaean civilisation. It was during this Mycenaean Era that arose the great fortresses of Mycenae and Tiryns, and the most majestic of the great beehive tombs. It was then that Mycenaean products were distributed all over the Mediterranean world.

The Mycenaeans were, therefore, a mixture of Achaeans and of the earlier 'Pelasgian' races on the Greek mainland. The Pelasgians were the more numerous, but the Achaeans supplied many of the leading spirits and an energising force, so that in time their speech and many features of their Aryan origin became dominant.

They firmly established their Zeus in the older seat of worship at Dodona (near Yannina) in Epirus, although the deity he replaced was, as in early Crete, a goddess. Into Crete also he was introduced by the Achaeans. Here he was born to the Earth-goddess in her own cave-sanctuary on Mount Ida, where he was given the Cretan symbol of sovereignty, the double-axe, with which the Cretan goddess had been honoured. Their Apollo captured Delphi by slaying the guardian serpent of the ancient oracle of the Earth-goddess there.

The energy of this Achaean-Mycenaean race in all its tremendous activities, and the monumental buildings which testify to its remarkable skill, demonstrates that it was a race of strong, capable and original people.

It was in 1876 that Heinrich Schliemann, discoverer of Troy, transferred the scene of his activities to Mycenae, and in the autumn of that year, lighted upon the circle of shaft graves just inside the Lion Gate. Buried with the sixteen corpses was found an immense treasure. Enough golden death masks, jewelry, vessels of precious metals, alabaster and copper, swords and spears, with hundreds of jugs and vases, were found to furnish a large museum. Their study revealed a new chapter in the history of ancient Greece and of the Mediterranean peoples.

Although the face under one of the golden masks was not that of Agamemnon as Schliemann thought, but that of a chieftain three

Fig. 66. Heinrich Schliemann

centuries earlier as we now know from the evidence of the pottery in the same grave, Schliemann's very real contributions to the progress of research are universally recognised, and his leadership in setting the course for the science of modern archaeology is universally admitted.

These six royal shaft graves consist of pits sunk as much as nine feet deep into the rock, and cover a period of about a hundred years from approximately 1600 to 1500 BC.

The warlike nature of the early Achaean leaders whose bodies rested

Map 3. Argolis and Corinthia

in them is confirmed by their other contents. Not only were the bodies surrounded by great swords and spearheads, but the precious objects that lay with them are ornamented with scenes of war and the chase. The leaping wild animals, the fighting warriors and the besieged towns are in striking contrast to the pacific art of Crete.

One innovation that ensured Achaean victory on the battlefield was the chariot. Already in use by the Hittites and Egyptians, it proved of the utmost value to the Mycenaeans for rapid warlike movements. Although the horse had been used for carrying loads in Greece from about 2100 BC, it was not used in battle until the introduction of the chariot during the sixteenth century.

What the Mycenaeans did not gain by war they acquired by commerce. They took an active part in the trade passing through the Mediterranean towards Egypt and the countries of the Near East. Their craftsmen were

skilled in the production of weapons and jewelry, and they exported
olive oil, wine, timber, hides and purple dye from murex shells to Egypt
in exchange for papyrus and rope, precious metals and linen.

The riches of the sixteenth-century shaft graves in Mycenae eclipsed
the splendours of anything found in Crete. Mycenae was in truth the
'city rich in gold'. The mere weight of the golden death masks, embossed
shields, brooches and goblets that have been excavated from the shaft
graves add up to a total of more than thirty pounds of gold. This great
concentration of wealth was not merely the spoils of war. Some of the
treasures bear evidence of close relations with Asia Minor and the
Caucasus. Another precious substance reached them from the north,
yellow amber from the Baltic and Russia.

Thanks, initially to the work of Schliemann, we now know that the
classical Greek was the product of an ancient race mixed with the blood
of wandering barbarian tribes who for a time had extinguished the results
of centuries of artistic evolution. Homer's stories of Achaean splendour
were no idle tales, but were founded upon solid fact. In his day, the old
Achaean order was a thing of the past, but legends of former splendour
were still transmitted from father to son.

Little but the foundations of the Mycenaean palaces and fortresses
remain today, so that we have to rely largely on diagrammatic recon-
structions to get an idea of what they were like. For us the originality of
the active Mycenaean civilisation shows itself principally in its funerary
architecture. Shortly after the shaft graves uncovered by Schliemann,
the great corbelled family vaults built into the ground came into use.
They are known as tholos tombs. The word tholos is applied loosely to
describe a circular building, but when applied to tombs it refers specific-
ally to the great burial vaults that were constructed during the Mycenaean
epoch from about 1500–1300 BC.

These tholos tombs are reached by a gently sloping unroofed corridor
or *dromos* cut into the hillside. To obviate falls of soft earth, these
approach corridors as well as the great circular beehive-shaped burial
chambers were lined with layers of stones with no mortar to join them.

In the vault itself the stones are placed in circles one upon another
gradually decreasing in diameter to form a majestic conical dome. They
are the most eloquent witnesses that remain to us of the Achaean power.
Archaeologists have so far excavated some nine of them just outside the
walls of Mycenae; one each at Dendra in Argolis, Vapheio in Laconia,
Orchomenos in Boeotia, Pylos in the south-west Peloponnese, Menidi in
Attica and many others.

They are almost invariably situated in the coastal areas where the
Greek Mycenaean centres flourished, and those at Mycenae show very

clearly their development from a comparatively modest vaulted construction of the late sixteenth century BC to the Treasury of Atreus built (as Professor Wace tells us) about 1330 BC, which ranks among the architectural wonders of the world. At ground level it is fifty-eight feet in diameter and forty-three feet high.

The walls of this great vault were decorated with a pattern of bronze rosettes, and may even have been lined with plates of bronze, which as one writer suggests may have been another reason for applying the epithet 'golden' to Mycenae. Over a doorway eighteen feet high and nine feet wide is a lintel-stone estimated to weigh more than one hundred tons or about five times the weight of the lintel-stone over the Lion Gate entrance to Mycenae itself. The massive simplicity of this vault has defied age and violence. Hardly a stone appears to have been moved from its place.

Mycenaean enterprise was less original in the domain of art. Here Cretan influence was very powerful, so powerful in fact that Cretan and Mycenaean decorative motifs often resemble one another to an extent that it is difficult to distinguish between them – more especially after the collapse of Cretan power in 1400 BC.

Not only Cretan art but the Mycenaean script – Linear B – was largely shared with Crete, as the recent discovery of a big store of clay tablets in the palace of Nestor at Pylos in the south-west Peloponnese by Professor Blegen has demonstrated.

About 1400 BC the supremacy of Crete was suddenly destroyed. Her palaces were sacked and burned, and her political organisation disrupted. That the invaders came from the mainland of Greece is probable though not absolutely certain. What is certain is that this disaster provided the opportunity for the Achaean power on the mainland to usurp the dominating position which Crete had enjoyed for centuries, with the result that Mycenaean power and wealth developed rapidly both inside and outside Greece. The tyranny of Crete removed, the Mycenaean world entered upon an age of remarkable expansion. Rhodes became a thriving seaport, Cyprus developed rapidly, Thessaly and even Thrace came under the Mycenaean influence.

The centuries which followed were ones of free intercourse with foreign countries, as we can see from the character of the Mycenaean pottery; painted in the same style whether we find it in Argolis, Boeotia, Crete, Asia Minor, Italy, Thessaly, Rhodes or Cyprus. By the thirteenth century Mycenae reached the zenith of her power. Her engineers, so skilful in building her fortresses, had endowed her with a well-organised road system radiating from Mycenae to carry her warriors to fresh conquests.

These stoutly built highways rest upon a substratum of Cyclopean masonry. They are carried over small streams by low culverts, and over deeper ravines by causeways built up of large stones. There are signs that the causeways were protected by guard stations at selected intervals. From the pictures upon Mycenaean pottery, it would appear that chariots were freely used for ordinary travel as well as for the chase and for war, although it cannot have been a comfortable experience to ride standing up in a springless chariot over the bumpy Mycenaean roads.

Homer depicts the Achaean princes as owning an allegiance to the overlordship of Mycenae. Whatever feudal relationship existed between them, it is clear that they shared a common civilisation whose centre of power was seated in the citadel of Mycenae.

There are two factors which bear witness to the extent of the Mycenaean empire in the thirteenth century BC. One is the Achaean dialect, in places so far apart as Arcadia and Cyprus. The other factor is the Mycenaean pottery.

As heirs to the Cretan tradition, the Mycenaeans produced their pots with the aid of a potter's wheel, and decorated them with motifs similar but simpler than those of Crete. These vessels are found in all parts of the Aegean. Although they have local variations, all show a common origin. Some shapes, such as the stirrup jar, some motifs like the stylised octopus, are found in the most widely separated localities in the Mediterranean. They cover a tremendous area which it would perhaps be premature to define as a Mycenaean political zone of influence, but which certainly denotes a commercial one.

These Mycenaean wares are not only to be found in the eastern Mediterranean. Large numbers have been found in Sicily and southern Italy. It would be reasonable to suppose that from there this commercial influence extended by way of Malta to Spain and the western Mediterranean, but it must be admitted that so far it has not seemed possible to find any actual Achaean pottery in Spain. Presumably the main stream of Mycenaean penetration was towards the wealthier east. All the same, it would seem that there are reasons for further examination of this matter.

In his book, *South from Granada* (Hamish Hamilton 1957), Gerald Brennan describes his visit to Louis Siret, a Belgian engineer and manager of some small silver mines at Hererias near Almeria. Siret, who has since died, was also an active and able archaeologist who had carried out extensive excavations in that region over the years. He had made, says Brennan, some surprising discoveries relating to the Copper and Bronze Ages. He had found and fitted into its place a new and unsuspected piece of the jig-saw of pre-history. Here in the remote third millennium BC the men of the eastern Mediterranean had possessed great mineral works where they smelted copper and extracted silver.

In Siret's opinion most of the silver used in Minoan and Mycenaean times had been mined at Hererias, and this was a proof of how early the trade routes to the west had been opened up.

Brennan, who had lived for years in southern Spain, also describes his visit to a number of Bronze Age settlements near Almeria which have been explored and yielded a number of finely worked flint and copper weapons. The best of these, he says, are at Los Millares, fifty miles to the west of the River Almanzora at the foot of the Sierra de Gador. Here one may see the stone walls and fosse that surrounded an early settlement, a conduit that brought water from a spring about a mile away, and – most remarkable of all – a large and impressive cemetery.

Its hundred or so circular tombs built to contain fifty to a hundred burials each, consist of beehive-roofed tomb-chambers approached by narrow passages of dry-walling roofed with stone slabs. Each tomb was covered with a cairn of earth and stones, while at its entrance stood a circular walled enclosure in which the funeral rites would have taken place. The person who is versed in archaeology will be reminded of the tholoi of Greece.

In the municipal museum at Almeria, says the author, one can inspect some of the objects that have been found here – bell-beakers of Andalusian type, as well as smooth pots of Egyptian ancestry, and plaque-idols of the Mother Goddess similar to those found in the Cyclades.

Achaean pottery has been discovered as far up the Nile as Assouan. Though it has been found in many sites on the coasts of Asia Minor, it does not appear to have penetrated far inland, possibly because that part of the world was then under the domination of the Hittites.

On the mainland of Greece, a great mass of Mycenaean pottery has been found. Even in the northern provinces of Thessaly and Macedonia, hitherto disposed to preserve their own identity, large numbers of Mycenaean stirrup jars and amphoras have been excavated.

At Thebes in Boeotia, stirrup jars have been discovered decorated in a style and painted with trade-marks similar to those found in Argolis, while the fine pottery is, if not imported from Crete, undoubtedly the product of Cretan craftsmen. In fact the industry of her potteries may well have been a principal source of Mycenaean wealth and prosperity.

Somewhere towards the middle of the thirteenth century, a huge military expedition was, according to Greek legend, dispatched by the Achaean confederacy against the coast of Asia Minor. It was the famous Trojan War. The *Iliad* gives a list of the forces engaged. On the Achaean side was the whole of Greece, from Thessaly in the north to Crete in the south. It is probable that the military power of the various vassal states owing allegiance to Mycenae is reflected in the Homeric catalogue of ships. On the Trojan side were the coastal peoples of Asia Minor, of Paphlagonia, of the Black Sea, of Lycia; and from across the European side of the Bosphorus, the tribes of Thrace. The war traditionally lasted for ten years and ended with the fall of Troy.

There is no reason to doubt the reality of the events which accords well with what we know of Achaean expansion. The difficulty is to discern the fundamental reasons for the war, which seems most likely to have occurred about 1250 BC.

It has been suggested that the campaign was undertaken for commercial reasons. The capture of Troy would have been an advantage to the Achaean fleet. Possibly the Trojans had been imposing vexatious restrictions upon Mycenaean traffic passing up and down the Dardanelles while engaged in trading voyages upon the shores of the Bosphorus and the Black Sea. It may, on the other hand, have been devised for purely destructive purposes with a view to sacking Troy and dividing the spoils, such as the expedition against Crete under Minos or against Egypt under Rameses III.

Another possible theory is that the Mycenaeans, already concerned about the advance southward of the Dorians, latest of the Greek invading tribes, and fearing that they might have to seek refuge in some new territory, were anxious to destroy the power that would provide an obstacle to their moving into the north-west of Asia Minor. Whatever were the fundamental causes that induced the Mycenaeans to undertake the Trojan War, the campaign was the last as well as the most spectacular of the great warlike undertakings of the Achaean confederacy, and as such it is the more clearly remembered in popular legend.

A Mycenaean vase of the late thirteenth century known as the Warrior Vase and now in the Archaeological Museum of Athens gives us an idea of the military equipment of the period. It is described in the section devoted to Myc. III C to which period it properly belongs.

Whatever the motive of the Trojan War, the Achaeans seem to have been unable to follow up their victory. There is no evidence of Mycenaean settlement in northern Asia Minor before the Dorian invasion.

In the Late Minoan period, during which were built the third and last of the great palaces at Knossos, Sir Arthur Evans believed that he could recognise the origins of all the characteristic elements of the mainland Mycenaean culture. He concluded, therefore, that the Mycenaean civilisation was directly derived from the Minoan, and that so influential a derivation could only have been effected by conquest and domination resulting from a large-scale invasion of the mainland by the Cretans. This theory prevailed for some time among other archaeologists, but as further excavation on Mycenaean sites in continental Greece proceeded, those responsible for the work found Sir Arthur's opinion on the matter less convincing.

The Mycenaeans certainly owed a great deal to Minoan influence, but the Achaeans had their own background of non-Minoan character derived as a legacy from their own racial evolution. It seemed to the archaeologists working upon the mainland sites that Achaean relations with Crete had begun by peaceful trade, and through Minoan artists and craftsmen working in continental Greece. From a culture much more highly developed than their own, the Mycenaeans certainly seem to have adapted and adopted for their own use much of Minoan origin.

With the passage of time, and as they became more powerful and warlike, the Mycenaeans built ships of their own. Inspired by the elegance and luxury of Knossos, they returned to their homes upon the mainland to build large palaces of their own, but in their own distinctive style. These mainland palaces were decorated in the Cretan manner, perhaps by Cretan artists and artisans. All the Mycenaean palaces found on the mainland of Greece belong to the Myc. III period, that is long after such ambitious structures had ceased to be built in Crete.

A great deal of further Mycenaean archaeological research was carried out between the two World Wars at both large and smaller centres which have yielded much new evidence for pottery sequence, while excavations in Rhodes and Cyprus and Syria have brought to light fresh Mycenaean pottery and other material which bears witness to the extensive Mycenaean trade, and possibly even colonisation round the eastern end of the Mediterranean.

It was during the war, in 1940, that Furumark's great work on Mycenacan pottery appeared, analysing and classifying all the available material published up till then. It fixed a chronological order of successive styles of shape and decoration of Mycenaean pottery, and forms a notable land-mark in the study of Mycenaean ceramics.

Since the war, many fresh archaeological discoveries of great interest have been made. The most important at Mycenae itself was the discovery of a second royal grave circle lying just outside the citadel. It was excavated by Professor Papadimitriou, that genial and charming scholar whose premature death in 1963 was a loss not only to his country, but to archaeology as a whole. Like other great archaeologists, he shared with Schliemann and Evans a sort of second-sight in locating the places where the most important discoveries were to be made.

The graves which he and Professor Mylonas discovered between 1952 and 1954 seem to have been of a somewhat earlier date than those excavated by Schliemann in 1876 inside the Lion Gate. For the sake of convenience the old circle excavated by Schliemann is now called Grave

Circle A, and the newly-found one outside the citadel is known as Grave Circle B.

Schliemann was, of course, the discoverer of Troy, but the mound of Hissarlik was composed of at least nine distinct layers of debris representing a succession of settlements, and he had difficulty in deciding which to identify as the Troy of the Trojan War.

At first he thought it must be the lowest and earliest layer, but when he found that it contained only the most primitive weapons of stone and bone and hand-made pottery, he realised that this was impossible. In his final campaign in 1890 with Dörpfeld, he exposed a quantity of Mycenaean pottery of a style with which he had become familiar at Mycenae. He realised at once that he must revise his ideas, and plan a new campaign of excavation; but his death in December of that year prevented him from realising this project. Dörpfeld, however, assuming his mantle, carried out the plan with striking success in 1893 and 1894 when he uncovered the magnificent fortification wall and great houses of Troy VI. As these were associated with much imported pottery of Mycenaean style, he concluded that this citadel must be recognised as the Homeric Troy of King Priam.

Between 1932 and 1934, however, an American team directed by Professor Carl Blegen re-examined the sequence of layers, as the result of which a further small change of identity was made. Professor Blegen decided that the ruins of Troy VI had been caused by a powerful earthquake, and not by human agency and fire. After the disaster, the fortification walls were at once repaired and many new houses were erected upon the ruins of their predecessors. This layer he called Troy VII A. Nearly every house, he found, was provided with large storage jars for wine, oil and food, varying in number from two to twenty according to the size of the house. They were sunk down beneath the floors and covered at floor level by flat stone lids. This was evidently a measure of precaution to withstand a siege.

This Troy VII A seems to have lasted probably no more than a generation, when it was destroyed by fire. Scattered among the ruins of the houses and streets were fragments of human bones showing that the destruction was a violent one due to enemy action. Professor Blegen concluded that this Troy VII A must, therefore, be recognised as the ill-fated city besieged, captured and burned by the Achaean invaders.

It is pottery sequence that forms the basis for dating, and although discoveries at one site or another lead to slight differences of opinion regarding a scale of absolute dates, many archaeologists are content to date Myc. III A from 1400 to 1300 BC, III B from 1300 to 1200 BC, and Myc. III C from 1200 to 1100 BC.

With several authoritative opinions settling for dates ranging between 1270 and 1230 BC for that of the Trojan War, we feel that until more concrete evidence is forthcoming it would be reasonable to say that Troy was sacked and burned by the Achaean forces about the middle of Myc. III B or say about 1250 BC.

It is a date confirmed, moreover, by other considerations and discoveries. Firstly, it seems reasonable to assume that the war against Troy by a large coalition of Achaean forces on an ambitious scale must have been waged long before the end of Myc. III B, while the Mycenaean world was still prosperous and powerful. It is unlikely that the Achaeans would have sent their military forces abroad if a threat of Dorian invasion had been imminent. If a large expeditionary force of Achaeans was assembled to cross the Aegean, with the intention of besieging the strong fortress of Troy, it must have been at a time when the Mycenaean world was itself prosperous and confident, and when the various vassal kings and princes were prepared to join their overlord with their armed contingents. This must have been at a time when the great Mycenaean fortresses still stood in their strength and splendour, at a time, as we know from the study of Mycenaean ceramics, when the pottery of Myc. III B was at the height of its vigour and popularity at home and overseas. It could not have been earlier, namely during the period of Myc. III A style of pottery, for the large Achaean palaces and cyclopean walls had not been built then, nor is it likely that the ruler of Mycenae had as yet established himself as supreme overlord of the Mycenaean confederacy.

Towards the latter part of Myc. III B, a remarkable change occurred in the conditions of the Mycenaean world. The Mycenaean fortresses were being more strongly fortified. In Mycenae, Tiryns and Athens steps were taken to ensure a supply of water inside the citadel walls. Also inside the walls, stores were constructed for provisions, and in some places walled refuges were built for the neighbouring populations. A great wall with towers was built across the Isthmus of Corinth.

In the past few years it has become generally recognised that the end of the ceramic period of Myc. III B was marked almost everywhere on the mainland of Greece by a trail of disaster and destruction. It was then that the Mycenaean palaces of Gla on Lake Copaïs, Iolkos near Volo and Krisa on the slopes of Parnassus were destroyed, leaving Myc. III B pottery as evidence for the date of the catastrophe; while the house of Kadmos at Thebes ended in disaster at the same period.

At Mycenae itself the palace and other buildings in the citadel were destroyed by fire, after which it was but feebly reoccupied during the period covered by the ceramic style of Myc. III C. Of these great

M

destructions, that of Mycenae seems to fall within Myc. III C, but if so it was only the last of several previous destructions which occurred in Myc. III B.

Tiryns suffered the same fate at the same time. The Palace of Nestor at Pylos also perished at this time in a great conflagration, and was never rebuilt or reoccupied.

Many of the smaller Mycenaean settlements also ceased to exist after the end of Myc. III B. From the town of Prosymna, excavated by Professor Blegen, were recovered more than twelve hundred vases from some fifty chamber tombs, nearly all of which belonged to the style of Myc. III B, but not one fragment of pottery datable to Myc. III C came to light.

The town of Zygouries, also excavated by Blegen, furnished a quantity of Myc. III B pottery, but nothing of Myc. III C. The same can be said of many other settlements in the Peloponnese, and it is clear that the Mycenaean world on the mainland of Greece suffered a grievous blow, and was reduced to ruin and poverty at the end of Myc. III B.

In the province of Attica alone did the Mycenaean civilisation continue, for we find abundant traces of the Myc. III C style both in Athens and the Mesogeia, that stretch of rich country between Athens and Cape Sunium. This confirms the tradition that the Dorians did not capture Attica. Nor, since a fair quantity of pottery of Myc. III C style, or a style akin to it, has been found in the Ionian Islands on the west, and in Rhodes, Cyprus and the Syrian coast on the east, does it seem that the Mycenaean culture in those regions was obliterated by the Dorians.

This means that the Trojan undertaking could not have occurred after the beginning of Myc. III C, when the Mycenaean centres which had provided the various contingents of ships and men comprising the Achaean expeditionary force were lying in ruins. Those settlements still remaining on the Greek mainland were undoubtedly too much concerned with the question of their own survival.

Professor Blegen gave it as his opinion in 1962 that Troy VII A was destroyed by enemy action some time between 1270 BC and 1260 BC, and that the Palaces of Mycenae and Pylos, as well as the other great palaces on the mainland, were pillaged and burned some two generations later near the close of the century about 1200 BC. Accepting Blegen's authority, we should not be far wrong then in dating in round figures the fall of Troy to 1250 BC.

In the Palace of Pylos a vast quantity of pottery was unearthed, more than seven thousand five hundred pots in fact, representing more than twenty-five shapes, some decorated, but for the most part plain. All this stock seems to have been stacked on wooden shelves in pantries at the time of the conflagration. Although they were for the greater part shattered in pieces, they have a chronological importance that lies in the fact that they represent the current style of the very day upon which the Palace of Nestor was destroyed.

They are all of a very uniform style, a style which marks them clearly as belonging to the latest phase of Myc. III B. Some vases found in other parts of the palace bear a painted decoration, which also indicates that they belong to the end of the Myc. III B, so that the whole consensus of evidence goes to fix the date of the destruction of the Palace of Pylos as having occurred at the very end of Myc. III B or say 1200 BC.

During the latter half of the thirteenth century BC there was a steady decline of the Achaean military civilisation. We do not know precisely what the factors were that contributed to the enfeeblement of the Mycenaean dominion and the break-up of the Achaean confederacy.

Was it that the vassal princes desired to free themselves from the over-lordship of Mycenae? Agamemnon had been murdered. Perhaps there was no prince of outstanding ability to fill his place. Was it due to the gigantic strain of the Trojan War? Possibly it was due to impoverishment through a loss of overseas trade during the long course of the campaign, for the Achaean ships which in those days would have been used indifferently for purposes of war or trade as occasion demanded, might have been too busy upon warlike pursuits, or too idle beached upon the Trojan shore, to be free for purposes of overseas commerce.

From excavations we do know that it was during this period that Mycenaean pottery imported into Syria, Palestine and Egypt was in fact mostly made in Cyprus, with a consequent diminution of trade between Greece and the eastern Mediterranean.

Although the last wave of Greek invaders, the Dorians, are traditionally supposed to have entered Greece early in the twelfth century BC, the style and execution of vase decoration becomes visibly impoverished before then.

Whatever caused the decline of Mycenaean power, we are aware of the sinister approach of the Dorians whose iron weapons gave Greece a shock that produced another series of migrations. Fifty years later the splendours of Mycenaean Argolis had finally passed away. Two hundred years of darkness followed. In the confusion of this epoch, it is only in legend that the brave deeds of the Achaeans are preserved, but Greece owes it to them that they gave a unity of Greek culture to the Aegean region, that they opened the roads which led Hellenism into Asia Minor and to the islands. They were the medium through which the Cretan artistic temperament, Cretan craftsmanship and Cretan religion were transmuted and transmitted to Greece. Without Mycenae the Greeks would perhaps have never received this valuable inheritance.

MYCENAEAN POTTERY

Our knowledge of the Mycenaean civilisation is to a great extent derived from its pottery which was produced so abundantly both in Argolis and in all regions subject to Mycenaean power and influence.

After two centuries of close contact with the Minoan civilisation, the Mycenaeans had inherited and developed a high degree of skill in the production of beautifully shaped pottery as well as a formal style of decoration that owed its origin directly to the designs of the later Minoan vase painters. During some four hundred and fifty years of the Mycenaean Era, this pottery underwent changes of style both in shape and decoration, but throughout the whole of these centuries its central directing source was the province of Argolis with its centre at Mycenae; and whether it was produced on the mainland of Greece, in Rhodes, in Cyprus or elsewhere, Mycenaean pottery found a ready sale in the markets of the Mediterranean.

Although of the Mycenaean style and period, most of the collections of 'Mycenaean' vases in museums outside Greece consist of specimens from islands like Rhodes, and are not from Mycenae or the mainland of Greece. In Greece itself, apart from Athens, the best collections are in the museums of Chalkis, Corinth, Nauplia and Thebes, while the British Museum has a small collection of vases from Mycenae and elsewhere presented by the Greek Government.

From the evidence of pottery, the Mycenaean world was united by close ties, for there is a remarkable uniformity of style prevailing all over the Mycenaean empire throughout the Mycenaean period. The centre of this empire was Mycenae itself. The Acropolis of Mycenae was little more than a fortified palace surrounded by Cyclopaean walls which protected the royal house, the great officers of state, their servants and households, and the soldiers of the royal guard to defend the walls in case of danger.

Pottery of the Mycenaean Era is well known from the enormous number of vessels which have been discovered. The Mycenaean potter was evidently in full command of his material, was a skilful craftsman, and could provide vases of high technical quality for almost any purpose, of all shapes and sizes both well constructed and well proportioned.

A noteworthy characteristic of the Mycenaean potters is their conservatism. In the earlier phases of the Mycenaean Era they made great use of Cretan models – in fact many of these potters may well have been Cretans working on the mainland. Towards the latter part of the era they created a few models of their own, but once included in their repertoire they continued to copy them with little variation in either shape or ornament.

In this they are in striking contrast with the early Cretan potters who constantly introduced new styles throughout the Minoan epoch. It is curious that this should be so, for while Cretan originality was most marked at the period of her greatest power, no such originality characterised the output of the Mycenaean potteries when Mycenae was the cultural and political centre of the Aegean world.

The explanation may be partly due to a greater expansion of export during the Mycenaean Era than during the Minoan, and that this called for greater industrialisation, and greater standardisation and mass production rather than the development of any latent artistic capacity. Whatever the cause, the Mycenaean potters were largely content to live on their artistic capital.

Yet although we do not find during the Mycenaean Era anything to equal the well-known terracotta masterpieces of the Minoan epoch, we do find a great deal that was created with exquisite sensibility.

We have no historical dates from Greece during the Bronze Age, but where examples of Mycenaean pottery have been found together with datable objects in the Orient, then we can allot a date with some accuracy to that pottery, and in time can compile an increasingly accurate chronological classification of Mycenaean ceramics.

The civilisation of the Mycenaean Era is archaeologically recognised as being divided up into five periods: Mycenaean I, Mycenaean II, and Mycenaean III A, III B and III C. Each of these periods is distinguished by its characteristic pottery.

Professors Blegen and Wace have designated these periods as Late Helladic I, II and III, but this description is not entirely accepted by other specialists on the grounds that the term Helladic implies that the civilisation is limited to the mainland of Greece, whereas quite a considerable amount of Mycenaean pottery was produced in Mycenaean areas other than Greece, which does not, therefore, come within the definition of Helladic.

As Glotz says: 'It is a vague and deceptive epithet with a purely geographical sense for long centuries during which there were no Hellenes in Hellas.'

Moreover the term Mycenaean is sanctified by long usage, and conveys to the mind a culture with its own peculiarities characterised by a certain general uniformity of style that prevailed throughout the whole Mycenaean Era. Hall, on page 219 of his book, *The Civilisation of Greece in the Bronze Age*, says: 'The main features of the Mycenaean period all over the Aegean area are the same, and we can speak of a universal

Mycenaean style . . . in ceramics as in all other branches of art. We cannot call it Helladic, because it is not Helladic, if all or any of the old individualistic pre-Mycenaean styles of mainland Greece are to be called Helladic. Its base is Minoan Cretan.'

Furumark, author of the monumental work on the analysis and classification of Mycenaean pottery, when discussing terminology says: 'The only good and unambiguous term for the Minoanised mainland culture . . . is the traditional term "Mycenaean". Mycenaean pottery should not be described as "Late Helladic" because this term has implications which do not agree with the origin and character of the pottery in question. . . . The term "Mycenaean" has a specific cultural sense and is absolutely to be preferred, the more so because Mycenaean culture and Mycenaean pottery spread to regions where the antecedents were not Helladic.' Sir Arthur Evans in his preface to Vol. IV of *The Palace of Minos* is equally emphatic in condemning the use of the term 'Late Helladic' instead of 'Mycenaean'. We have, therefore, chosen to use the expression 'Mycenaean' for these reasons.

It is generally recognised that the five periods of the Mycenaean Era are chronologically divided up as follows:

Mycenaean I	1580 to 1450 BC		
,, II	1450 to 1400 BC		
,, III A	1400 to 1300 BC		Mycenaean III represents the
,, III B	1300 to 1200 BC		whole three centuries after
,, III C	1200 to 1100 BC		the fall of Minoan power.
and Sub-Mycenaean	1100 to 1000 BC		

These dates are subject to constant minor rectifications with new discoveries, but within reasonable limits they are generally accepted.

There are no sharp divisions between one period and another, but the culture of one period or phase as exemplified by its pottery evolves gradually into the next period.

It has two main phases: firstly the era of Minoan cultural domination during periods Myc. I and II (1580–1400 BC) corresponding to Minoan periods LM I and II, and secondly the era of independent development covering periods Myc. III A to III C (1400–1100 BC) corresponding to Minoan period LM III.

Mycenaean pottery of all periods is characterised by great standardisation and uniformity of style, characteristics that affect all pottery within a given period whether produced on the Greek mainland or in other places subject to Mycenaean influence. Pottery characteristic of the Mycenaean civilisation was made at a number of local centres, and has been found throughout the mainland of Greece and the islands of the

Aegean. It has also been found on the coasts of Macedonia, Thrace and the Troad, as well as in the west and south of Asia Minor.

Attic and Argive pottery, though made locally, are closely related to one another in shapes and decorative patterns, although some vessel shapes made in Attica are not found in Argolis. Local potters to some extent evolved styles of their own, particularly towards the end of Mycenaean III as the power and influence of Mycenae itself waned.

Considerable quantities of Mycenaean pottery have been found in southern Italy, Sicily and the Aeolian Islands dating back as far as the sixteenth century BC, a time when the Mycenaeans may have been obliged to expand westward owing to the control of the richer eastern markets by Crete.

It was, however, during Myc. III when the maritime power of Crete had been broken, that the greatest Mycenaean expansion into Italian lands took place. Mycenaean pottery dating from Myc. III A has been found as far west as the island of Ischia off Naples. Although it is unlikely that the Mycenaeans established colonies on the Hellenic model, it is probable that they had trading posts for the convenience of merchants belonging to the lands of the Mycenaean commonwealth, as Rhodian, Cypriot and mainland wares have been found among the vases excavated. Although Mycenaean pottery had been exported in considerable quantities before the destruction of Knossos in 1400 BC, this export trade greatly expanded after the power of Crete shifted to the mainland.

In some islands, particularly in Rhodes and Cyprus, Mycenaean pottery was also made locally, but in Syria, Palestine and Egypt it was almost certain to have been imported. We do not know for sure what was exported in these jars, but it may have been some sort of oil or unguent.

Judging by the great quantity of pottery of the Mycenaean style discovered there since 1870, Rhodes must have been an important centre of Mycenaean civilisation. Its history, however, during the Late Bronze Age is still obscure. Nearly all the sites where Mycenaean pottery has been discovered in Rhodes are near the coast, which reflects the maritime and commercial interests of the Mycenaean settlers. The discoveries of Mycenaean products of the fourteenth and thirteenth centuries in the tombs of Ialysos are so abundant, while native Rhodian products are so poor and so scarce, and the graves are so full of weapons, that it would seem to indicate an armed invasion of Mycenaeans preceding the establishment in Rhodes of an important Mycenaean centre.

It is clear from American excavation at Troy that Mycenaean pottery was also known there throughout the Mycenaean Era, being imported in Mycenaean I, II and III. It seems probable that this imported ware came from the mainland of Greece.

Hitherto the dates of the Trojan War have been a matter for some speculation, but it should not perhaps be too much to hope that with increasingly precise knowledge of dates of Mycenaean finds, it will be possible to interpret these traditions with greater accuracy and to relate them to historical data derived from other sources.

The relations of Minoan Crete with Egypt are well attested from very early times, and form in fact the foundations of Aegean chronology.

It is now thought that of the Mycenaean pottery discovered in Cyprus, some was imported and some locally made, and that in their commerce with Cyprus, the Mycenaeans may have established trading posts in the island with Mycenaean potters working in them. In Cyprus an increasing output of Mycenaean ware was accompanied by a gradually perceptible independence of style.

There is nevertheless strong evidence of the unity of a Mycenaean culture, whether the pottery discovered around the coasts of the Levant in Syria, Palestine and Egypt came from Cyprus or Rhodes or from Mycenaean Greece itself. So much so that it is quite difficult at times to decide whether a Mycenaean pot came from Rhodes or Cyprus or from Greece, a difficulty which only emphasises the homogeneity of the Mycenaean ware and thus the very frequent intercourse which must have existed at this period between all parts of the Mediterranean world. At other times, although Mycenaean pottery from Greece, from the Cyclades, from Rhodes, Cyprus or Crete developed local peculiarities of their own, they all bore the stamp of a common Mycenaean style.

The inhabitants of Mycenae lived mostly in villages or communities upon the slopes of the hills upon which Mycenae is built. It is probable that they lived in clans or groups of families, and that they continued in their tombs the clanship they had maintained in life, for we find that the tombs which have furnished the great mass of Mycenaean pottery to the archaeologist are arranged in groups of eight to fifteen lying in definite localities, the groups clearly separated from one another.

These tombs are hewn out of the conglomerate rock of the hillside, nearly always with an approach-corridor or dromos leading to the burial chamber. The burial chamber itself was closed with a door of stones while the dromos was filled up with earth on every occasion of a burial.

A number of kylikes or stem goblets have often been found mixed with the earth close in front of the actual door of the burial chamber which do not correspond with the fragments of pottery found in the chamber itself.

These, it is thought, are connected with the funeral rites. When the doorway was walled up, the members of the family may have gathered together in the dromos before the doorway to drink a farewell toast or pour a last libation to the dead, and shattered the cups they had used before the corridor was filled up with earth again. J. T. Bent, describing a funeral in the island of Mykonos in 1885, in his book *The Cyclades*, says that 'it was customary to spill some water from a jug when anyone was going upon a journey, as an earnest of success; in the case of funerals it was customary to break a jug of water upon the threshold, for now that the traveller had gone on his last long journey, the jug itself was broken'.

The custom of burying the dead in coffins was excessively rare on the mainland, and even then only introduced towards the end of the Mycenaean period. In the contemporary cemeteries of Crete in Late Minoan times it was quite common as we can see from the great number of clay larnakes which have been recovered from the tombs of Knossos and other sites. These clay coffins were used in Early Minoan times in Crete, but the practice which seems purely Cretan, was not adopted on the mainland.

When a tomb was reopened for a fresh burial, it seems to have been fumigated with incense burners. Such burners have been discovered in several tombs. They were probably filled with glowing charcoal and some aromatic gum. A number of long-handled scoops have also been found in tombs which may have been used for carrying the glowing charcoal into the tomb for use as incense burners. Again J. T. Bent, in describing funeral customs in the Cyclades of 1885, says that when a death occurred in a house, the house was thoroughly purified by fumigation. If the agony of death was prolonged, his relative knew that the sufferer had been unpardoned for some injustice to another. In this case the injured man was summoned to forgive, or if he was dead, the dying man must be fumigated by burning a portion of the injured man's shroud.

A type of vessel found in large numbers in the tombs of Mycenae is the squat alabastron. Its use is not certain. As it is much more rarely found in contemporary Cretan tombs, it is possible that it may have served some special purpose in connection with mainland funeral rites.

The greater part of Mycenaean pottery, whether made in Argolis, Attica or elsewhere, is made of well-levigated clay with a smooth slip, and decorated with a paint which when fired has a glossy surface. There are, however, variations in colour and texture, some of which are due to accidental causes and some which are not. The commonest accidental variation is in colour, for the same clay and paint will turn either red or black according to the conditions of firing. This we can see in certain pots where the paint is black on one side and bright red on the other. Again, where a vase has long been buried in the soil, the colour of the clay itself, especially on the surface, is affected.

As a criterion of date, not only the shape and style of decoration must be considered but also the fabric itself. Early Mycenaean III pottery, for instance, usually has a fine smooth biscuit, generally light buff in colour, decorated with glossy red paint. Late Mycenaean III ware such as the 'Granary' class is generally of a gritty and less well-refined clay with black or purplish-brown paint. These two extremes show the general tendency of Mycenaean fabric to deteriorate in quality, and the decorative paint to change from red to purplish-brown or black.

Generally speaking, Mycenaean pottery was of two main categories: fine ware and common ware. The fine ware was of well-purified clay usually buff coloured. Its walls were thin and hard. The vases are usually covered with a smooth, well-polished slip which made them better adapted for holding liquids. They were well baked in kilns of the period, some of which have been found at both Tiryns and Mycenae. They were also nearly always wheel-turned on discs, some of which have been found near the kilns. The finer vases are nearly always decorated with a lustrous paint of one colour which varies between black and red with occasional details in white.

In the Mycenaean I and II periods, matt decoration was also sometimes used. The decoration is largely of linear or curvilinear designs conventionalised from natural objects both floral and marine. On many vases also occur representations of birds and fish and of animals, mostly oxen and horses. They also have conventionalised men and women driving in chariots or marching in single file. These may have been inspired by frescoes painted on walls.

The other category, the common ware, comprises the greatest part of the earthenware for domestic and kitchen use. It was plain and undecorated, though some of the large storage jars or pithoi, which were often of great capacity, were strengthened with bands of clay applied outside the vessel and decorated with simple incised relief patterns. Almost every kind of vessel for domestic and kitchen use can be found in Mycenaean pottery, and many of their shapes are derived from or influenced by metal prototypes.

This common ware is made of reddish, coarse and relatively porous clay, and is sometimes hand-made. Big vessels of both categories and cooking pots as a rule contain grit, added no doubt intentionally to prevent cracking and warping. In some cases the same shape of vase is found both decorated and undecorated. Apart from this relatively coarse ware, there is a progressive tendency to apply decoration to vases of all kinds.

In the case of stemmed cups, there is a slight difference in shape between those which are decorated and those which are undecorated.

Vessels common to all Mycenaean Periods

SHAPES. Among the shapes which persisted throughout all Mycenaean periods from Mycenaean I to Mycenaean III C were (Fig. 67):

1. *The pithoid jar* sometimes called a piriform jar. It is also sometimes called an amphora for want of a better word, but this is a misnomer, for the word implies a pot with two handles, and which can be carried from both sides, whereas the pithoid jar is nearly always provided with three handles, either vertical or horizontal, symmetrically spaced on the shoulder. Pithoid jars were made in Crete during the MM II period, but it is from those made in MM III and in LM I and II that the Mycenaean pithoid jars are derived. These jars are very characteristic of Mycenaean pottery in Rhodes, which were influenced by the Palace Style jars of the LM II period in Crete.

2. *The wide-mouthed jug* with a handle joining the top of the neck to the shoulder of the jug is another shape that appears in all Mycenaean periods. It is not as a rule found in Crete except in some late example of Mycenaean derivation. It almost certainly originated in a metal prototype, and was the most common form of all Mycenaean jugs.

3. *The squat alabastron* is another shape that was represented in all Mycenaean periods. It is not certain whether it was introduced from Crete, which in turn received it from Egypt, or whether it was from the Greek mainland that it was transmitted to Crete.

In the early examples when they were hand-made, some of these squat alabastra had an elliptical horizontal section, but after the introduction of the wheel, this naturally had to be circular. This strange shape of jar is common in Myc. I and II, and becomes one of the most popular forms of vessel in Myc. III. It is almost invariably fitted with three small equally spaced handles. There are two types of these squat alabastra, one known as the baggy alabastron which has a curved profile. The other has straight, and even slightly concave sides. This latter type is sometimes classed as a Pyxis (see Myc. I). Examples of both curved and straight-sided types are found throughout all Mycenaean periods.

4. *The cup* with a single handle, very similar in shape to our tea-cup, has an origin which goes back a long way, and similar types have been found in Minyan ware of about 2000 BC, themselves possibly derived from a neolithic origin. Its use continued after Mycenaean times, and it is found in Protogeometric times.

Besides this semi-globular type of cup, there are two other types which run right through the Mycenaean Era: one is the *straight-sided cylindrical cup* and the other is the *concave cylindrical (or carinated) cup* which might

b. Straight-sided cup (Myc. II)

a. Cup (Myc. I)

c. Mug (Myc. III A)

d. Pithoid jar (Myc. III A)

e. Kylix (Myc. III B)   f. Wide-mouthed jug (Myc. II–III)   g. Squat alabastron (Myc. II)
Mycenae

Fig. 67. Shapes common to all Mycenaean periods

more appropriately be called a mug – it generally has a broad band round the middle.

5. *The two-handled kylix*, also common to all Mycenaean periods, is sometimes called the 'champagne cup'. It varies considerably in style and decoration.

In Crete kylikes are comparatively rare, so that the origin of the vessel is not in Crete, but rather is developed from a single-handled bowl in the Minyan ware repertoire. Its evolution in Argolis can be traced fairly continuously. As none found in Crete seem to date before LM I they may have been introduced from the Greek mainland. The clay Myc. II goblets were also inspired by metal prototypes, of which early specimens were found in the shaft graves of Mycenae. This clay goblet with painted decoration of a single flower or other motif on one side of the bowl is the type called 'Ephyraean' (see Fig. 73).

There are no specially metallic traits in the later Mycenaean stemmed kylix, but it was one of the most graceful and popular earthenware shapes developed by the Mycenaean potters, and was one of the most characteristic vases of Myc. III. As a general rule the stem is tall and slender while the cup is rather shallow, but some variation in proportions is occasionally seen. The handles are thin and small, bending in a narrow vertical loop from the rim down to the middle of the body. Many of these kylikes are extremely well made, and their slender, graceful proportions produce a pleasing effect.

The stem is often ornamented with a number of painted bands, a fact which helps to confirm the derivation of the Myc. III kylix from Minyan ware, for these painted bands seem to be a graphic representation of the rings executed in relief upon the stems of the Minyan goblet. As, however, there were no raised rings or painted bands upon the stems of the Myc. I and II kylikes, it is a theory that needs further investigation.

Another common form of decoration on the kylix is a degenerate rendering of the murex or triton shell. In a few cases the kylix is covered with monochrome paint.

A variation of the stemmed kylix is one with highly raised handles, which might be called a kantharos-kylix. The kylix shown on Fig. 67 properly belongs to Myc. III B. The stemmed goblet of Myc. III A from which it evolved and the kylix of Myc. III C into which it developed are shown in Fig. 92.

DECORATION. The decoration of Mycenaean pottery derived its inspiration almost without exception from Crete, and in particular from the Cretan LM I style which itself was the outcome of a thousand years of evolution. Even during the Mycenaean II and III periods, it was Cretan decoration of the LM periods which continued to influence the Mycenaean, and provide prototypes for the Mycenaean vase painter. The Mycenaean vase decorator was much less original than the Minoan and was inclined to continue a mechanical repetition of motifs invented in Crete, but without the Minoan force and refinement.

Few purely naturalistic designs were used during the Mycenaean Era. The most lifelike of the decorative motifs are the animals – fishes, birds, deer and bulls. Birds and fishes occurred occasionally in Minoan vase decoration, but they never assumed the important position that they occupied during the Mycenaean Age. It has been suggested that in cases where they appear together they are symbolical of the heavens and of the sea.

The class of design most characteristic of the Mycenaean Era is that type of motif which conventionalised natural objects, as for instance the palm.

Fig. 68. Conventionalised palm motifs

The most conventionalised object in the Mycenaean repertoire is the octopus, so lifelike during the Minoan and early Mycenaean periods but which degenerated in the later Mycenaean periods into a continuous series of curves.

It will be seen that there is little originality of design or invention of new motifs, but rather a progressive conventionalisation and debasement of naturalistic motifs. This system of decoration showed that the spirit of originality, which was never the strong point of the Mycenaean vase decorators, gradually disappeared, and so left the field clear for the purely Geometric Style of the early Iron Age.

Vessels characteristic of each Mycenaean Period

Apart from the above vessels, which were common to all Mycenaean periods, the sections which follow show the shapes and decoration which were characteristic of each Mycenaean period. In the case of the shapes an indication is given in each case to show whether the shape was:

(C)	of Cretan origin.
(MH)	of Middle Helladic origin.
(MC)	of Mycenaean Creation.

It will be seen that of these, Cretan Minoan sources provide about half the models adopted by the Mycenaean potters. There is, however, a noticeable difference between those of Minoan origin and the others.

The majority of forms of Cretan origin are those which were typical of the better class of Cretan ware, whereas the others consist largely of vessels made for domestic and kitchen use.

Generally speaking, the shapes derived from Minoan models covered the whole of Myc. I and II except for a short period at the end of Myc. II when there was evidently less contact between Crete and the mainland. Although some of the vessels found on the mainland may have been importations from Crete, the bulk of them are of Mycenaean manufacture, even though a substantial number may have been made by Cretan potters working on the mainland of Greece during Mycenaean I and II.

The forms of Mycenaean creation which had neither Minoan nor Middle Helladic prototypes are not very numerous, but in some cases owe their inspiration to Rhodian or some other oriental influence. With one exception they belong to Myc. III.

The F. number against each pot corresponds to the classification number given in *The Mycenaean Pottery* by A. Furumark.

Jars are taken to include vessels which are too small to be termed pithoi, but which seem to have been used for storing rather than for pouring. They were found everywhere in large quantities. The jug is a vessel primarily for pouring, but the class sometimes overlaps that of jars.

MYCENAEAN I 1580–1450 BC

A. SHAPES CHARACTERISTIC OF MYC. I. No neolithic pottery has been discovered at Mycenae, but early Mycenaean is plentiful (see Figs. 69 and 70). We said that, in general, Mycenaean fine ware was wheel turned. There are, however, some exceptions, in that a few fine ware vases were hand-made in Mycenaean I which were survivals of the old process. Among these are a squat jug with one vertical handle, and the early spouted cups. As well as these a number of miniature cups and jugs were hand-made.

Matt paint decoration similar to that in the Middle Helladic period appears in the Myc. I period, although in fact vases with lustreless decoration are occasionally found in nearly all Mycenaean periods. The colour of the paint of the designs varies from black through all shades of brown to red. The black paint is apt to flake off. On the earlier vases dots and lines were often added in matt white paint which is fugitive and easily wears off. In a few examples of stemmed goblets, a coat of

a. Shallow cup

b. Hole-mouthed jar

c. Ostrich-egg shaped sprinkler

d. Straight-sided alabastron

e. Brazier

Fig. 69. Mycenaean I vessels

uniform greyish pigment seems to have been applied after the firing.

Vases of similar appearance have been found in Crete. Sir Arthur Evans suggests, in discussing finds from the prehistoric tombs of Knossos, that this coating may have served as an undercoat before applying a polychrome decoration which has since been washed away.

Although vases of the Myc.I period are mostly wheel-made, they are often somewhat uneven in execution, although the clay is well refined.

The principal shapes introduced in Myc.I are given below with their derivation, i.e.:   C = Cretan,   MH = Middle Helladic,
                  MC = Mycenaean Creation.

1. *The shallow cup with raised ring handle* (C) (F.237). This shape, sometimes called a phiale, is not found in Crete, but is common on the mainland, both in clay and metal (Fig. 69a).

It stands on a low ringed base, and the rim splays outwards, forming a sharp angle with the shoulder of the cup. Sometimes the flat handle has a metallic-looking knob at its base.

2. *The deep cup with two raised handles* (MH) (F.240). This is an early form of 'Kantharos' which became in classical times associated with Dionysos, the God of Wine (similar to Fig. 65d).

3. *The ostrich-egg ritual sprinkler* (C) (F.76) is derived from a Cretan MM model which itself was derived from an Egyptian prototype. These latter were actual ostrich eggs fitted with a metal mouthpiece and outlet (Fig. 69c). The clay model is one of the most characteristic Myc.I shapes which continued into Myc.II.

4. *The conical filler* (C) (F.199), sometimes called a rhyton, is derived from a Cretan MM form (Fig. 70a). Its purpose is not quite clear, but it may have been a libation vessel. The Mycenaean shape is similar to the Minoan. (See note on Conical Wine Filters on p. 287.)

In the earlier types the handle is S-shaped and flat, joining the upper side of the lip to the side of the vessel. In later vessels it forms an oval loop with both ends joining at the lip.

5. *The hole-mouthed jar* (C) (F.100) has an old history dating back to the Early Minoan period. The mainland forms of Myc.I have a graceful outline and a piriform shape, with in some cases an outward turn towards the base (Fig. 69b).

Even though some of the specimens are ornamented with the Cretan double-axe pattern, they do not appear to be made in Crete, but are rather imitations of Cretan vases, or vases made on the mainland by Cretan potters.

6. *The jug with cut-away neck* (MH) (F.135) derives its name from the

N

a. Narrow-necked jug

b. Jug with cut-away neck

c. Conical filler

d. Handled goblet

Fig. 70. Mycenaean I vessels continued

fact that the rear part of the neck is cut down at the point where the upper part of the handle is attached (Fig. 70b). The body and neck are made separately and joined together by hand, so that the fabric is considerably thickened at the base of the neck and presents a rough surface on the inside. The shape is very rare on the mainland in Myc. I. The best-known specimen is from one of the tombs near Mycenae. It is of piriform shape and the cutaway of the neck is not particularly noticeable. The ribbed handle with two 'rivets' at the point where it is attached to the neck, and the knob where it is attached to the shoulder as well as the ring at the base of the neck indicate the metallic origin from which it is derived.

7. *The brazier* (C) (F.312). This, as mentioned previously, may have been used with glowing charcoal and incense for the fumigation of tombs. It is bent up near the middle to protect the hand from the heat (Fig. 69e). In later types the handle is bent downwards.

Although of Minoan origin most specimens have been found at Mycenae, and vary in periods from Myc. I to Myc. III B.

There is still some diversity of opinion regarding the purpose of this vessel. Furumark described it as a brazier. In *B.S.A.*, XLVII, pp. 269 and 271, it is described as a lamp.

8. *The side-spouted jug with basket handle* (MH) (F.158) has a narrow tubular spout standing up from the shoulder. It usually has a ring foot. Side-spouted jugs are sometimes referred to as 'feeding bottles'. Somewhat similar ones are made in Rhodes today for use as drinking vessels or for pouring water over a person's hands. There is a more developed form in Myc. III (Fig. 77d).

9. *The narrow-necked jug* (C) (F.117). This narrow-necked conical vessel with concave neck, flat tip and ring mouldings at the base of the neck and foot comes from the shaft-graves of Mycenae (Fig. 70a).

10. *The straight-sided alabastron* (F.89) is sometimes described as a pyxis (Fig. 69d). It is another version of the squat alabastron with the curved profile. The origin of the shape is doubtful. It does not seem to be native either to the mainland or to Crete.

A Levanto-Mycenaean version has concave sides and a convex bottom. These have a collar neck for the accommodation of a lid. Like other squat alabastra, these vessels usually have three handles on the slope between the shoulder and the neck. They are well made with fine regular wheel marks showing on the inside.

11. *The handled goblet (early type)* (MC) (F.262). This graceful shape is derived directly from Minyan ware, and the rounded profile is one of the favourite shapes of Myc. I and II (Fig. 70d). It is shown with the description of Ephyraean ware when it reaches its most graceful form. It

is a drinking vessel which, through Myc. II, gradually evolves into the long-stemmed champagne cup shaped drinking vessel of Myc. III.

Unpainted ware. In addition to these decorated shapes, a great quantity of unpainted ware belonging to Myc. I has been found. Among the shapes are the stemmed goblet with rounded profile, a jug with cut-away neck, a dipper or ladle, a deep bowl with small side-spout, and a handleless cup with flat bottom.

Monochrome ware. Instead of being finished with a fine slip, these vases are completely covered with a smooth coat of good quality black or red paint. In many cases, uneven firing has caused the red paint to turn to black in places, thus producing a mottled effect.

Shapes found were stemmed goblets, deep bowls and large bowls of heavier fabric with a spout on one side between the handles.

Domestic pots. These include a variety of large, coarse vessels made of unrefined clay. Among shapes were high-necked water jars, deep bowls, urns on a heavy stem, small jars on a small raised base and various cooking pots with one or two handles.

B. VASE DECORATION CHARACTERISTIC OF MYC. I. During Myc. I, vases were sometimes made by hand, but in general they seem to have been made on a wheel; where the wheel-marks are not very clearly visible they would have been made on a slow wheel, so that there appears to have been a touch of carelessness in execution. The fabric is good. The clay is finely sifted and free from gritty particles; baking is generally well done and the surface of the vase covered with a smooth slip similar in colour to the clay.

The paint is lustrous and of good quality, although in a considerable number of cases it has partly flaked off. The most usual colour of the paint is a lustrous black, varying to brownish on vases of yellowish-green clay, while on vases of buff clay a good red is most frequently used. It is the black paint which shows a tendency to flake off. On the earlier vases, subsidiary details were often added in white.

The patterns are to a great extent, but not exclusively, linear (Fig. 71). The majority of Myc. I style motifs are also found in LM I ceramics, and in fact the two are virtually indistinguishable. The stock of patterns, however, used by the vase decorators of Myc. I was more limited than that of LM I which may be partly due to the fact that many of the motifs of the Kamares tradition which were included in the stock of LM I were not transmitted to the Mycenaean potters.

Floral designs in particular are much rarer than in LM I.

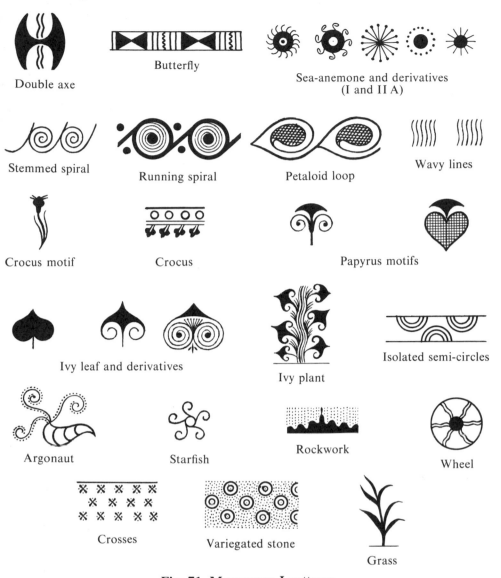

Double axe

Butterfly

Sea-anemone and derivatives
(I and II A)

Stemmed spiral

Running spiral

Petaloid loop

Wavy lines

Crocus motif

Crocus

Papyrus motifs

Ivy leaf and derivatives

Ivy plant

Isolated semi-circles

Argonaut

Starfish

Rockwork

Wheel

Crosses

Variegated stone

Grass

Fig. 71. Mycenaean I patterns

There are certain instances where Minoan motifs have been transformed under the influence of Mycenae. The most notable example of
this is the 'double-axe' of Crete which becomes the 'butterfly' of Mycenae.
The conventionalised double-axe with curved blades was also used. In
the central space between the blades, both above and below, are two or
three vertical dashes or parallel lines. This motif was repeated several
times round the vase.

Another example is the Mycenaean conventionalised 'sea-anemone',
although in fact several of these circular motifs bear a close resemblance

to the seeds of certain wild flowers in Crete and on the mainland.

There was also a taste for abstract designs inherited from the Middle
Helladic period, but the favourite motif of Myc. I is the spiral, and particularly the running spiral and its variations. It is usually well drawn in
a rather fine line starting from a large central disc, making some five or
six revolutions before ending in a broad line forming the circumference.
In later examples, the drawing is less careful and the central disc is
often missing, but the number of revolutions remains about the same.
These spirals are generally arranged in a belt running round the upper
half of the vase. They are connected by tangents of single or double
lines which usually join the base of one spiral to the top of the
next.

Typical of these running spirals of Myc. I vases are two large round
dots placed one above and one below the tangent connecting each pair
of spirals. These dots and the central discs are often painted with small
white dots, and a row of small white dots is often added to the tangents
connecting the spirals.

Derived from the spiral is a pattern with a series of pear-shaped leaves
filled in with cross-hatching which are connected by curved lines into a
spiraliform system.

Groups of parallel lines are often the only ornament running in a
horizontal or a vertical direction.

The majority of the vases of this period carry their main decoration in
a zone round the upper part of the vessel, while the lower part is occupied
by broad bands of paint varying in number from one to six.

During Myc. I ornaments were mostly drawn free-hand, and the
unevenness of the horizontal lines shows that the vases were painted on
a slow wheel or even after they were taken off the wheel.

The parallel lines running vertically are arranged in several different
ways. In some cases they are short so as to fill a zone round the upper
part of the vase, while the lower part has the usual horizontal bands. In
another type they are longer and usually wavy, and occur in groups of
four, five or six at intervals round the body of the vase, or else fill the
whole available space. This type of ornament is probably related to the
so-called 'ripple' motif which reaches its finest development in the
tortoise-shell cups of Myc. II.

Festoons sometimes occur between pairs of parallel lines. Naturalistic
designs are much rarer than these linear patterns.

The most common motif of this class is the ivy-leaf. A chain of ivy-
leaves was a popular ornament in Crete during LM I and consequently
also in Mycenaean vase decoration.

Among the flowers used were the iris, as well as sprays of grass and conventionalised papyrus heads.

The crocus has its prototype in Minoan decoration, but did not play a large part in the ornamentation of Mycenaean vases.

A few very conventionalised marine motifs such as the argonaut, the starfish and rockwork are also represented.

MYCENAEAN II 1450–1400 BC

SHAPES CHARACTERISTIC OF MYC.II. The pottery of Myc.II is technically almost identical with that of Myc.I so far as slip, clay and paint are concerned. The vases are on the whole perhaps better fired and have a smoother slip, while the patterns, especially the horizontal bands, are more carefully drawn. Most of the shapes used in Myc.I continued to be used in Myc.II which should be regarded as a developed phase of Myc.I rather than as a new period with a new style. Squat alabastra are much more numerous than in Myc.I. The strongly marked Cretan influence in these vessels may be the work of Cretan potters working on the mainland. Changes of shape do, however, appear, and the principal new ones characteristic of Myc.II are given below.

1. *The bridge-spouted jug* (C) (F.103) is of Minoan origin. Mycenaean specimens have been found at Mycenae, Aegina, Thebes, Chalkis and other places (Fig. 72d). The shape is depressed ovoid, with the handle laid from rim to shoulder. It has an open and tapering bridged spout. Here again, although ornamented with the Cretan double-axe and sacral knot, it is probable that this vessel was made on the mainland by Cretan potters.

2. *The tall amphoroid jar* (F.71). This vessel is of elongated conical piriform shape with a short concave neck and the mouth pinched in on either side by the handles which run from rim to shoulder (Fig. 72c). Vessels of this shape have been found at Mycenae and Kakovatos (see pages 271–2). The shape is well known in Crete and has also been found at Phylakopi in Milo. From fabric and decoration they suggest a Cycladic influence.

3. *The baseless askos* (MH) (F.194). The askos is an old Mediterranean shape with a wide distribution. In Mycenaean pottery there are two types: baseless and based. Some of the baseless askoi have a low elevation along the back deriving from a seam in the leather prototype (Fig. 72e). This is sometimes even decorated with lines representing the stitching. Its use is uncertain, but it is not likely to have been used as a lamp. See based askos (F.195).

4. *The perforated bowls* (MH) (F.314), sometimes referred to as braziers

a. Perforated bowl

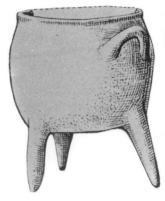

b. Tripod cauldron

c. Tall amphoroid jar

d. Bridge-spouted jug

e. Baseless askos

f. Based askos

Fig. 72. Mycenaean II vessels

or incense burners, are common furniture of Minoan and Mycenaean tombs, to provide 'for the comfort of the cold dead' and for fumigation with resinous matter (Fig. 72a). They are dated between the latter part of Myc. II to III C.

5. *The beaked jug* (C) (F. 143) is a very common form with traditions that date back to the Early Minoan I period (Fig. 73e). There are two varieties, one with a low and wide, and the other with a higher and narrower neck. It is the latter which belongs to the Mycenaean Era. There is usually a clay 'rivet' at the lower end of the handle where it joins the shoulder.

This jug is of much finer fabric than the ordinary jugs of the period, with thin and well-baked clay notable for the regularity of the lines on the inside, formed while the vessel was being made on the wheel. A smooth, even slip covers the exterior. From the top of the neck a ridged ribbon handle bends down to the shoulder. Opposite the handle a spout projects and points upwards at an angle of about 45 degrees. The junction of the body with the neck is sometimes marked by a raised ridge with a sharp profile. This feature, the rivet-like knob at the base of the handle, and the neck decoration of vertical linear pattern of elongated festoons point strongly to a metal prototype. Vases of this shape have been found at Korakou near Corinth, in Attica, and at Thebes in Boeotia.

6. *The based askos* (MH) (F. 195) has a body with an outline similar in shape to the squat alabastron (Fig. 72f). This shape, although it occurs in the Middle Helladic period, is not common in Myc. II, but is more popular in Myc. III (see baseless askos (F. 194)).

7. *The tripod cauldron* (MH) (F. 320). Tripod cauldrons overlap in shape, and presumably in use, with jars (Fig. 72b). Unevenness of the floors may explain their popularity since they must have stood more firmly than flat-based vessels. Although there were many cauldrons, they were not necessarily used for cooking, as many have been found with no signs of blacking on legs or bases. The legs were always added separately, the surface of the base being scored across to give a rough surface to which they could adhere. Cauldrons were generally flanged to receive a lid.

8. *The ladle or scoop* (C) (F. 311). This ladle resembles the brazier (F. 312) of Myc. I but is not bent up near the handle (Fig. 74e). On the other hand the handle is bent downwards to support the vessel when standing still, and to protect the hand from the heat of the contents.

9. *The handleless stemmed bowl* (C) (F. 307) is very rare. The only known specimen hitherto found at Mycenae is probably of Cycladic origin although derived from a Minoan prototype (Fig. 73a).

Another was recently discovered during his excavations at Kato Zakro in Crete by Professor Platon who published a picture of it in the

a. Handleless stemmed bowl
or 'fruit stand'

b. Ephyraean goblet

c. Ephyraean goblet

e. Beaked jug

d. Squat alabastron

f. Squat jug

Fig. 73. Mycenaean II vessels continued

a. Pithoid jar

b. Pithoid jar

c. Ewer

d. Pear-shaped ritual sprinkler

e. Ladle or scoop

f. Spouted cup with raised handle

Fig. 74. Mycenaean II vessels continued

Illustrated London News of 20th February 1964. It is also known as a 'fruit stand'.

10. *The pear-shaped ritual sprinkler* (F.202) is an elongated development of the ostrich egg type of Myc.I (Fig. 74d). It is fitted with a small ring-handle attached to the under side of the lip. Some specimens of this type have a peg-top shape and are elongated into a spout. There is a small handleless jar similar in shape, also derived from the ostrich egg sprinkler, belonging to Myc.II.

Parallel with this Mycenaean peg-top type is the gracefully shaped elongated oviform type of sprinkler, but this really forms part of the repertoire of the Minoan series of ritual sprinklers.

11. *The spouted cup with raised handle* (C) (F.253). Sometimes referred to as a ladle. The body is a shallow globular bowl and the handle a high flat loop (Fig. 74f). In the centre of the base is a small projection carefully turned as a kind of foot. The form occurs in Crete and Greece in MM and MH periods. Some varieties have a small spout at the side. The shape is common in Argolis and rare in Attica. In Attic tombs, their place was taken by a simpler, more domestic-looking ladle. A painted example is given in Furtwängler and Loeschke (Plate XVIII, No. 132).

VASE DECORATION CHARACTERISTICS OF MYC.II. This period marks the culmination of a process of development that had been going on since Middle Helladic II, namely the fusion of Minyan with Mycenaean art, and the completion of this process gives the best results achieved in the Mycenaean Era.

During Myc.II vases were made on the quick wheel, and horizontal lines were drawn while the vase was revolving on the wheel as can be seen from their evenness as compared with those of the preceding period.

Big vases were sometimes made up in sections or remodelled by hand after turning. The smaller vessels were made in graceful shapes, and naturalistic designs are seen at their best, especially on Ephyraean ware from Korakou near Corinth (see below). Although at the beginning of Mycenaean II it may be said that the style was derived entirely from Crete, and was introduced on to the mainland fully developed rather than deriving from Mycenaean I, it does not mean to say that all the Mycenaean designs of this period have an LM counterpart. Moreover, where a motif used on both Minoan and Mycenaean vases had a common prototype, it usually developed along different lines in Crete, and on the mainland.

The result was that towards the latter part of the period the style became more characteristically Mycenaean with a lesser degree of Cretan influence than hitherto.

The fabric of Myc.II is identical with that of Myc.I, while the paint is

ndant crocus

Spiral and papyrus

Running spiral

Ivy derivative

Octopus

Rock pattern

Rock work

Pendant

Papyrus

Papyrus

Rosettes

Lily

Palm

Ivy derivative

Argonaut

Scale and ivy leaf

Curved stripes

Shield

Ogival canopy

'Ephyraean' lily

Double axe

Arcade

'Adder mark'

'Ephyraean' nautilus

Fig. 75. Mycenaean II patterns

of the same colour and the same good quality. The use of white as an accessory colour became more common. Ornaments were mostly drawn free-hand but more carefully than those of the preceding period.

In the decoration, linear patterns take second place to naturalistic designs. There is, however, sometimes a more artistic combination of spirals in the formation of the heart-shaped ivy-leaf or in the formation of a more complicated spiraliform design such as the motif that combines the running spiral and papyrus (Fig. 75).

In Myc. I the dashes branch directly off the horizontal lines to suggest that the design is derived from a foliate spray. In the cups of Myc. II, however, they are not attached to the central stalk and simply run in lines parallel to it. The best vases of this period are decorated with naturalistic designs of which most are either floral or marine.

Among some of the patterns used we may specially notice the following:

Rockwork decoration of which there are two kinds: one with rounded outlines, chiefly convex curves, the other with concave curves joined by projecting knobs.

The papyrus motif which is derived from Egypt.

The rosette, very common in Minoan vase decoration, was also largely used in Mycenaean. For space filling there are a great many varieties, some of which evidently take their model from the wild flower seeds of Crete and the Peloponnese.

The lily was among the most popular subjects. It derived from the Minoan lily decorations which themselves were inspired by the Cretan lily that still flowers in the island in September. It first appeared in Myc. II in a fairly naturalistic form that became more conventionalised in the succeeding period. In both periods it was conventionalised into a design similar to the top of a fleur-de-lys.

The palm was also a favourite motif with an immense number of conventionalised variations.

Among other floral designs were the iris, the crocus, daisies, ivy-leaves and other plants, while the chief elements in marine designs were the octopus, the nautilus and seaweed.

In some cases the whole surface of a vase is stippled so as to produce a speckled effect in reddish brown or brownish black.

A very effective decorative motif characteristic of this period is called by Sir Arthur Evans the Ogival Canopy. It seems not impossible that it may have been inspired by pieces of ribbon seaweed attached to a stone.

The shield pattern is met with again and again, not only on vases, but also on a large scale in frescoes on the walls of Bronze Age palaces.

EPHYRAEAN WARE. In the excavation which he undertook at Korakou near Corinth in 1915, Professor Blegen discovered a style of pottery which belongs to the Myc. II period. As Korakou may have been the Homeric Ephyra, he gave it the name of Ephyraean ware. Besides the specimens found in Corinthia, others have been discovered at Mycenae and Tiryns, in Boeotia, and at Phylakopi in the island of Milo, where they were evidently imported from the mainland. Imitations have also been found in LM II contexts at Knossos and elsewhere in Crete, but of inferior quality both as regards fabric, shape and decoration (Figs. 73a and c). Some specimens of both Minoan and Mycenaean Ephyraean ware have also been identified in Rhodes.

With a single exception, namely a jug with a cut-away neck from Prosymna (Blegen, *Prosymna*, p. 415, Fig. 681), Ephyraean ware seems to be limited to one shape, the deep two-handled goblet on a short stem, a form which is clearly derived from vessels of metal. Like goblets of the same shape belonging to Myc. I and II, this goblet is a direct descendant of a characteristic Middle Helladic Minyan goblet, and as such, Ephyraean is essentially Minyan ware treated in Mycenaean technique. The whole surface of the vase, both inside and out, is coated with a smooth glaze-like slip of the same tone as the clay. Apart from this it is rarely painted on the inside, although occasional examples are coated inside with a deep brown paint. The smooth slip forms a ground for designs in lustrous paint of a rich orange-red or purple-brown, or nearly black. The black has a tendency to flake off more easily than the other colours. Some of these colour variations may be due to the firing, for the decoration on a vase has sometimes been found to shade from one colour to another. As a reliable date mark for Myc. II, Ephyraean ware has a particular importance.

A special attraction of the Ephyraean goblet lies in its proportions. The body and foot form a most graceful curve, crowned by a lip of the right width to suit the size of the vessel. In size and shape and position, the handles are perfectly suited to the curve of the body. The decoration of the Ephyraean goblet is simple and restrained. There are no zones to confine the painter in the placing of his decorative pattern, which is limited to one motif on each side of the vase.

Ephyraean decorative motifs are of two classes only, floral and marine. It is the floral patterns which are the more common, and of these the favourite is a lily of some sort, but so much stylised as to consist of only two spiraliform petals and three or four stamens. At the bottom of the stalk, roots are conventionally represented, sometimes carried up in graceful curves of two or three strands on each side of the flower.

Another flower may represent a budding crocus with a swelling bud in the centre and five narrow leaves on either side. Roots are indicated by short wavy lines at the bottom of a short stalk.

The large rosette on another goblet may be meant to represent a daisy, but it has no stalk to make identification certain. Some of the petals have a rotary twist as they approach the centre which gives the design an added attraction, almost a sense of movement.

Among the marine designs on Ephyraean vases, the favourite is the argonaut whose tentacles wave in spiral curls in a pattern admirably suited to the shape of the vase.

Although the main design on Ephyraean vases is really limited to a single motif, a small rosette is sometimes added between it and the handle when the flower was felt to be insufficiently decorative. Another feature of this ware is that both rim and base are left quite plain, apart from the lustrous slip that covers the whole vase. Altogether these Ephyraean vases have a special charm due to their harmonious shape and decoration which combine simplicity with graceful proportion.

Before leaving Mycenaean II, we ought to give a word of mention to Kakovatos. It is a place so small that it does not appear in the usual maps of Greece but it lies on the west coast of the Peloponnese, six miles north of the mouth of the river Neda and fifteen miles due south of Olympia as the crow flies.

Some forty miles to the south lies the Bay of Navarino sheltered from the sea by the remote and desolate island of Sphacteria, which as Pausanias observes (iv. 36.4) is an example of 'how human fortunes can confer renown on places previously unknown' – in this case the tale is told by Thucydides (iv. 2.40) of the military operations between Athens and Sparta which lasted for over two months in 425 BC. More important, however, for the fortunes of modern Greece was the battle fought in the Bay of Navarino on 20th October 1827 AD.

Just north of the island of Sphacteria lies the rocky promontory of Coryphasium, 450 feet high, crowned by the remains of a Venetian castle, as well as much older walls built, some in polygonal and some in Cyclopean style. For Pausanias, the promontory of Coryphasium was the site not only of the Pylos of classical times but was the abode of King Nestor of the Trojan War, nearly eight hundred years earlier.

Strabo, however, argued (vii. 3.22–29) that the Pylos of Homer lay somewhere in Trifylia, north of the River Neda, and following this clue, the German archaeologists Dörpfeld and Müller excavated at Kakovatos in 1907, and there discovered some tholos tombs with a series of fine pithoid jars among other Bronze Age objects. For the next thirty years archaeologists were prepared to place the Pylos of King Nestor at this spot, and even to associate one of the tombs at Kakovatos with the hero of the Trojan War.

It was not until shortly before the Second World War that the American archaeologist Carl Blegen revealed a new Pylos, not at Coryphasium but a few miles inland to the north-eastward at Ano Englianos, where he uncovered the foundations of a great building which archaeologists now assume to be the remains of what was once the real palace of Nestor.

The account of the excavations at Kakovatos, however, is of interest to us in view of the fine series of great Palace Style jars which Dörpfeld and his colleague unearthed. They belong to Myc. I and Myc. II periods. Drawings of one or two of them have been included in Sir Arthur Evans's *Palace of Minos*, but the report itself by Dörpfeld and Müller illustrated with the dim photographs of the period lies hidden away in obscure corners of archaeological libraries in Vol. 33 (1908) of the periodical with the formidable title: *Mitteilungen des Kaiserlich deutchen archaologischen Instituts Athenische Abteilung.* (Reports of the Imperial German Archaeological Institute. Athenian Section.)

MYCENAEAN III 1400–1100 BC

Mycenaean III may be said to have begun with the ending of active Minoan influence in Greece. It lasted for three hundred years (1400–1100 BC), as long a time span as separates us from the reign of King Charles II, whereas only about a century has been allotted by archaeologists to Myc. I and Myc. II.

During the Myc. I and Myc. II periods, Minoan forms and Minoan designs had been modified by mainland Greek Influence, but it was at a date which we may associate with the fall of Knossos in 1400 BC that mainland influence became predominant.

The Minoan spirit was one of freedom and naturalism; the Mycenaean of restraint and formalism. The flowers and animals which we find upon the Mycenaean vases have not got the free vivacity of the Cretan decorations.

A change in shape from that of Myc. II is noticeable. New types are seen in the kylix on a high stem, and the typical Mycenaean bowl and the stirrup jar, all of which became very popular as the period progressed.

The decoration of Mycenaean vases was nearly always fairly sober in style. The vase painter left the pot in its natural colour upon which he drew in red, brown or black, his designs drawn from the Cretan repertoire. It was only when he had the guiding hand of the Cretan artist that he had the courage to make experiments of his own, and when his designs acquired some originality of style and more forceful expressiveness. When this was withdrawn and the production of Mycenaean pottery expanded so much as it did in Myc. III, the vase painter had no time to create original patterns and was content largely to repeat the motifs of the earlier periods. Vase-making tended to become an industry rather than an art.

Design during Myc. III showed a progressive tendency towards

o

conventionalisation and stylisation, a tendency which lasted until the Geometric period of the early Iron Age.

In Myc. III the interior of the vase was almost always painted, usually brownish black in colour. This differs from the custom of the preceding period, when in almost every case the inside of the vase was left unpainted.

The Mycenaeans of Myc. III added little to the artistic heritage of Crete; on the contrary, with rare exceptions, the Minoan patterns were steadily reduced to stylised symbols which can hardly be recognised as representatives of the originals from which they evolved.

Although further removed from metal prototypes than the vessels of Myc. I and II, there are still in Myc. III a number of features in form and decoration which are deliberately suggestive of metal vases. The process of making metal and clay vessels is dictated by the material used. A clay vessel is made from one lump of clay except for the spout and the handle. A metal pot may have to be made in several sections; and where, for instance, the neck and body join, there will be a seam or ridge. The base of the clay pot is usually all one piece with the body. The base of a metal pot may be a separate piece, folded over and welded into the body, thus producing a more distinct base-ring than is usual in pottery. Clay handles are most commonly made from strips of clay, round in section. The handles of early metal vessels were frequently made of flat strips riveted to the vessel. These and other features of metallic origin may be seen in the ceramics of Myc. III. In pottery they have no functional purpose, and can only be explained as imitations of metal work, deliberate at first, but later traditional.

Even the colour and smooth finish of clay vessels may be intended to represent silver or gold or bronze. In Myc. III occur a number of pots painted all over with glossy red or brown or black paint. This seems to be a way of suggesting a shiny metal surface, and occurs most commonly on vases of metallic form. It should be borne in mind, however, that most of the known pottery of Myc. III comes from tombs, so that many of the pots which imitate metal prototypes may have been substitutes used for funeral purposes only.

Although the potters introduced scarcely any new types of vessel or even any new decorative patterns during the first half of Myc. III, this does not imply that they were bad craftsmen. Technically they were skilled craftsmen, but they were not creative artists. It was an age when more attention was paid to technical improvements than to artistic innovation. Generally speaking, the pottery of Myc. III was better made and better fired than that of Myc. II and I. This can be seen from the refinements of the clay and by the thin walls of the vases. The surface is covered with a slip of smooth, even texture, which varies in shade from buff with a slight greenish-yellow tint to a pale brick-red. There was a greater variety of shapes, partly because the period was longer than either of the preceding ones, and partly because more pottery seems to have been made.

In fact, Mycenaean III, at least in its earlier phases, may be said to mark the highest point attained during the Bronze Age on the Greek mainland in so far as the technical side of pottery manufacture is concerned. At no time before was the potter so skilful in fashioning vases of the most varied shapes with walls of nearly uniform thickness. His dexterity is particularly well illustrated by the slender high-stemmed kylikes so common in this period. The surface of the vase is usually coated with a smooth even slip, and the decoration carried out in lustrous paint generally applied in a coat of uniform thickness. Vases were made in countless numbers, and it is evident that the output of the potter had become industrialised to such an extent that it had become mass produced.

Myc. III is often referred to as a period of decline and decadence. It is true that the freshness of the preceding age had been lost, but in fact there was no real decadence until the end of Myc. III. Pure form was the aim of the potter's effort and he strove to obtain it through a refinement in the drawing of his decoration.

We also see a successful effort to refine the shapes of the vases not only in the graceful high-stemmed kylikes but also in vessels of other shapes. It is easy to recognise a striving for elegance of form in the long series of three-handled piriform jars with their slender shapes and curving shoulders. It is also evident in the varied shapes of the stirrup jars first introduced in Myc. III A. In so far as vase decoration was concerned, however, more attention was given to the mechanical rather than to the aesthetic side. This resulted in a growing spirit of restraint which eventually culminated in the almost mathematical exactitude of the Geometric Style of vase decoration which characterises the pottery of the Early Iron Age.

The freshness and freedom of design which were seen at their best in the Ephyraean ware of Myc. II vanished in Myc. III. The old zonal system of ornamentation came back into fashion again, and the decoration itself shows a tendency to use very conventionalised geometrical patterns.

These patterns are frequently arranged in panels on each side of the vase, separated from each other by groups of vertical lines. These lines are often fringed, while within them is in many cases a vertical space filled with figures. This panelled system of decoration is sometimes known as the 'Metope style'. It is chiefly associated with the typical krater or

a. Spouted bowl

b. Stand

d. 'Pilgrim' flask

c. Jug with cut-away neck

e. Piriform three-handled jug

Fig. 76. Mycenaean III A vessels

deep bowl, and it is well adapted for the decoration of vases of this form. But the panelled system of decoration was also extended to vases of other shapes, the high-stemmed kylix and jugs.

The spiral and its derivation again play a part in the decoration. Floral and marine motifs also occur but debased and highly formalised.

A large number of household vessels in the shape of domestic pots and pithoi were used in Myc. III. These were generally made of unpurified brick-red clay, often very thick and heavy. They have no painted decoration. A peculiar shape was found during the excavations by Blegen at Korakou with a thick incurving rim, evidently to prevent the contents from spilling or boiling over. It has no handles or lugs and was hand-made. Because this domestic pottery was not considered suitable for funeral purposes and so not found in tombs, few whole specimens have been discovered.

It was during Myc. III that Mycenaean pottery attained its widest diffusion. It has been found at many places on the mainland, in the Aegean Islands, at several places upon the coast of Asia Minor, in Cyprus, Syria and Egypt, in Sicily as well as in Sardinia – in fact, throughout the eastern Mediterranean zone from Sicily to Palestine. Within this wide range of time and space, there was naturally a considerable variety of both shape and decoration, partly due to the passage of time and partly due to differing materials and traditions in different localities. It thus appears that at this period there existed a wide-spread active seaborne traffic throughout the Mediterranean, a trade in which the towns of Argolis and Corinthia with their favourable situation took an active part. It is a point worth noting that no Mycenaean cemetery has been discovered in Athens except the Sub-Mycenaean graves excavated by the German Institute at the Kerameikos.

Archaeologists have agreed to divide the Mycenaean III period into three phases, Mycenaean III A, III B and III C, which are contemporary with the XVIIIth, XIXth and XXth Dynasties of the Egyptian New Kingdom and can be dated within certain limits. Phase A lasts from 1400 to 1300 BC, Phase B covers the thirteenth century BC and Phase C covers the twelfth.

So far as ceramics are concerned, these prehistoric phases are each distinguished by pottery characteristic of that phase. Generally speaking, the three successive stages of Myc. III ceramic development are associated respectively with the names of Tel-el-Amarna on the Nile (192 miles above Cairo); Zygouries near Corinth; and the Granary at Mycenae; as well as some Mycenaean-inspired Philistine ware from Palestine.

Mycenaean III A 1400–1300 BC

SHAPES. Generally speaking, Myc. III A is typified by a quantity of pottery found at Tel-el-Amarna in Egypt, most of which seems to come from Rhodes and some from the mainland of Greece. It dates from about 1380 to 1350 BC. The decoration of the style is fundamentally a degenerate form of LM ornament, so that the naturalistic designs of octopus, triton shell or flowers of Late Minoan became so stylised as to be hardly recognisable (Figs. 76, 77 and 78).

It is strange to think that Mycenaean Greek pottery of this very remote period should be principally associated with a deposit found at a small place on the Nile about two hundred miles above Cairo, where it provides the best clue we have for dating pottery of this period. It was in fact a large city in antiquity, the city of Akhenaten, and the Mycenaean pottery found there among the Egyptian is uniformly of Myc. III A date. It is mostly of the usual Rhodian-Cypriot type which is also comparatively common in Argolis. Most of the shapes found there, or rather the sherds, for whole vases were rare, belong to such vessels as the pilgrim flask, the stirrup jar and an amphora, all of which were small and suitable for travelling, since it was the contents of the vases rather than the vases themselves which were important. A few sherds from cups, bowls and fillers were also excavated, showing the presence of an Aegean community among the Egyptian.

Two sherds from a big water-jar were also unearthed, probably a stirrup jar, bear so strong a resemblance to examples found by Blegen at Zygouries near Corinth, that it is reasonable to suggest that the vessel was almost certainly brought up the Nile on a barge, and probably contained water or wine for the crew.

The motifs on sherds found at Tel-al-Amarna are very few, and consist mostly of chevrons, spirals, U's, wavy lines, a very conventionalised palm flower, and bands, thick or thin, encircling the pot.

Mycenaean III A began when the formalising tendency became a dominant feature. Few new pottery shapes made their appearance; those in Myc. II continued, but reduced to a more restrained style of shape or design.

Curiously enough, the Myc. II style had not been much influenced by Crete, whereas a new Cretan influence appeared in Myc. III A, implying a closer relationship between Crete and the mainland.

With the pottery found in Wace's excavations at Mycenae, and those of Schliemann as published by Fürtwängler and Loeschke, we get an excellent picture of the ceramic art of Mycenae throughout the Myc. III period.

a. Stemmed goblet

b. Deep krater with two
vertical handles

c. False-necked or stirrup jar

d. Feeding bottle

Fig. 77. Mycenaean III A vessels continued

We have already mentioned the kylix as one of the vessels which are common to all Mycenaean periods, but as an instance of the changes in style during the three phases of Myc. III, we cannot do better than use it as an example.

During Myc. III A, the shape was half-way between the Ephyraean goblets of Myc. II and the high-stemmed champagne cup kylix of Myc. III B. The body is deep, and borne by a relatively short stem resting on a slightly domed foot. It is a form which goes back to Myc. I and may be taken as an imitation of the more costly metal ones, such as the four gold goblets in the National Archaeological Museum in Athens. We shall see how the shape and decoration alter in Myc. III B. Some characteristic Myc. III A shapes are given below.

1. *The stand* (MC) (F. 336) was often used with a small-based deep krater so as to give it more stability. The one shown has a concave cylindrical shape with three ogival openings which thus form three wide legs (Fig. 76b).

2. *The pilgrim flask* (C) (F. 188) has a globular body slightly flattened, with a ring foot, a very narrow neck and two vertical loop handles which stand on the shoulder and join the neck about half-way up or sometimes a bit higher (Fig. 76d). The pilgrim flask is often found in the Mycenaean ware of Cyprus where it is almost twice as common as elsewhere, and where it was probably adapted from Syrian or Syro-Egyptian models. It must have been fairly common in Myc. III A since it is a frequent shape in the Tel-el-Amarna sherds.

The earliest Minoan models have short necks and flattened lentoid bodies decorated with concentric rings or spiral coils said to imitate the grain of a wooden original. If one examines the old wooden pilgrim flasks to be found in Rhodes, however, it is not the grain of the wood that one sees, but the circles made by the tool of a lathe. Some pilgrim flasks were made with only one handle.

3. *The deep krater with two vertical handles* (C) (F. 7) may almost be regarded as a large version of the early type of stemmed goblet, a Mycenaean creation of Myc. I. (Fig. 77b). Where, in some cases, these deep kraters had a very small base, and therefore little stability, they were mounted on a stand like the one described above (F. 336).

4. *The tall piriform jug with three handles* (F. 151). A number of specimens of this graceful jug with narrow concave neck, short beak and three perpendicular handles have been found in Rhodes, while some have been found at Mycenae and Argos (Fig. 76e). The shape is known as 'advanced piriform', for the foot tends to become narrower than in Myc. II. Another version of this class of jug has only two handles.

5. *The spouted bowl* (F. 290) has a wide mouth and narrower base

a. Basket vase

b. Conical filler

c. Conical filler

d. Stirrup jar

Fig. 78. Mycenaean III A vessels continued

(Fig. 76a). The sides are contracted in a hollow or double curve. Two rounded loop-handles are usually set horizontally below the lip. On one side between them is a spout, sometimes bridged and sometimes an open trough. Decorated examples are rare before the Myc. III A period.

6. *The feeding bottle* (MH) (F. 159) has a basket handle spanning the lip, and a tubular spout projecting from the body (Fig. 77d). It is possible that it may have appeared before the end of Myc. II, deriving its origin from a Middle Helladic or even an early Helladic shape, but it is common in Myc. III A. This is a shape characteristic of the mainland, but very rare in Crete. It is really a drinking flask, but the name 'feeding bottle' is convenient to distinguish it from other shapes of pouring vessels.

7. *The basket vase* (MC) (F. 319) is a simple open globular shape with an arched handle (Fig. 78a). Some specimens are fitted with small legs.

8. *The false-necked or stirrup jar* (C) (F. 182 etc.). Although deriving from the Middle Minoan period in Crete, the false-necked or stirrup jar did not appear, save for a few isolated examples, in the Mycenaean repertoire, before Myc. III A, but it became the most characteristic shape of Myc. III, and persisted right through the remainder of the Mycenaean Era (Figs. 77c and 78d). Since stirrup jars are found at nearly all Mycenaean sites, they provide valuable dating evidence.

The jar has many varieties of globular form: ovoid, spherical or more or less depressed, as well as tall with a contracted foot, and squat with a flat shoulder. Many of these shapes, however, were in use at the same time.

On top is a short closed central stem (the 'false neck') across which a low flat 'stirrup' handle is arched. As a general rule the stirrup jar has a ringed foot.

Perhaps the stirrup jar was invented in Gournia in eastern Crete, for the early examples seem more common there than elsewhere; but although it originated in Crete, it is far more common on the mainland in Myc. III than in Crete in LM III.

The later ones sometimes have an air-hole at the foot of the false neck to increase the rate of flow of the contents, as well as an elongation of spout and handles.

These stirrup jars vary so much in size and shape that they cannot all have been used for the same purpose. The small ones may have contained some precious liquid, but the largest ones must have been treated as storage jars.

The scheme of decoration for stirrup jars of Myc. III A and B is fairly general. The usual design on the body of the jar is a succession of broad encircling bands enclosing a varying number of thin bands. On the

Ivy derivative	Flower	Argonaut	Running spiral
Stemmed spiral	Murex shell	Cuttlefish	Cuttlefish and flower
Octopus	Octopus conventional	Papyrus	Flower
Arcade	Triglyph	Running spiral	Rosettes
Man	Tri-curved arches	Fish	Chariot
Robed figure	Horse	Bull	Bird

Fig. 79. Mycenaean III A patterns

shoulder, the most common motif is a stylised flower or some variation, while a subsidiary zone of decoration occurs below the shoulder.

The stirrup jar was exported in thousands during the fourteenth century BC to Egypt where it is constantly found in Egyptian tombs of the XVIIIth and XIXth Dynasties. It was even imitated in Egyptian blue faience with Egyptian designs in black.

VASE DECORATION CHARACTERISTIC OF MYC. III A. The ornamentation of the Myc. III A style derived not only from Cretan LM II and III but also from Myc. II with a few additions of Mycenaean creation, particularly that of horizontal stripes which may have been inspired by veined stone (Fig. 79).

Conventionalisation of natural motifs continued to such an extent that the ivy-leaf became a chevron, while the shell of the argonaut disappeared to leave only three spiral coils. This tendency would probably have evolved into an almost geometric style of decoration had it not been for the adoption of new Minoan motifs which checked evolution in that direction.

As in the preceding period lustrous paint was used for vase decoration, but more often red than black owing to the use of higher temperatures for firing in the kiln. Linear decoration was more exactly drawn, and reached its acme of technical skill during this period. The Myc. III A spiral, however, is not as well made as in Myc. I. The centre disc is frequently missing, and there is a relatively coarser effect in this motif.

A new element was introduced into Mycenaean vase painting in Myc. III A. This was the pictorial element which up to 1400 BC was extremely rare in the Aegean, but from then on it became more common, especially on pottery made and decorated for the Cypriot market. This style, both in its figure drawing and composition was Mycenaean, but the style itself was probably created to satisfy the oriental taste which always leaned towards exuberance in decoration and to which pictorialism exercised a strong appeal. This Cypro-Mycenaean pictorial style of Myc. III A, of which chariot scenes form the favourite theme, continued throughout the fourteenth century BC, and although a common style of shape and decoration is evident, many of the centres of manufacture developed their own variations, particularly in Rhodes and Cyprus.

In drawing human beings, the artist did not draw the ear but left a space where the hair curves round it. In the earlier examples he drew the eye in the shape of an oval touching the forehead. In later examples it was drawn round with a dot in the centre, so that it looks like the eye of a chicken.

Men are always shown standing, either in a long robe, driving a chariot, or naked. The robe was derived from a fashion introduced from the east which became increasingly popular. These robed figures are generally shown wearing a sword, a feature which does not appear in Minoan figures of the sort. The swords are sometimes drawn with a tassel hanging from the end which shows that it was housed in a sheath. The naked men are warriors, attendants or grooms who would presumably be wearing only the Minoan loin-cloth.

Nearly all these human figures are from Rhodian or Cypriot vases of the Mycenaean period. Drawings of men from the Greek mainland are more often shown wearing a kilt which is sometimes fringed, or a belted chiton.

Chariot groups which formed so favourite a subject during the Mycenaean III periods, were specially popular in Cyprus, where Mycenaean ware is known as Levanto-Mycenaean. In the early examples an effort was made to show two horses, but later on the body of one horse only was shown, equipped with two tails and four legs to indicate the two horses of the chariot.

In the early examples the artist tried to show the two heads in profile, but with further conventionalism these two heads tended to grow into one which was turned to show full face with round eyes and a dot in the centre which gives them an air of astonished surprise.

Bulls were another favourite subject of vase decoration during Mycenaean III. Generally the whole body is shown, but sometimes the artist drew only the head and forefeet. As a rule the head is shown in profile, but occasionally it is turned so as to show full-face with the usual little surprised circles for eyes. Sometimes the patches on the hide are represented by a trefoil motif along the outline while circles or crosses or zig-zag lines ornament the body of the animal as if they were inspired by a cross-stitch pattern. These drawings of bulls are not derived from Egyptian or Assyrian ones but are of independent Minoan inspiration.

Birds, partly derived from the decorative motifs of the Cycladic potters, with whom they had been very popular, appear and gradually deteriorate.

During Myc. III A motifs taken from the sea were popular. A kylix from Aegina and in the Aegina Museum is ornamented with murex shells swimming diagonally across the cup. Another favourite motif from the marine world is the cuttlefish (Fig. 77a). In particular, a goblet from Rhodes and now in the Copenhagen Museum shows a powerfully stylised cuttlefish. Its body is divided into two parts connected only by a thin stalk. The top part has a profile like that of the goblet itself out of which wavy arms emerge. In these kylikes of Myc. III A, the pattern is always confined between horizontal strips. Octopus and argonauts also occur frequently on Myc. III A vases as effective decorative motifs.

As for the patterns taken from the plant world, they derive from a few prototypes, mostly the papyrus head in a number of variations. Sometimes these have stems, but more often they are without a stem, in which case they consist of single or double chevrons with the angle filled in by concentric arcs.

A characteristic of the earlier part of Myc. III A is the simplification of motifs by the omission of details, with a greater tendency, therefore, towards conventionalisation. This tendency is often carried to such lengths that some of the stylised designs of this period bear little resemblance to the objects from which they are derived. For instance:

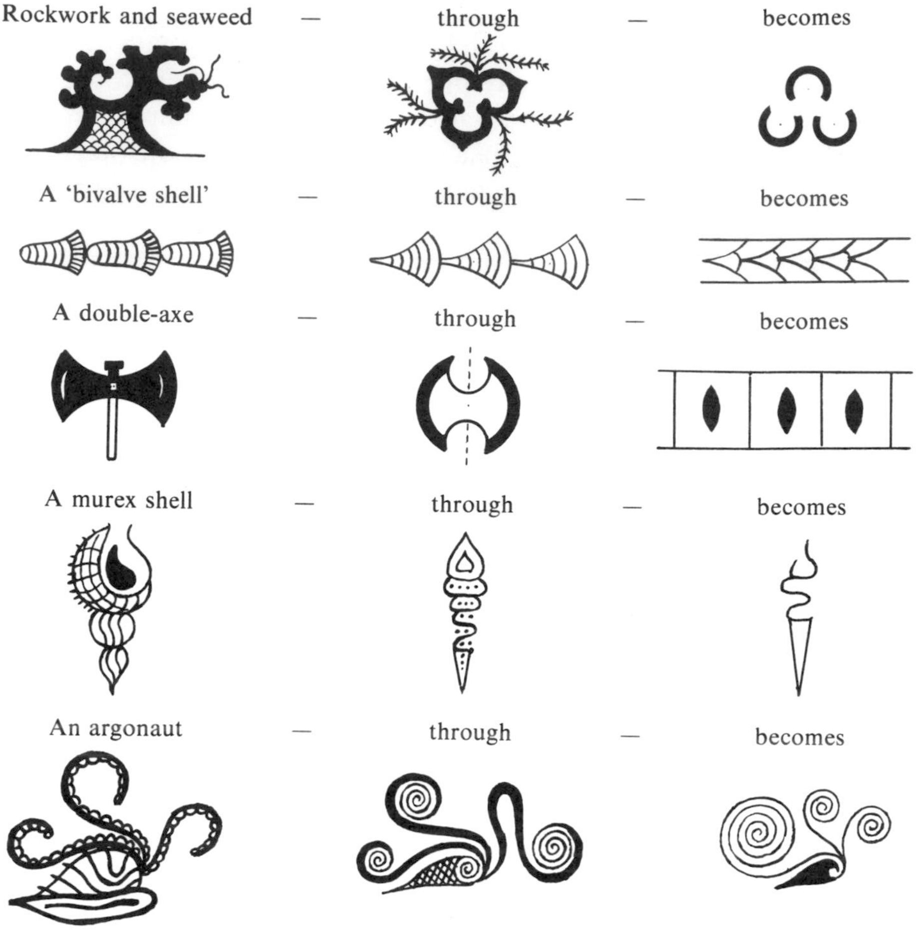

Rockwork and seaweed   —   through   —   becomes

A 'bivalve shell'   —   through   —   becomes

A double-axe   —   through   —   becomes

A murex shell   —   through   —   becomes

An argonaut   —   through   —   becomes

Fig. 80. Progressive simplification of motifs

At this stage the two contemporary styles began to diverge, so that whereas Myc. III is to some extent a continuation of Myc. II, the Cretan LM III is a continuation of the Palace Style. In the latter part of Myc. III A, there is a reduction in the number of designs from stock patterns, and a further standardisation with a tendency to reduce still more the ornamental motifs to very simple, almost curvilinear forms:

Palm   Argonaut   Papyrus

Fig. 81. Standard motifs

The ornamental repertoire was reduced to a limited number of simple standard designs till they became mechanically repeated formulae, a process almost essential with the improvement in communications and the consequent need for mass production to meet increased demand.

The style of the period was a further stage in the process of separation of the Mycenaean from its Minoan parent. Although there was a lack of novelty and originality in the ornamental designs, the linear decoration was as a rule reasonably well executed.

In discussing the octopus as a decorative motif, an interesting point is made in *Asine 1922–1930* by Frödin and Persson (Stockholm 1938), page 402.

The authors say that some of the designs on Myc. III vases attributed to a derivation from the octopus are in reality derived from a species of cuttlefish known as the Loligo which has an elongated shell and ten rather short tentacles. Nor are these motifs, they say, conventionalised palm trees.

The point is illustrated as follows:

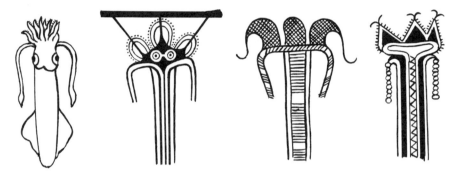

Fig. 82. Loligo and Loligo patterns on Mycenaean III pottery

Mycenaean III B 1300–1200 BC

SHAPES. Of the three phases of Myc. III, the most widespread category is that of Myc. III B. A much greater quantity of pottery of this period has been found than that of Myc. III A, including a great variety of bowls, kylikes and jugs, as well as pilgrim flasks, pithoid jars and necked kraters.

From the pictorial style of much of the decoration, it seems that the greater quantity of the pottery, although Mycenaean in style, was of local manufacture. There was no great difference between the pots of mainland Greece and those of Cyprus or Rhodes, and this similarity implies an active trade in the pottery itself (Fig. 83).

The style is noteworthy for its remarkable uniformity all over the

Mycenaean world, which included the Peloponnese, Attica, Boeotia, Phocis and Locris, part of Thessaly, and the islands of the southern Aegean. It also embraced parts of Asia Minor and southern Italy, as well as ports upon the coast of Syria, and the island of Cyprus.

Among Professor Blegen's finds at Zygouries were a number of high-stemmed kylikes, which from ornament, shape and stratification date from III B (Fig. 83a).

Among the contents of a tomb at Episcopi in Cyprus were a high-stemmed kylix, a flat vase and a conical filler of similar characteristics as well as an Egyptian scarab of the time of Rameses II (1296–1230). Thus we have a pointer for dating Myc. III B.

Pottery of this period is also found in quantity in Rhodes, but with local variations which rather tend to cling to the traditions of Myc. III A. It has also been found in isolated deposits at several sites such as Phylakopi in Milo, and in the island of Paros. Owing to this great homogeneity, it is not always possible to say with certainty where the imported pottery came from.

As far as style is concerned, it is mostly typified by pottery found in the 'potter's shop' and the tombs of Zygouries near Corinth, as well as by that found in the earlier strata near the Lion Gate of Mycenae, and near the west wall of Tiryns. We may in fact date the Lion Gate at Mycenae as belonging to Myc. III B or late III A from the many sherds found nearby and underneath.

The type of vase which represents the most noticeable difference from that of Myc. III A is the kylix which has changed from the goblet form and become nearer to that of the champagne cup. The body, however, is still fairly low, but the stem is taller and slenderer than the shape of Myc. III A.

The commonest form of vessel in Myc. III B was probably the open bowl, though the most important vessel found in tombs is the stirrup jar where the globular type becomes more squat, and the shoulder patterns more linear.

A noteworthy feature of Myc. III B is the popularity of the round loop handle.

It occurs on three new forms of vessel which came into frequent use:

  i. The large bowl.
  ii. The deep bowl.
  iii. The bowl with foot.

The first two forms were especially common.

The technique of vase formation during Myc. III B was of high quality with finely prepared clay covered with a slip. More and more quickly

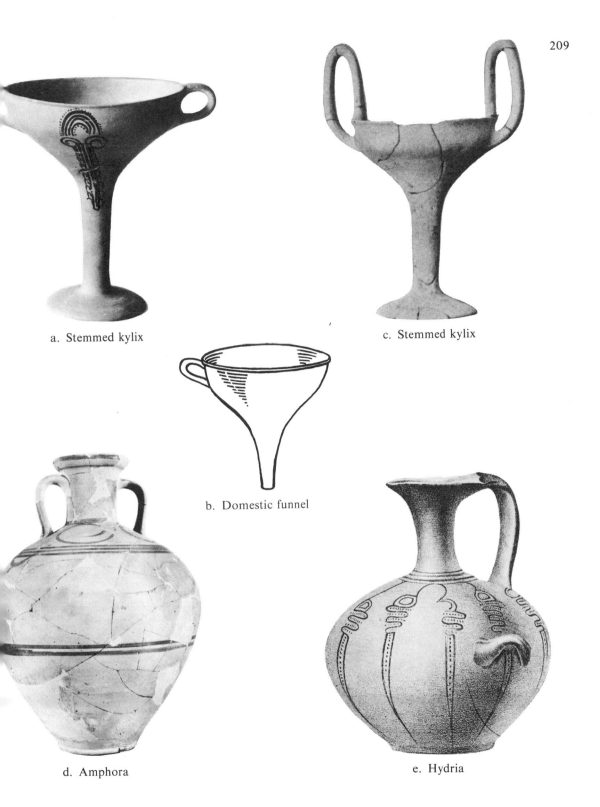

a. Stemmed kylix

c. Stemmed kylix

b. Domestic funnel

d. Amphora

e. Hydria

Fig. 83. Mycenaean III B vessels

revolving wheels were used, and kilns for firing at increasingly higher temperatures, while skill in forming and painting the vessels gradually attained a high degree of precision.

Although pottery was not, of course, all made in one district, and distributed from there to others, it would appear as if the style in both shape and decoration originated in one district, and was accepted and adopted by the potters of other areas throughout the period. Although of Minoan inspiration, the style was a creation of mainland Greece, and its place of origin was almost certainly Argolis with its capital at Mycenae.

With the extension of Mycenaean culture and art, itself of Cretan and Minoan origin, over the whole Greek world, the great period of the Greek Bronze Age drew to an end. A common static civilisation managed to maintain an equilibrium from about 1350 BC to 1250 BC when warlike convulsions broke out in the Mediterranean lands, convulsions which seriously affected the security even of Egypt and brought devastation to Greece and the speedy decline of her ancient civilisation.

In the pottery of the period we can trace a decadence that seems to have set in during the thirteenth century BC and produced various local styles which were eventually supplanted by the Geometric pottery of the early Iron Age. On the development of the Geometric Style of pottery decoration, these local styles appear to have exercised a considerable influence, so that even in the eighth and seventh centuries BC there are still traces of Mycenaean ceramic art. The technique of vase painting remained the same. The old Minoan tradition was never entirely lost.

The following are some specimens characteristic of this period:

1. *The domestic funnel* (MC) (F.198) shaped like a modern funnel with curved convex-concave outline, and a handle from the rim to the side (Fig. 83b).

2. *The deep bowl or krater* (C) (F.281) with two horizontal handles (Fig. 84a). It could be used as a mixing bowl, or fitted with a lid and used as a storage jar.

It is an early form of krater derived from similar Cretan shapes of the LM II period. The best-known example is the warrior vase which belongs to Myc. III C.

3. *The ritual peg-top filler* (C) (F.201). The type shown here (Fig. 84b) has an egg-shaped upper part, and like the domestic funnel, has a convex-concave outline ending in a spout with a hole in the bottom. A Cretan vessel of almost identical shape dating from about 1500 BC (LM I) was found at the Palace of Phaestos.

4. *The stemmed kylix* (MC) (F.273) has a great variety of shapes, and is common to all Mycenaean periods from I to III C. The type with the

a. Deep bowl or krater
Cypriot Mycenaean

c. Triple jug

b. Ritual peg-top filler

d. Cylindrical narrow-necked
jug with trefoil mouth
Cyprus

Fig. 84. Mycenaean III B vessels continued

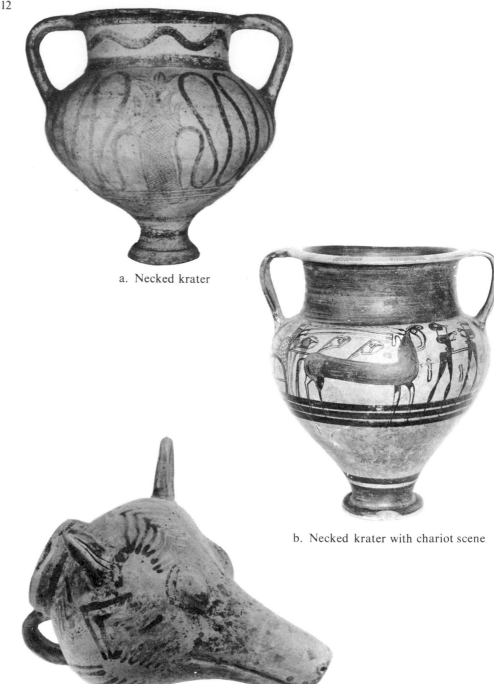

a. Necked krater

b. Necked krater with chariot scene

c. Fox's head rhyton

Fig. 85. Mycenaean III B necked kraters

two raised handles occurs in III A, B and C, but is rare by comparison with those shapes having horizontal handles (Fig. 83c).

5. *The double jug* (MH) (F. 325) is an example of several different kinds of composite vessels, some with two, some with three or more cups joined together by clay connections (Fig. 84c). The example shown here has a high inverted U-shaped handle.

6. *The amphora* (C) (F. 69). The amphoroid jar (Fig. 83d) is a common Mycenaean form which probably originated in MM II. It persisted in a great number of variations in all Mediterranean countries throughout the centuries and is still in use today. The shape shown here, however, is a new one which appears first in Myc. III B.

7. *The cylindrical narrow-necked jug* (F. 139) is common in Cephalonia and Cyprus (Fig. 84d). It is a Cypriot oenochoe, of Levanto-Mycenaean type and may have originated from a Syrian prototype.

8. *The hydria* (MC) (F. 128) is a vessel of tall neck and roughly globular body with an old mainland tradition (Fig. 83e). It is a variant of the ordinary jug, usually plain or very simply decorated.

9. *The necked krater* (F. 55). A characteristic vessel of Myc. III A and III B is the 'necked krater' (Figs. 85a and b). It is a type rare both in Rhodes and the mainland of Greece and is primarily a Cypriot type of vase. The great majority are decorated in a style peculiar to Cyprus. The broad zone round the upper part of the pot normally bears a frieze of animals or birds, or most typical of all, a chariot scene. It is a lively and imaginative style of pictorial decoration, and the designs on the better examples have fascinating drawings of animals, birds and chariot scenes.

VASE DECORATION CHARACTERISTIC OF MYC. III B. Nearly all the decorative motifs of Myc. III B were derived from those of Myc. III A. There are a few exceptions to this rule, and amongst them are:

The chequer board

Certain variations on
the zig-zag

A variation on the
tassel pattern

and due to influence from contemporary Cretan style (LM III):

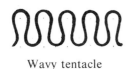

Wavy tentacle

Panelling

Fig. 86. Mycenaean III B special patterns

In the thirteenth century, the pictorial style which began in Myc. III A about 1400 BC may have begun to lose some of the vigour of its earlier compositions, but on the other hand it became more decorative.

Animal figures drawn in outline formed favourite decorative subjects

Fig. 87. Mycenaean III B patterns

(Fig. 87). Bodies were filled in with motifs that look like embroidery which give a pleasant decorative effect. The bodies of others are filled in with parallel wavy lines. It is not impossible that these new features derived their inspiration from embroidered textiles imported from the Near East.

Stags and goats became popular subjects for vase decoration while birds were very much stylised, generally without wings and with the body filled in with small crosses or parallel wavy lines. A comparison with the birds of Myc. III A shows quite a different manner of treatment.

To turn to the decoration of the stemmed kylikes of this period, we find that murex shells appear in a more stylised form than in Myc. III A. They no longer swim obliquely through the water. They always hang vertically on the side of the vase, sometimes in pairs back to back or front to front. The tail is sometimes ornamented with a line of dots as before, but even here a short-cut is used sometimes in the form of a line down the middle, or the tail is even left empty or painted plain black.

The complicated cuttlefish that used to ornament the kylix of Myc. III A has also undergone a metamorphosis. Of the original eight, only two curving arms are left with two eyes floating detached below them. The body hangs down like a long cigar. The argonauts or nautili have lost their shells; only the arms remain, ending in spirals.

Turning to the plant ornaments, we find a further stylisation of the same motifs as in Myc. III A.

In Myc. III A the papyrus head was represented by single or multiple chevrons closed by an arc of radial leaves and containing a curved headed stamen. In Myc. III B it becomes a four-sided geometrical figure. Two sides of this are formed by a single, double or triple chevron, while the other two sides are composed of a row of short dashes. The stamen in the middle has become a small hook. The progress from Myc. III A to III B appears as follows:

1–4 – Myc. III A; 5 – Myc. III B

Fig. 88. Progressive stylisation of papyrus head

One of the most characteristic forms of ornament of Myc. III B, although it begins in Myc. III A and continues into III C is known as the Panelled or Metope Style of decoration. It occurs principally on deep bowls in the space between the rim and the lines which encircle the lower part of the pot. This panelled style is not limited, however, to deep bowls, but is also found in mugs, large bowls, footed bowls, squat jars, stirrup jars and jugs. The earliest examples of the Panelled Style were inspired by the double-axe or butterfly motif, and other patterns of the system are known as the Wavy Border, the Triglyph and Half-Rosette, the Horizontal Wavy Line pattern and the Chequers pattern.

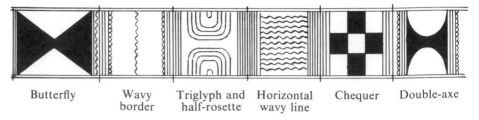

| Butterfly | Wavy border | Triglyph and half-rosette | Horizontal wavy line | Chequer | Double-axe |

Fig. 89. Mycenaean III B panelled or metope style ornaments

In the case of the Half-Rosette, the pattern looks much like the later Protogeometric Style, but the Myc. III B style was done by hand whereas the Protogeometric semi-circles and straight lines were usually done with compass and ruler.

We have not so far mentioned the animal rhyton in this survey of Mycenaean pottery. A lifelike example in the form of a fox's head found at Tiryns and dated to Myc. III B can be seen in the Ashmolean Museum at Oxford (Fig. 85c).

Mycenaean III C 1200–1100 BC

The breaking up of the Mycenaean world in Myc. III C was already foreshadowed in III B by the fact that pottery of the Mycenaean type imported into Syria, Palestine and Egypt was in fact mostly produced in Cyprus rather than in Argolis, until the time arrived when imports of pottery into those countries from the Greek mainland ceased altogether.

Up to now we have no definite chronological grounds such as dated tomb discoveries for the Myc. III C period. We are, however, given a hint by drawings representing stirrup jars in the tomb of Rameses III (1198–1167 BC) which bear a strong resemblance to the Myc. III C specimens with high slender false necks and handles which slope inwards as they join the shoulder of the vase. Moreover in a tomb at Mouliana in Crete were found stirrup jars of the LM III C period as well as swords similar to those found in Egypt and inscribed with the name of Seti II (1209–1205 BC).

Myc. III C is principally associated with two styles of vase decoration known as the 'Granary Style' and the 'Close Style', which we will deal with separately after listing some of the vase shapes otherwise characteristic of Myc. III C.

Another example of Myc. III C ware has been found in South Palestine. It is Mycenaean-inspired Philistine ware dating from about 1190 BC. It is interestingly discussed and illustrated by Mr Desborough in his book *The Late Mycenaeans and their Successors*. It is, he says, locally made, but has strong stylistic affinities with Cyprus.

SHAPES. Some shapes characteristic of Myc. III C are:

1. *The storage jar* (MH) (F.63). A large storage jar of ovoid shape with a slightly raised neck designed to take a lid (Fig. 90a).

2. *The squat jar with concave sides* (F.97). The squat jar with concave sides is sometimes referred to as a pyxis, but it is more appropriately considered as a development of the straight-sided alabastron (F.89) of Myc. I. The type has been found in Tiryns and Rhodes.

3. *The stamnos with vertical handles* (F.58). This ovoid type of storage amphora is common in Myc. III C (Fig. 90b). It has a concave neck with or without a short lip. Finds are widely distributed, i.e. in Mycenae, Milo, Rhodes and Athens.

4. *The pithos* (MH) (F.13). Pithoi must have been used, as they are today, for storage jars and water-butts. Sometimes the dead were buried in them, but this did not necessarily imply the creation of a special funerary type. Pithoi are always of coarse clay, and were made up in sections. Some have been found split apart showing how one edge was finished with a groove and the other with a tongue to facilitate attachment. A band, generally with some form of moulded or incised decoration, was applied over the join to conceal and strengthen it. The rim, if thick, was added in the same way. The general shape is tall for its width. As a rule there is no very pronounced curve on the sides, but sometimes there is a definite shoulder. Handles, which are usually vertical, may be attached at the rim, on the shoulders, or below the widest part of the body.

An interesting and beautiful handleless specimen comes from Mycenae and is in the museum at Nauplia (Fig. 90c). It is described by Furumark as a burial pithos of tall ovoid shape tapering to the mouth which has a thick horizontal lip. The broadest part of the body has three zones each containing three parallel undulating bands with transverse incisions. Between and above these zones, and separated from them by moulded bands, are narrower ones containing finely incised running spirals, and below the lowest broad zone is a series of four narrow mouldings. The neck is decorated with vertical ribs between which are moulded curved bands. The rich and finely executed relief decoration is unique.

5. *The ring vase* (MC) (F.196) is classed as an askos (Fig. 90d). Ring vases also occur in Egypt, Anatolia and in the Cyclades. A good selection of them is to be found in the little archaeological museum on the island of Mykonos. Some have small round handles at the base of the neck, others have ones which span the ring.

6. *The pyxis* (MC) (F.12). Pyxides must have been used like present-day ornamental boxes to contain jewelry or other valuables or cosmetics They presumably all once had lids. The Mycenaean one in Fig. 90e

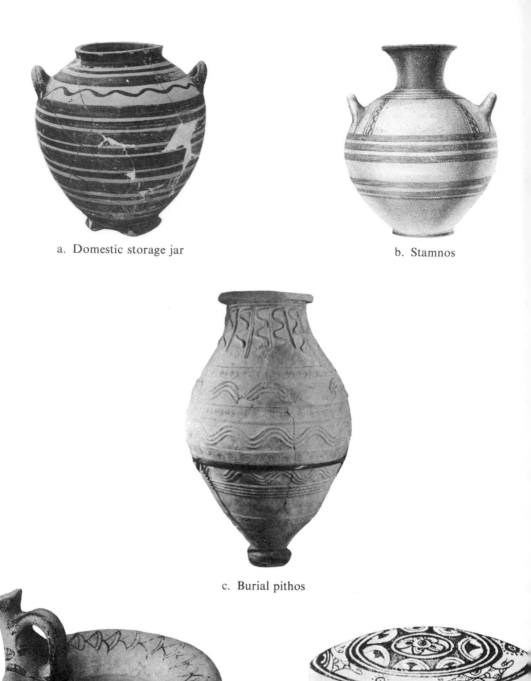

a. Domestic storage jar

b. Stamnos

c. Burial pithos

d. Ring vase

e. Pyxis

Fig. 90. Mycenaean III C vessels

is nearer the Cycladic than the Minoan form and may be a ceramic version of an old form made of other materials.

The 'Granary Style' ware. During his excavations at Mycenae in 1922–23 Professor Wace unearthed a distinct class of pottery to which he gave the name of 'Granary Style' because much of it was found in the corridors of a building just inside the Lion Gate which was assumed to have been a granary.

With it was found some pottery decorated in what is known as the 'Close Style' which will be referred to later.

It is thought that the Granary Style pottery began about the middle of Myc. III C, but generally speaking it seems to have been characteristic of the period, and is that variety of pottery which was in fashion at Mycenae at the time of its destruction by the Dorian invaders. Specimens of this class have also been found at Pylos in the south-west Peloponnese and at Ialysos in Rhodes.

The Granary Style pottery is inferior to the earlier Myc. III ware, and the vases seem to have been more hastily made; the clay is less well refined, and has a poor surface, while the decorative paint is washy and not very shiny (Fig. 91). In fact this pottery is more crudely made, and is painted with sketchy and unskilful designs. It is even sometimes made without a slip. The paint is usually black or brown, and sometimes red. It is wheel-made, but the wheel marks are somewhat uneven. The patterns are almost exclusively linear, and comprise mostly bands, dashes, S-shaped ornaments, concentric semi-circles and antithetic spirals.

It may not sound of much importance, but in fact it is a style which was the basis for later stylistic progress, if progress it can be called. Moreover, it has enabled the destruction of certain Mycenaean centres to be dated to the latter part of the twelfth century BC by its presence in the burnt layers.

It probably originated in Argolis, and appears to have survived until it merged with the sub-Mycenaean and later the Protogeometric style of pottery.

Although few kylikes decorated in the Granary Style were found by Wace at Mycenae, numerous examples were discovered at Korakou and Asine. From them we see the last Mycenaean shape of the high-stemmed kylix. Through continuous degeneration it has evolved into a stiff shape with conical bowl, less well-shaped handles, a small foot and inferior decoration. Further development of the kylix was almost exhausted, and in most regions it is missing after the Mycenaean Era.

In his essay, *The Last Days of Mycenae*, written in 1956, Wace points out that the final destruction of Mycenae was a crucial event in the

a. Bowl

b. Deep bowl

c. Three-handled jar

d. Krater

e. Krater

Fig. 91. Mycenaean III C 'Granary Style' vessels

Fig. 92. Stemmed kylikes

early history of Greece, and that if it were possible to date it with some approach to accuracy we should possess a fixed point of great value both historically and archaeologically. The archaeological date, he says, can be deduced with some degree of accuracy in terms of sequence dating of Mycenaean pottery. Archaeological sequence dates are best derived from a study of the pottery from inhabited sites rather than from tombs. It will be understood that the passage of time can be measured with some accuracy by the gradual and natural accumulation of debris which is characteristic of the undisturbed deposit of very early inhabited sites.

Moreover on any inhabited site the process of slow development and change can be read in the evolution of pottery. Pottery style does not change suddenly but gradually.

Evidence from a tomb, which is a closed deposit, provides a view of pottery only at a given time, and is, therefore, less reliable for sequence dating than that from the successive strata of an inhabited site where the process of development and change can be read in the evolution of the pottery.

Unfortunately at Mycenae itself, owing to the steepness of the citadel, and to consequent erosion by wind and rain as well as various human disturbances, there was little opportunity for an accumulation of debris.

There is, however, one small area between the west wing of the Lion Gate and the east wall of the granary where stratification was preserved, and which is the main basis for trying to date the fall of Mycenae. The pottery from this section, which was excavated in the early twenties, was placed in the Nauplia Museum, but during the war it was lost, and the only record of this important stratification is that given in *B.S.A.*, XXI (1922–23).

The excavators divided the stratification into levels. The lowest ones from I to V contain pottery of Myc. III B. At level VI the pottery began to change from III B to III C. Level IX was identified as the level of the destruction of the Granary, which itself was destroyed by fire at the same time as most of the other buildings within the citadel of Mycenae.

Levels X and XI contain debris dating from after this destruction, and include pottery of the Granary Style (but not of the Close Style). Level XI even contains some Orientalising sherds which belong to a post-Mycenaean period. It will be seen that Mycenae was destroyed when Myc. III C was nearly at its end.

The Granary Class was already established before the destruction of Mycenae, and survived its destruction for some little time. It forms the overlapping link between the two periods, pre-destruction of Mycenae and post-destruction. Although it was inspired from Argolis, it was not limited to that province alone. It spread to other parts of the Mycenaean world, where it developed into a number of regional diversities which characterised the ceramics of Myc. III C.

The principal shape on which Granary Style decoration occurs is the deep bowl which continued uninterrupted through Myc. III C. It is the most familiar kind of Mycenaean bowl, with handles set horizontally and of the loop type proper to pottery. There is no specially Granary Style stirrup jar.

The 'Close Style' ware. Schliemann's excavations at Mycenae in 1876 unearthed a special kind of Mycenaean pottery characterised by a carefully drawn, detailed pattern covering the whole surface of the vessels. In their magnificent publication, Fürtwangler and Loeschke called this form of ornamentation 'Style IV'.

When the exploration of Mycenae was continued in 1921–23 by the British School of Archaeology, many other specimens of this style were discovered, and it was then called the 'Close Style' of decoration (Fig. 93). These were found in the same layers as the pots decorated in the Granary Style. Both styles are also represented among the finds from Korakou and Asine and both seem to have been widespread in Argolis.

In spite of the general degeneration of style, and the general uncertainty of conditions, it was in early Myc. III C that was devised in Argolis this Close Style of decoration, beautiful, elaborate and delicate. It contrasts strongly with the rather coarse Granary Style and with the simple Ephyraean Style goblets of Myc. II. Strangely enough, it was not only contemporary with the Granary Style, but was also found in the same strata just inside the Lion Gate at Mycenae.

The Close Style is characterised by an elaborate overall style of decoration of conventional perfection. This tendency applied not only to the design as a whole, but also to the desire to use a number of ornamental details. The decoration fills all the available space on the surface of the vase with complicated geometrical patterns, frequently elaborated with rosettes and fishes and strange aquatic birds.

a

b

c

d

Fig. 93. Mycenaean III C Close Style vessels

The intricate delicacy of the Close Style suggests that although it had a fairly wide distribution, it was the production or at least the inspiration of one workshop, probably in Argolis. It was a style that may have been produced under foreign influence, perhaps from Egypt. The subject of the decoration became of secondary importance or almost lost in the elaborate ornamentation that covered the vase, and it is interesting to notice that the same phenomenon occurred again four hundred years later in the profusion of ornaments that covered the great funerary vases of the Dipylon Style belonging to the Middle and Late Geometric periods.

It would be wrong to describe the Close Style of Myc. III C as degenerate, for in its own way it is a remarkable artistic achievement, and although it was adopted in Athens and Thebes, its home was evidently in Mycenae itself. It is mainly found on stirrup jars and deep bowls, with rare examples on large jugs and hydriai. In the Argolis it does not seem to have survived the destruction of Mycenae.

The 'Octopus Style' ware. A particular version of the Close Style was evolved in the islands of the Dodecanese with the highly conventionalised octopus as its main decorative theme, particularly on stirrup jars (Fig. 94).

In Crete, too, there was a local version of the Close Style belonging to the end of LM III called the 'Fringed Style' which on stirrup jars takes the form of an octopus decoration (Fig. 95) and of a particularly elaborate panel decoration on pyxides.

Sherds of Argive Close Style have been found in Corinthia, Laconia, Attica, Delphi, Amorgos and the Dodecanese, and approximations to it have been discovered in Messenia, Achaea, Cephalonia and Cyprus.

There are indeed few districts in the south Aegean where stirrup jars with the Close Style conventionalised octopus have not been found, and in fact they have been found still further afield at Pharsala in Thessaly, South Italy and Tarsus in Cilicia.

The Warrior Vase. Perhaps the best known of all vases of the Mycenaean period is the deep bowl or krater found at Mycenae known as the Warrior Vase (Fig. 94c). It is now in the National Archaeological Museum in Athens. It dates from about 1200 BC and, therefore, belongs to Myc. III C.

On either side are double handles formed by long arching horns rising out of the moulded heads of bulls. Unfortunately it has had to be reconstructed from fragments, many of which are missing. Nevertheless, the decoration gives us an idea of the military equipment of the period.

On one side is a woman with raised right arm, evidently waving fare-

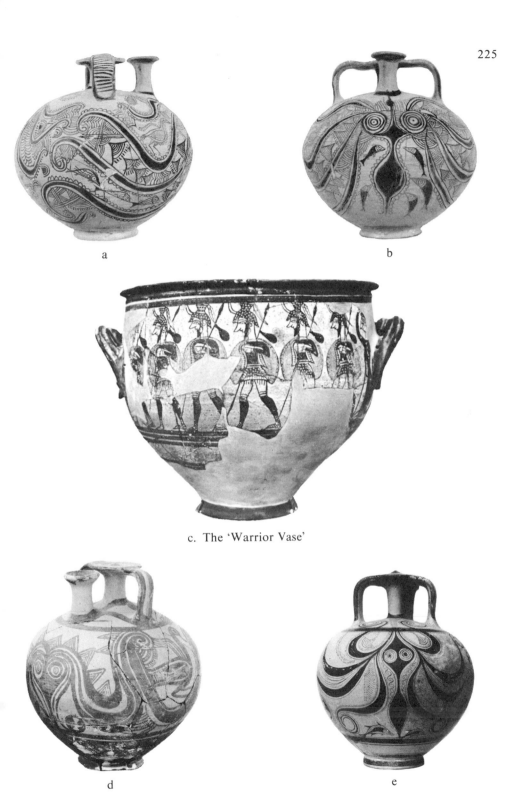

a

b

c. The 'Warrior Vase'

d

e

Fig. 94. Mycenaean III C 'Octopus Style' stirrup jars, and the 'Warrior Vase'

well to a file of six soldiers marching to battle. On their heads are plumed metal-horned helmets. In their right hands they carry the long thrusting spear which in the thirteenth century superseded the sword as the main weapon of attack. A bag is attached to each spear, perhaps to carry their rations. On his left arm each man carries a small round shield with a segment cut off the bottom. The upper part of the body is protected by a leather corselet and below it is a fringed kilt. The legs are protected by leather leggings.

Much is missing from the other side of the vase, but it too evidently showed a file of soldiers, but with raised spears and wearing helmets of the 'hedgehog' type.

VASE PATTERNS CHARACTERISTIC OF MYC.IIIC. The twelfth century saw the end of pictures of human beings and of chariot scenes but there was a great conventionalisation of natural objects (Fig. 95).

Of animal motifs there were plenty, including bulls, goats, dogs, snakes, insects, fishes and birds. The hedgehog and some other animals come from late examples of Levanto–Mycenaean pottery. Birds are shown in large numbers and of many different species. Sometimes they are shown with folded wings, sometimes they are shown in flight.

Quicker wheels were used together with higher kiln temperatures, while the skill of potters and painters reached a high degree of technical perfection in vessels decorated in the Close Style of ornamentation. In the ordinary Granary Style there was deterioration in both shaping and decoration. Some of the motifs of this period were derived from a style developed in Rhodes.

The end of Myc. III C marked the end of the Mycenaean Bronze Age. Apart from some tombs used again in classical times, the last burial had been made, the doorway walled up and the dromos filled in. The grave remained undisturbed and its position forgotten in the troubled times which followed. Then unless a peasant trying to till the rough slopes below the citadel accidentally stumbled upon it, it lay undisturbed till the archaeological exploration of recent times, for the very existence of these people was unsuspected till Schliemann began his work at Mycenae.

With the arrival of the iron-using Dorian tribes, the Aegean for some two or three centuries became the scene of constant invasions and migrations. During this chaotic period the old civilisation was swept away and forgotten. Minoan Crete became a thing of the past, and the splendour of Mycenae vanished.

When the influx of northern tribes ended, and the Aegean had ceased to be the battleground of nations, we find the intruders sharing the land

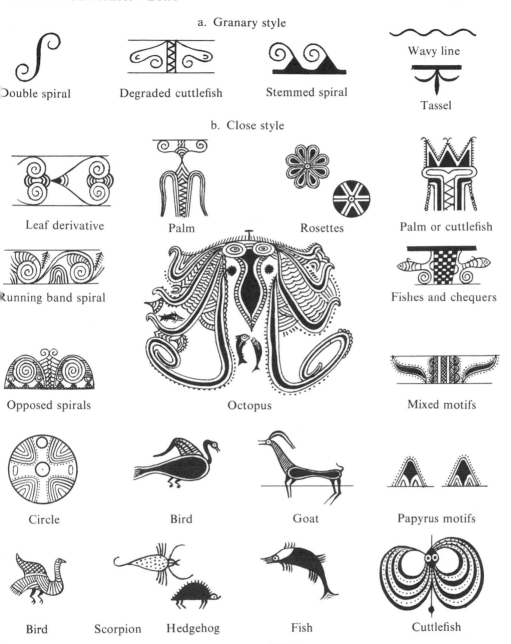

a. Granary style

Double spiral   Degraded cuttlefish   Stemmed spiral   Wavy line   Tassel

b. Close style

Leaf derivative   Palm   Rosettes   Palm or cuttlefish

Running band spiral   Fishes and chequers

Opposed spirals   Octopus   Mixed motifs

Circle   Bird   Goat   Papyrus motifs

Bird   Scorpion   Hedgehog   Fish   Cuttlefish

Fig. 95. Mycenaean III C patterns

with the remnants of the ancient populations to form a new people. It was then that the artistic and original spirit inherent in the Minoans began to revive in the mixed race, and drove it to the amazingly rapid development of classical Greece, a development which seemed so inexplicable before the spade of the archaeologist lent its aid to the historian.

CHAPTER FIVE

The Cyclades and Cycladic Pottery in the Bronze Age

The beginning of the Iron Age seems an appropriate time to go back and have a look at the ceramics of the Cyclades during the Bronze Age, which as we have seen, began in 3000 BC and ended in 1100 BC.

The Cyclades are those islands in the south of the Aegean lying in a circle round the rocky island of Delos. When we speak of the Isles of Greece, it is generally the Cyclades that we think of.

Before dealing with the pottery of the Cyclades during the Bronze Age, let us first have a look at some of the more important of these islands.
DELOS is the most famous of them. In antiquity it was the centre of the worship of Apollo, the radiant god of youth and the arts and the harmonious development of man. The island, only three miles long and less than a mile wide, first appears in history as the scene of a great festival to which the various Ionic states, including Athens, were accustomed to send each year a sacred embassy on the anniversary of the birth of the god. A four-yearly festival there, attended by people from all parts of the Greek world, was celebrated with games which rivalled those of Olympia and Delphi.

The island has been systematically excavated by the French Archaeological School of Athens since 1877. The sacred precinct of Apollo has been uncovered as well as the commercial quarter of Hellenistic times, so also have the theatre and the temples of foreign gods, including a great deal of sculpture, and a vast number of inscriptions.
TENOS today is in a way the successor of Delos as the religious centre of the Aegean. Every year it is the scene of the great festival of the Annunciation (Evangelismos) on 25th March, the anniversary of the Greek Declaration of Independence, and again on 15th August.
PAROS and NAXOS are the two largest of the Cyclades. Both are famous for the white marble which was used for Greek sculpture not only in classical times but also for making the strange marble figures that are so characteristic of the Bronze Age Cyclades.

Naxian marble was used to make the sphinx at Delphi and the colossal Apollo at Delos; but the Parian which has a finer grain came to be preferred, and was used in the great age of Greek sculpture; the Hermes of Praxiteles, for example, is of Parian marble.

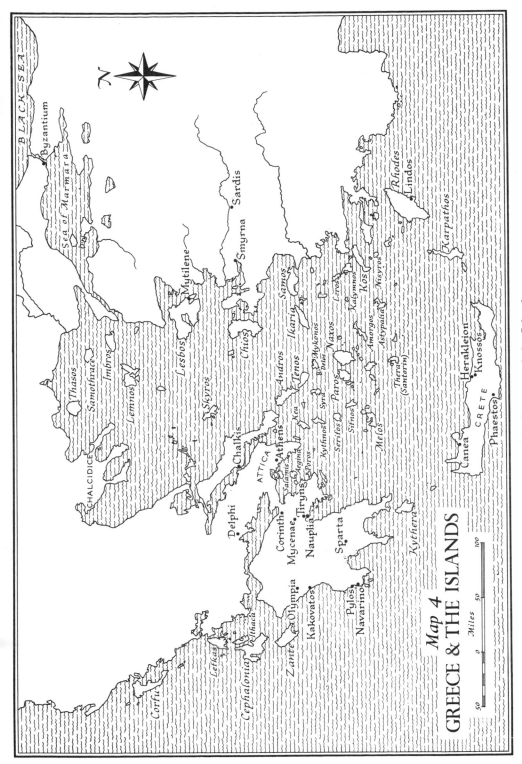

Map 4. Greece and the Islands

MILO. The fine harbour of Milo is the crater of an extinct volcano. The island is mountainous and rich in all kinds of volcanic products. In the Neolithic and Bronze Ages it had a great export trade in obsidian, which was mainly shipped from the early settlement of Phylakopi, which has been excavated by the British School of Athens.

Between the entrance to the harbour and the landing-place is the site of the ancient city of the classical period which is remarkable for the statues that have been found there – the Venus of Milo discovered in 1820 and now in the Louvre, the head of Aesculapius in the British Museum, the Poseidon and an archaic Apollo now in Athens.

Milo has Hellenic and Roman remains, as well as catacombs, the only ones in Greece, which served as refuges for Christians during the early persecutions.

THERA or SANTORIN (*Saint Irene*) is also the crater of a volcano, but of an active one. It has a fantastic appearance, as a great part of the island is a mere rim round its circular crater on which the town is built. This rim forms a crescent for about two-thirds of the circumference, and the little island of Therasia fills part of the gap. The walls of the crater are almost perpendicular to a height of about a thousand feet, and continue to descend below the sea to a depth of two hundred fathoms or more.

In the southern part of the island, pre-historic stone buildings have been found, underneath the volcanic ash. Between the stones of the buildings are beams of wild olive branches, a method of building still in use in the island to resist earthquake. This was also the system used, but on a much larger scale, in the Palace of Knossos in Crete.

Vases of imported Cretan pottery date this settlement to the Middle Minoan period, and connect the volcanic explosion with the earthquake which wrecked the first Palace of Knossos.

High on the shoulder of Mount St Elias are the remains of Thera, the ancient capital, in which it is easy, thanks to the excavations of the German, Baron Hiller von Gärtringen, to trace out the streets and buildings; a theatre, a temple of Dionysos and the Ptolemies, later dedicated to the Caesars, and a temple of Apollo. Here, punched on the rock, are the earliest known inscriptions in the Greek alphabet, perhaps as early as the eighth or ninth century BC. Outside the town a number of early tombs have been found, and vases from them are to be seen in the museum at Thera.

SYRA is the principal port of the Cyclades. It played little part in classical times, but its prehistoric importance is attested by the large quantity of Bronze Age Cycladic antiquities which have been found there.

ANDROS is the most northerly of the Cyclades. It is mountainous, with many fruitful and well-watered valleys.

The ruins of Palaeopolis, the ancient capital, are on the west coast; the town possessed a famous temple dedicated to Dionysos. In the seventh century BC Andros founded a number of colonies on the shores of the Black Sea. In 480 BC it sided with the Persians and supplied ships to Xerxes.

SIPHNOS lies some thirty miles south-west of Syra. In ancient times it was colonised by Ionians from Athens. It refused to pay tribute to Xerxes in 480 BC and sent one ship to fight on the Greek side at Salamis.

Siphnos was immensely wealthy in classical times due to her gold mines. She built a beautiful stone treasury at Delphi to house the precious offerings she made to Apollo. This was remarkable for its fine sculptured frieze, and also for its elaborate marble façade, of which a complete reconstruction was recently to be seen in the Delphi museum.

The potters of Siphnos are celebrated throughout Greece. In the springtime they start on their travels far and wide and settle in towns and villages for days and weeks until the place is supplied with large well-made amphorae and cooking utensils; it is an ancient art which has never left the island. In Pliny's time and before that, their ceramic art was celebrated.

Cycladic is the name given to the Bronze Age culture of the Cyclades. For archaeological purposes, the expression Cycladic also embraces Euboea and other Aegean islands which do not geographically form part of the Cyclades group.

As for periods, although it has been agreed that the Cycladic periods shall correspond as far as possible with the Minoan and Mycenaean periods, it is difficult, owing to lack of sufficient material, to be quite so precise in the allocation of styles and shapes to one or other period as is done with Minoan and Mycenaean wares.

It is not surprising that the Cyclades from early times played an important part in the Bronze Age civilisation. Placed as they are between Asia Minor in the east, European Greece in the west, and the great island of Crete in the south, they were at the crossing of the sea lanes of international commerce.

Several of them had valuable products of their own – obsidian in Milo, marble in Paros and Naxos, minerals in Seriphos, gold in Siphnos – but cramped as they were for space, they necessarily became traders and the middlemen for the larger centres of production. Syra became the commercial centre of the archipelago, and the ships propelled by oars which ornament the Bronze Age vases of that island form a pictorial record of her early mercantile marine.

The excavation of the Germans in Thera (Santorin), the English in

Milo, the French in Delos and the Greeks in Rhenea have produced evidence to show that throughout the Bronze Age the pottery of the Cyclades was not merely a local extension of that of the mainland, but that it had its own independent styles of vase-shapes and decoration, more especially during the Early and Middle Cycladic periods.

Hardly any pottery earlier than the Bronze Age, has so far been found in the Cyclades, although pottery with linear decoration has been found in all the principal islands of the Archipelago: Syra, Delos, Siphnos, Antiparos, Naxos, Amorgos, Thera, Euboea and Milo.

The beginning of the pottery industry in the islands would seem, therefore, to have coincided with the beginnings of the Bronze Age early in the third millennium BC. It seems more than probable, however, that the Cyclades were inhabited in Neolithic times, and we need not doubt that before long the perseverance of the archaeologist will produce evidence to this effect. Already indeed in 1964, excavations on a small scale were undertaken on the island of Antiparos which were rewarded with some neolithic finds. A few neolithic discoveries have also been made on the island of Mykonos.

Even if these finds do not reveal anything very sensational, the birth of a Bronze Age civilisation among the islands of the Cyclades does not necessarily seem to have owed its appearance to the intrusion of a new race. It is probably to be explained by the beginnings of inter-island traffic, the discovery that marble could be carved into figures, that clay could be used to make pottery, and above all to the valuable obsidian in the island of Milo. These reasons are enough to explain the rise of a new civilisation that appeared simultaneously in all the islands of the Aegean.

The rise of the Cycladic civilisation exercised a considerable and wide-spread influence. Inter-island commerce gave a big impulse to shipping. From then onwards wealth increased with trade. Vessels plied their way between Europe and Asia, between Crete and Troy, with the result that the island products became widely distributed. At different periods, one or other of the islands played a more important role than the others. During the Bronze Age it was Milo that was the richest owing to her export of obsidian. At the beginning of the Iron Age it was Euboea that showed the most commercial enterprise, while later on it was Delos, as treasury of the Delian Confederacy that held the centre of the stage. Nevertheless, in spite of a fundamental unity of style within the Cycladic framework, there was a diversity sufficient to give a character of its own to some of the islands. This was partly due to their local importance at different periods and partly due to the deposits of clay whose nature varied from island to island.

The population of Milo alone, thanks to the wealth acquired by her active export of obsidian, was in a position to construct solid houses and even a relatively sizable megaron, and to display sufficient artistic taste to have their walls decorated with frescoes, and to import the finest Cretan vases.

The last centuries of the second millennium and the beginning of the first saw a great social change in Greece and the islands.

We do not know exactly what occurred during the events known as the Dorian invasion and the Ionian migration, but there is no doubt about the destruction and confusion that reigned during that period. The Mycenaean world collapsed under the blows of the rough invader, and all that was left of the once wealthy and complicated Cretan civilisation disappeared for ever.

As for the islands, their remoteness and relative poverty no doubt gave them some partial protection, but the many links which had been forged over a long period of peace and prosperity between them and the mainland were broken. The whole system of trade created and developed during the course of the second millennium was dissolved. In the general state of insecurity there was no thought as formerly of accumulating wealth, but only of self-preservation. The various isolated communities preferred to rely upon their own resources, and to seek in isolation some protection against the evils that threatened them. Even for those islands which managed to remain apart from the general disturbance, it must have been a period of artistic sterility. Why indeed should they try to create anew when the future was so uncertain?

In one respect alone was this period marked by any progress. It was towards the end of the second millennium that the use of iron was introduced into the Aegean world. But even this became a factor that contributed to the decadence of the islands. Milo lost the privileged position which she had occupied during the Bronze Age due to her possession of obsidian. Instead of being the centre of international trade she sank to the position of an island no different from the others.

CYCLADIC POTTERY

Let us now look at the Cycladic decorative motifs and chronology of the Bronze Age. In the early Cycladic periods, the vase decoration was of such primitive simplicity that it is easiest to treat both shapes and decoration together.

Cycladic pottery was different from that of the mainland; each had its own character, more particularly in the earlier part of the Bronze Age. Their course of development was somewhat different, for the island ware came earlier under Cretan influence which hastened its development, while the mainland ware pursued a more independent and less rapid evolution.

Just as the finds at Knossos in Crete provide the chronological standard for Minoan pottery, so it is the finds at Phylakopi in Milo which principally furnish the chronological sequence of Cycladic ware. The spelling Milo is used instead of Melos, for it is as Milo that the island received her crown of immortality in 1820 when her soil yielded up the Venus of Milo for the admiration of the world.

Phylakopi is the only excavated site from which as yet we have the necessary stratigraphical data on which to found a chronological scheme that covers the whole Cycladic Bronze Age. From no other site has there been discovered a more interesting collection of Cycladic pottery, which ranges without any apparent break from the beginning of the earliest to the end of the latest Cycladic periods. It provides examples of pottery over the whole Bronze Age of the Cyclades from its earliest beginning to the era of decline.

The island owed its wealth during the Bronze Age to its immense stores of obsidian, a volcanic glass of great value during pre-historic times. It was used for making blades, scrapers, knives, razors, arrow heads and stone tools. It is found in irregular lumps varying from the size of an egg to that of a man's head, which lie embedded in the yellow pumice like currants in a pudding. Though brittle, it could be re-sharpened by flaking.

Milo was the only source of this useful substance for the peoples of the Aegean, and it was exported not only to the other islands of the Cyclades, but also to the mainland of Greece, to Asia Minor and to Crete.

The wealth so acquired enabled Milo to develop a pottery more advanced in technique and decoration than any other island of the Cyclades throughout this early period. Nowhere else have finds been excavated that compare with it in completeness and variety. These excavations were carried out in 1896–99 under the successive direction of Duncan Mackenzie, Sir Cecil Harcourt Smith and D. G. Hogarth of the British School of Archaeology at Athens in the first years of the new century.

It is true that representative examples of different periods have been found in other islands. Thus in Syra and Naxos, apart from incised ware, only lustre painted pottery has been found, while at Amorgos only matt painted pottery.

At Paros and Milo both types of decoration have been found; but there seems little doubt that Milo was the most active centre of Cycladic pottery production. There alone did the workshops show a spirit of originality and invention. Little has been found in the other islands which has not been found in Milo. Their potters seem mostly to have been inspired by vases produced in Milo.

From the immense quantity of pottery found there, Phylakopi was evidently densely populated at that early period, and a site which has at some time been densely populated is unlikely to yield much unbroken pottery. A factor which made reconstruction difficult there was the corrosion caused by the salt spray that saturated the soil and damaged much of the buried painted ware. The result was that of the earliest remains, it was not possible to obtain complete specimens at Phylakopi, but complete or nearly complete examples have fortunately been found at the neighbouring cemetery of Pelos and from other sites in Milo.

Even so we must remember that no neolithic pottery was discovered at Phylakopi, whereas at Knossos the neolithic deposits reach down for some fifteen feet below the Bronze Age deposits before they reach virgin soil. Thus the neolithic inhabitants of Knossos had already passed through a civilisation of some four thousand years before the settlement at Phylakopi was so much as begun. If we bear this in mind, it will help us to assign the earliest settlement at Phylakopi to its proper historic place in the long line of Minoan, Cycladic and Mycenaean civilisations.

If the evidence afforded by the deep neolithic strata at Knossos immediately below those of the Bronze Age is sufficient to establish a continuity of race in Crete, we may expect similar evidence to be forthcoming some time of a neolithic ancestry to the peoples of the Cyclades.

The examples of Milo were followed for the most part by the other islands with one exception, namely that during the Middle Minoan period when Minoan pottery led the way in the design of shapes and decoration, and Milo made great efforts to compete with Cretan pottery, the other islands did not follow the example of Milo in emulating Cretan design, but continued instead to follow, generally speaking, their early insular tradition.

The brilliant development of civilisation in Crete in the second millennium was obviously not without repercussion among the Aegean islands, and Cretan pottery must have been studied with care and admiration by the island potters, particularly in the southern islands nearest to Crete.

Nevertheless, although the potters of Milo and Thera may have learned lessons from Cretan pottery, they did not slavishly copy it. Right up to the end of the Bronze Age, the production of pottery with linear decoration continued in the islands without interruption.

Moreover, although pottery with linear decoration was almost universal among the islands, pottery embellished with ornaments of Cretan inspiration was limited to only a few of the islands. The explanation is no doubt an economic one. Until the mass import of Minoan ceramics, pottery with rudimentary linear decoration, capable of being quickly drawn, was no doubt the cheap ware for ordinary use in the islands situated far from the normal trade routes.

Pottery decorated in a manner inspired by Cretan motifs required more skilful craftsmen, and it remained the monopoly of a comparatively few workshops. But even in Milo when Cretan influence was strongest, the Melian potters retained an independence of style, known as Creto-Cycladic, which is distinguishable from that of Crete itself. Cretan pottery which was of a high standard and definitely superior to Cycladic pottery of local manufacture, always remained an expensive article of luxury. With their considerable skill, the local Melian potters could hold their own, but after the collapse of Crete and the supremacy of Mycenae it was another matter.

The Argolis produced an immense quantity of pottery which, although it did not reach the high standard of Minoan ware, was nevertheless of good quality and agreeably decorated. Moreover, Argolis had a great export trade of Mycenaean ware. Nothing could stand up to this mass production, doubtless delivered at a low price.

The local workshops of Milo were gradually swamped, so that by the end of the second millennium, Mycenaean pottery was almost the only good class pottery used in the island. Of local manufacture, only two classes managed to survive. One was represented by the large pithoi and small cups, the other by ordinary household ware with linear decoration.

Thus we can see one of the results of the collapse of Cretan power when Crete ceased to have any influence overseas, and her place was taken among the islands by the continental power of Mycenae.

As regards Cycladic ceramics, although Cretan influence played an important part, it was only a temporary one, and the islands still held on to their local insular style. Of the various Cretan phases such as the naturalistic and the polychrome styles, not a trace remained after the collapse of Cretan power. It seemed as if the island potter was not sufficiently sure of his skill to mark and learn any of the lessons which he might have done from Cretan practice.

We now know that the potters' workshops in the islands were no less active and original than those elsewhere, and it is possible to speak of the Cycladic Era with the assurance of a wide knowledge of vase forms and decoration in the islands of the Cyclades.

One might suppose that each island formed a small independent society developing its own pottery under its own special conditions. This was not really so. If in a sense the sea formed a barrier between the islands, it also formed a link. The hazards of wind and storm were compensated by the ease of transport as compared with that of a rough path on dry land. Even a small boat can carry the loads of many donkeys.

Instead of shipping their breakable produce to its destination, many of the potters probably found it more convenient to ship the clay in bulk to wherever it was needed, and then with ovens erected locally, to make their pots on the spot. This in fact is what is done today by the potters of the island of Siphnos. They go from island to island with their clay, and stay there till the needs of the inhabitants are satisfied. It is probable that this procedure was also used in antiquity, and thus the sea became a unifying element that made for community of technique and of decorative style.

At first the pottery was made by hand, but later on with a wheel. The earliest decoration was incised, then painted on a plain background. At first the decoration was in the form of straight lines, then came curves with occasional spirals and gradually these linear motifs were varied with other motifs which drew their inspiration not only from nature but also from daily life. A boat propelled by oars and steered by its coxswain has been found among the early Cycladic decorative themes.

Incised Cycladic pottery has even been found in the heart of Arcadia. For the first time we see a truly Aegean civilisation, a civilisation with a general sense of unity – perhaps even speaking the same language.

The simplicity of Cycladic art was imposed by the slender resources of the population. No discoveries have been made in the Cyclades of palaces or elaborate tombs. The luxurious splendours of Crete were never adopted in the islands.

In spite of the excavations at Milo and the researches of archaeologists in other islands, our knowledge of Cycladic Bronze Age pottery is still insufficient to draw up a chronological table with any degree of accuracy. It has not been possible to unearth any Cycladic pottery in Mesopotamia or Egypt which could help us to elucidate dates as was the case with Crete, nor have Asiatic or Egyptian objects been found in the Cyclades.

Owing to the volcanic explosion of Thera (Santorin), it is not easy to follow the sequence of development of the various styles which prevailed there. Fortunately it has been possible to make some approximation due to finds of Cycladic pottery at Knossos, while a further aid has been provided by the Kamares ware found at Phylakopi. Pottery found at Paros, Antiparos and Despotiko has no painted decoration. Is it older than painted pottery? We may think so, but we cannot be sure.

Nevertheless, in spite of these great difficulties, it has been possible to gather some facts which throw a light upon this long era of some twenty centuries, which help to establish some sort of chronological division.

One discovery which has given a very clear date is that of a great number of Cretan Kamares fragments in the same levels as those of Cycladic painted rectilinear decoration, and a few in those of the style which immediately succeeded it, namely the painted curvilinear.

We can, therefore, state that Melian incised pottery is older than that of the Kamares style, and that the end of the incised style coincides with the rise of the Kamares style in about 1800 BC.

We can also say that the beginning of the painted curvilinear style coincided with the end of the Kamares style but that the greater part of it came after the Kamares style period. The manufacture of Creto-Cycladic ware began at the end of LM II (1700 BC), attained its height towards the end of LM III (1600 BC) and then faded into the Mycenaean Era.

Convenient as it would be to make Cycladic chronology correspond exactly with Minoan, we are not yet in a position to do so with any certainty. One of the principal difficulties is that in these remote periods a style of decoration may last for centuries. This is the case, for instance, with incised decoration, the use of which continued from about 3000 to 2000 BC.

There is no doubt, however, about the wisdom of dividing the Cycladic Era into three general periods: Early, Middle and Late, and to do our best in the matter of further sub-division in the hope that later excavation will reveal new discoveries to amend our present somewhat tentative ascriptions.

The following, therefore, gives a rough list of Cycladic ware in the different general periods. It is admittedly incomplete, but better to have some chronological basis than none at all.

EARLY CYCLADIC (3000–1900 BC)
Simple incised herring-bone decoration.
More complex incised rectilinear designs and stamped circular patterns.
Incised curvilinear designs.
Matt painted light-on-dark rectilinear designs.

MIDDLE CYCLADIC (1900–1600 BC)
Lustrous painted dark-on-light rectilinear designs (MC I).
Matt painted dark-on-light rectilinear designs (MC I).
Minyan Ware (MC I).
Matt painted ware dark-on-light in curvilinear designs influenced by Cretan MM II ware (MC II).
Matt painted ware dark-on-light in naturalistic designs influenced by Cretan MM III ware (MC III).

Matt painted ware dark-on-light in naturalistic designs with highlights in
   burnished red or brown circles of Cycladic creation (Melian 'Black
   and Red' style) (MC III).

LATE CYCLADIC (1600–1100)
Local 'Red and Black' style ware of the Creto-Cycladic style with lustrous
   paint (LC I and II).
Imported LM I and II ware (LC I and II).
Imported LM III ware (LC I and II).
Imported Myc. I and II ware (LC II).
Imported and locally made Myc. III A and B ware (LC III A and B).
Locally made and imported Myc. III C ware (LC III C).

THE EARLY CYCLADIC PERIOD 3000–1900 BC

It cannot be said with certainty whether marble or stone vases were made
before clay ones, or whether pottery was made before stone vessels in
the Cyclades. It was, however, during the first stage of Cycladic pottery
that the island workshops displayed their most distinctive powers of invention. Many of the islands had ample deposits of clay, and the manufacture of pottery in the Cyclades was very abundant, judging by the
number of vases and the amount of fragments discovered there. These
bits of pottery take us far back to some of the origins of the Greek race,
but of the men who made this ware and whence they came we know little
or nothing. We are almost as ignorant of them as they were of us, or
knowing them at most through some few wares transmitted to us after
lying for long centuries in the dark womb of time.

   The earliest Cycladic pots, such as the clay vessels with high shoulders
and incised decoration, bear some resemblance to those found at Cilicia
in the south of Asia Minor just north of Cyprus. This resemblance, however, is limited to their shapes. Their decoration more closely resembles
that of the early cities of Troy which also had a comb or herring-bone
form of ornamentation. It might be said with some degree of probability
that the inhabitants of Troy II were among the forebears of the early
Cycladic population.

   Owing to its position on the road from Asia Minor to Europe, and its
proximity to the islands of the Greek archipelago, Troy early occupied an
important position on the eastern trade routes. It was the centre of exchange between the islands, continental Greece, and the coasts of the
Aegean Sea. The similarity between Trojan vases and pyxides and those
of the Cyclades seem to make it possible that the Trojans were among
other Anatolian peoples who carried the first seeds from Asia Minor of

what later became the Cycladic culture. Close as may have been the links
between the people of the Cyclades and the sources from which they
derived, and however closely they followed the styles by which they were
inspired, they soon developed their own artistic style, particularly in the
creation of the remarkable marble figures which so clearly distinguish
Cycladic art from that of all its neighbours. Whatever their origins, they
displayed great activity, and soon set themselves to create an indigenous
civilisation which undoubtedly showed itself most distinctively in the
Early Bronze Age.

Archaeologists have noted that on more than one occasion this Cycladic
civilisation expanded on to the mainland of Greece during the Early
Helladic period. In the neighbourhood of Corinth at Korakou and
Zygouries, at Kokkinia in Attica, and at Eutresis in Boeotia, thin layers
of incised Cycladic sherds with the spiral and the stamped decoration of
Syra have been discovered.

By the great variety of its shapes and proportions, the extensive repertoire of its linear motifs, the increasing freedom and complexity of its
designs, the island pottery was marked during the Early Cycladic period
by a distinctive Cycladic style. The principal sources of Early Cycladic
pottery are the cist tombs of Milo, Naxos, Paros, Antiparos, Amorgos,
Syra and Siphnos. One would like to think that in emptying these early
tombs of the offerings deposited in them with such loving care four
thousand years ago, the same kindly rule was observed as is enjoined
upon the bird's nester, namely that he should leave two or three eggs in
the nest; but as a rule every scrap is removed to furnish the shelves of a
museum or to hide away in the drawers of the 'reserve'.

Although Milo alone has yielded a complete Bronze Age sequence of
pottery, it would be a mistake to assume that the spirit of inventiveness
was confined to that island alone. Paros, Naxos, Amorgos, Siphnos and
particularly Syra have all yielded high-class and original pottery styles.
None the less, apart from the 'Frying Pans' of Syra, examples of every
style from these islands have also been found in Milo, whereas not all
the styles found in Milo have been found in the other islands of the
Cyclades.

Whereas in Milo and Thera the vase painters strove to emulate the
finest productions of Crete, those of the other islands were for the most
part content to limit themselves to the linear style of decoration and of
very much stylised human and animal forms.

This Early Cycladic period lasted from the beginning of the Bronze
Age till a time when Cretan and, particularly, Kamares ware was
imported into the islands and exercised such an influence as to change,
at least for some considerable time, the Cycladic ceramic style. It was

a period which lasted from about 3000 till about 1900 BC, during which the islands displayed a marked individuality.

The decoration of very early Cycladic pottery may be divided into two categories: incised first and then a simple painted decoration.

Early Cycladic I

The earliest incised decoration was of a herring-bone pattern – almost universal among the islands except in Syra (Fig. 96). The early date of this style is confirmed by a similar type which was characteristic of the Early Bronze Age in Crete and on the mainland of Greece. At Phylakopi in Milo it came at the lowest level, resting on bed-rock.

The pots were incised before they were baked. This incising is generally divided into zones in which the incised lines slope alternately one way and the other into the herring-bone pattern. This simple style of ornament formed the first category of incised decoration. It never extended beyond the simple line, and never developed beyond the simplest form of rectilinear decoration.

The special interest of this early ornamentation is that it gradually led up to the motifs of the rectangular system of decoration, a system which was never really lost in the ceramic art of the Cyclades, and which ultimately was to develop into the universal style of vase decoration all over the Aegean world seventeen hundred years later.

Its decorative repertoire which the inhabitants of the Cyclades knew how to practise with an innate sense of composition was taken up and amplified by the Dorians. By then the Bronze Age had been superseded by the Iron Age, and the style is known as the Geometric Style of decoration.

The idea suggests itself, therefore, that the Cyclades were at any rate one of the principal sources from which the Iron Age Geometric Style originated, a style adopted by the whole Greek world at approximately the same time. If this is so, even the workshops of Athens derived some of their early inspiration from the island potteries, a debt which was later repaid by the Dipylon potters of the Kerameikos with the inventive genius for composition and design which they displayed in so marked a degree.

This, however, touches upon the larger question of the origin of the Geometric Style, which itself is linked with the geometric styles of Italy, Central Europe and the Balkans. It is enough to suggest here that the islands of the Cyclades may have played an important part in the generation of the Geometric Style of ceramic decoration.

The earliest Cycladic pottery was hand-made, of coarse imperfectly baked clay containing sand and bits of stone, and which varied from one

R

a. Cylindrical-necked jar
with simple incised lines
Paros

b. Incised narrow-necked jar
Naxos

c. Jar with high-pedestalled foot
Siphnos

d. Incised globular pyxis
Paros

e. Incised cylindrical pyxis
Antiparos

Fig. 96. Early Cycladic I vessels

island to another: black in Paros, grey in Antiparos, brown in Siphnos and Naxos, and reddish in Amorgos. In some cases the surface remained rough; in others it was smoothed and given a burnished surface, red or brown. Baking seems to have been done in ovens, but not sufficiently hot to allow the potter to give his vases ordinary handles. The oldest Cycladic jars and pyxides have in fact not got them, but only little pierced lugs for suspending the pot by means of a string.

The regularity of shape of some of these early vessels does not necessarily indicate the use of a potter's wheel, even of the most primitive type, for in Crete, Cyprus and elsewhere one may see vessels of superb regularity of shape made today entirely by hand, in a manner which has descended unchanged since neolithic times.

During this Early Cycladic I phase the shapes were comparatively few. The following were the most characteristic:

1. *The cylindrical-necked jar* (Figs. 96a and b) is the most common form of early vessel with incised herring-bone decoration. The body is shaped rather like the shell of a sea-urchin after the needles have been removed. These globular shells are very common in Greek waters as bathers sometimes know to their cost. Even now the contents of a sea-urchin's shell form a substantial part of an islander's meal, and in the earliest times the shells themselves might have been used as drinking vessels. However that may be, most of these clay jars have a wide funnel-like neck narrowing slightly towards the top, and spreading shoulders with two or four suspension lugs pierced vertically. Where the jars have four suspension lugs they are not close together in pairs as in some later examples from Syra and Tiryns. The base is small in proportion to the full width of the jar, and is flattened. This characteristic type is very common, but instances have been found of suspension lugs pierced horizontally and the rim of the neck turned slightly outwards. These come as a rule from Naxos and Antiparos.

Incising was confined to the body of the jar, and was not applied to the neck except very occasionally when a simple motif was engraved upon the lower part.

2. *The pedestalled jar* (Fig. 96c) is a similar vessel to the above, but much less common. It is fitted with a hollow-pedestalled foot.

3. *The cylindrical pyxis* (Fig. 96e). Cylindrical pyxides are comparatively rare. In all cases they are fitted with lugs at the sides which take the form of vertical hollow tubes. In some cases the holes of the tubes were to enable the lids to be tied on, in others they were for suspension. It is curious to note how many of the pots produced by African tribes today have similar arrangements for suspension.

4. *The globular pyxis* (Fig. 96d) is a vessel of flattened globular shape. It

has two suspension lugs and a low collar, over which a cap can fit. A similar shape but of later date has been found in Syra.

In both types of pyxis the incised decoration almost invariably covers the whole surface of the jar including the lid. It is interesting to note that an effect similar to the Early Cycladic herring-bone incising is obtained today in the decoration of pots in Africa by the use of a wooden four-sided roulette.

Fig. 97. Roulette

There are no vessels similar in shape to the pyxis in the ceramic range of either Egypt or the regions of the Danube. Nor does it appear of the same shape in the Early Minoan repertoire. It may, therefore, be considered as a shape of Cycladic creation, inspired perhaps by examples from Troy. As most of the above examples came from tombs, it is possible that in some places the types continued for the use of the dead after they had ceased to be used for the living.

Another similar example was also found in Milo, without ornament of any kind, but with four equally spaced suspension lugs, pinched out of the body and not separately moulded, which in spite of their solidity can hardly have been meant to resist a direct strain. When hung up the weight would be borne by cross strings under the body, the lugs being merely guides to keep the strings in place.

Early Cycladic II

The second category of pottery, which we may call Early Cycladic II, was a technical development of the first (Fig. 98).

It has a lustrous surface, red, brown or black. With some exceptions, the lustre was not produced by the old method of burnishing, but by a refinement of the clay slip with which the pots were covered. It is a sheen which is not at all brilliant.

Whereas the almost universal decoration of vessels of the first category consists of bands of herring-bone decoration, those of the second category show a fair variety of rectilinear designs.

In this second category of Early Cycladic pottery decoration, the designs, although still very primitive, consist mostly of simple incised geometrical figures such as hatched triangles, circles and lozenges, and sometimes of triangles filled with dots. Besides these motifs, sherds have been found with small isolated spirals, a Greek cross, or a field of dots.

As a rule the ornamentation is divided up into two or more horizontal bands; sometimes the same pattern is repeated upon the different bands, sometimes it differs.

As the decoration became more elaborate, so new vase forms were introduced. It is particularly interesting to note that the whole range of forms and decoration introduced in this second category is found throughout all the neighbouring lands – Crete, Attica, Argolis and the Troad – in all are found similar shapes and similar decorative motifs.

In many cases there are traces of a white filling in the incised lines, and in other cases it is probable that it existed at one time, but has now disappeared. In fact the numerous incised designs of this phase were probably for the most part picked out in white gypsum, when the designs would have been much more distinctive than they are now.

The earlier incised pottery of the first category does not have this white filling; in fact it could never have had any, for the grooves are too shallow to have held it.

Besides the incising, a number of fragments of this period have been found with impressed patterns of zig-zags, rows of triangles and other simple geometric schemes. Small stamped circles and dots are also common features of this early class of Cycladic pottery.

Incised pottery, although made of unrefined clay, and with a very simple ornamentation, gives the appearance of having been made by men who had long practised the art of making pottery. The beautiful and symmetrical outlines of the vases, the comparative smoothness of their surface, the simple but charming designs, all indicate a developed Cycladic taste.

Each workshop, however, maintained a certain individuality, and the islands were alone in utilising real objects such as ships or human beings as a form of decoration during this early period. Thus it is that although the development of the second category developed spontaneously as a logical development of the first, it would seem evident that some communication existed between the various centres of production. The islands, however, and Milo in particular, were notable for their greater fertility of original invention.

Some characteristic vessels of the second category are:

1. *The conical pyxis* (Fig. 98c) which in this phase narrows slightly towards the top. It is without suspension tubes, having merely a hole on each side a little below the top. It has a low rim over which to fit a lid.

2. *The globular pyxis with a foot.* This is virtually of the same shape as that shown in Fig. 2c but increased skill is shown in the curve of the foot, the thinness of the walls and a symmetry preserved between the upper and lower halves of the body which pass into one another almost at right

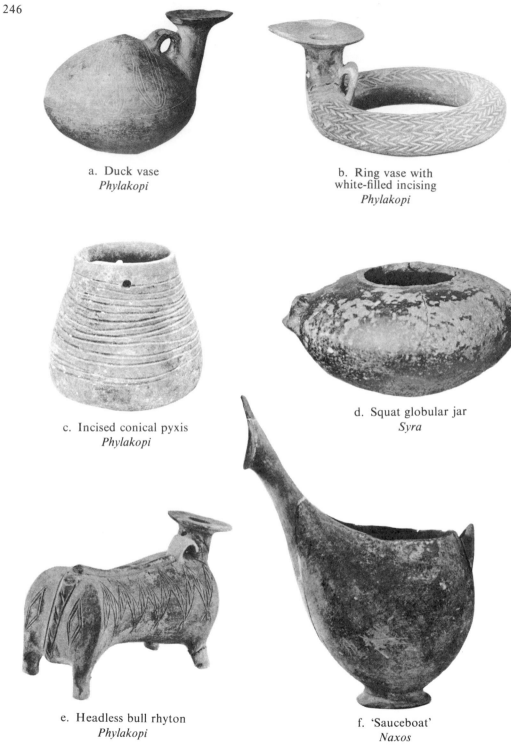

a. Duck vase
Phylakopi

b. Ring vase with
white-filled incising
Phylakopi

c. Incised conical pyxis
Phylakopi

d. Squat globular jar
Syra

e. Headless bull rhyton
Phylakopi

f. 'Sauceboat'
Naxos

Fig. 98. Early Cycladic II vessels

angles. The mouth with its rim to hold a flat lid, marks the pot as a storage vessel and not a drinking cup. On the shoulder of one example is a tubular projection to which the lid was probably tied. Older vessels have four such handles for the double purpose of suspension from the roof of a primitive hut which had no cupboard and of fastening the lid to exclude the smoke.

3. *The duck vase* (Fig. 98a). Contemporary with these pyxides was the early form of duck vase. It consists of a rough sphere, pointed at the top with a flattened base, and a short spout ending in a broad, flat leaf-shaped rim with pointed nose. A small ring-handle joins the spout to the sphere. Some of the larger examples of these duck vases have suspension handles on either side.

4. *The ring vase* (Fig. 98b). Another early form is the ring vase which bears a suggestive resemblance to a serpent, a resemblance which is sometimes enhanced by the incising that recalls the overlapping of scales. It has a spout of the same shape as the duck vase, and a small suspension handle on the neck.

The idea of making vases in the shape of a hollow ring with an upright spout is a very old one, for the form is found in the archaic pottery of Egypt. Its popularity lasted right through the Bronze Age.

5. *The sauceboat* (Fig. 98f). We have described this distinctive and graceful vessel elsewhere, but the examples found in Naxos (as well as in Syra) are characterised by a foot slightly higher than those found elsewhere. They are rarely decorated.

The sauceboat has a remarkable number of varieties, and though a great many examples have been found on the mainland of Greece and regarded as Early Helladic, it seems probable that it was mainly produced in the Cyclades. Its specific purpose is not clear, but it seems likely that its remote prototype was a leather vessel.

An example found in Naxos is shaped somewhat like a boat with the spout forming the prow, but as a rule the general shape of the sauceboat gives the impression of a waddling bird, but a bird that one feels is as extinct as the dodo.

6. *The animal rhyton* (Fig. 98e). In this case a bull with a leaf-shaped rim at the top of the neck instead of a head. It has a minute handle at the base of the neck, and sometimes a small suspension hole at the top of the tail. The incised decoration is in the form of hatched lozenges and hatched double zig-zags. The form though strange is not at all uncommon.

As the vase decorator of this early period progressed, his angular incised patterns tended to become curved by more hasty execution until the rectangular style of incising gradually merged into a curvilinear style.

Although incised ware did not stop suddenly with the end of the Early Cycladic period, it did not survive into the Middle Cycladic period except in coarse household varieties.

7. *The squat globular jar* (Fig. 98d). Although this jar was found in Syra, it is not typically Syriot. It has a low globular body with flattened shoulders on the edge of which on each side is a pair of string suspension tubes modelled in astragal or knuckle-bone form. This is not uncommon in early Aegean pottery and what makes it more remarkable is that some early Chinese vases of similar form also have similar twin suspension tubes. This vase is very small of dark reddish clay with a black polished surface which has partly perished. The colour is produced by a pigment and not in firing.

Early Cycladic III

It is likely that the incised vases with white fillings suggested the use of painted pottery. Painting was easier than incising, and allowed for more complicated patterns. For this reason the earliest forms of painted pottery were for the most part white on a dark background. When it was found possible to paint a white design on a dark ground instead of filling incisions with white, incision was found to be superfluous and fell into disuse.

An important factor in this process of change from incision to paint was the tendency which began to develop from rectilinear to curvilinear patterns. Incision does not readily lend itself to curvilinear motifs, and when the first attempts were made to produce them we find a transitional stage of doing so by stamping impressed designs into the clay. It was, however, a stage which did not last long, and the development of curvilinear design was continued with the use of the brush alone.

Although slow, this progress is very noticeable with the passage of time. But it needed time to develop, and in fact after the introduction of painted pottery, there was a noticeable improvement in the preparation and baking of the clay. The contours of some of the vases also indicate some sort of primitive mechanism for making the pots.

In the case of white designs on a dark ground, the surface was covered with a lustrous brown, black or red slip, sometimes burnished. The designs were drawn with a fugitive white paint.

This technique of burnishing a pot was used by the Cycladic potters as well as by those of the mainland. It was commonly used in the Early Cycladic period, particularly for incised wares, and also as a suitable background on which to paint patterns in white.

The amount of pottery decorated with white designs is not very abundant by comparison with the dark-on-light style, and no shapes can be regarded as being specially characteristic of this style of decoration. Rather did the shapes form part of the categories that were characteristic of the designs drawn in a dark paint on a light background which belong more properly to the next period, the Middle Cycladic period. The light-on-dark style has few original motifs though it did produce some human forms.

Two interesting examples are given on Plate XIII (17 and 19) of *J.H.S.* Supplementary Paper No. 4, 'Excavations at Phylakopi in Melos'. The first is on a sherd and shows a man standing beside a tree in an attitude of worship of the sun. The second is on a pithos showing how this design was transformed into a conventionalised pattern.

Fig. 99. Early Cycladic III motifs of man worshipping the sun

The white paint used on Cycladic ware is of poor quality and cannot compare in brilliance with some Cretan vases decorated in white on a dark ground.

The Pottery of Syra

Before going on to the next Cycladic stage let us pause to take a look at a group of pottery from Syra which occupies a special place of its own in the ceramics of the Cyclades (Fig. 100). Its different shapes and decoration distinguish this pottery from that of all the other islands. The greater part of it was excavated from a large group of tombs by Tsoundas in 1898, although some earlier finds had been unearthed in 1861 by Papadopoulos.

It is not easy to assign a definite place to this group in Cycladic chronology, although we can perhaps hazard some sort of estimate. Its developed style, the general technique of its vases, the thinness of their walls, the elegance of their shapes, and the complexity of their incised ornamentation by the use of the spiral in a great variety of forms, make it virtually certain that this pottery is later than Early Cycladic.

Lustrous varnish, sometimes red and sometimes black, and white matter in the incising, are common to incised pots in all the islands, but in the case of Syra, although the motifs are limited in numbers, they have a sureness and precision greatly superior to the rudimentary work at the beginning of the Early Cycladic period.

Moreover most of the vessels show a high technical standard in the polish of their surfaces and in the grace of their shapes which indicate that they were made by experienced and highly qualified potters, much more so than those who produced the Early Cycladic incised jars.

A peculiarity which is rarely found elsewhere except on a small scale, is the very general use of a stamp for impressing the designs on the clay. This stamp is used for three types of motif:

a. Small triangles arranged in rows so as to form a zig-zag.
b. Concentric circles.
c. Spirals.

The stamp was probably carved in wood and pressed into the soft clay.

The principal ornamental characteristic of the pottery found at Syra is the adoption of linked spirals as the main decorative pattern. What is the explanation of the prominent part played by this linked spiral in the decoration of Syriot pottery? Syra was rather far from Crete for her pottery to be greatly influenced by Cretan products, and yet this particular pattern bears a striking resemblance to that which decorates some of the large pithoid jars unearthed by Seager at Pseira in Crete and belonging to the LM I period. Whether the Syriot design was borrowed from Pseira or the Pseira design borrowed from Syra it is difficult to say. It seems that they were contemporary.

The Northern Cyclades including Syra were in close touch with Mycenae whose power and wealth were steadily growing at this time. It is believed that one of the motifs used for the decoration of the golden jewelry of Mycenae was the linked spiral. It seems, therefore, more than likely that this was the source from which the Syriot potter got the idea of decorating his pottery in the same way, and that the idea was transmitted to Pseira.

Among the vessels which are particularly characteristic of Syra are:
1. *The pyxis.* There are three pyxides found in fairly large numbers:

a. The globular pyxis (Fig. 100b) is of similar type to those of the other islands, but of a rather more gracefully curved body fitted with suspension lugs. Some are decorated with incising, others painted.

b. The globular pyxis mounted on a foot. This is similar to Fig. 100b but for the foot.

c. The cylindrical pyxis (Fig. 100a). This has a circular lid and a very

a. Cylindrical pyxis and cover

b. Globular pyxis and cover

c. 'Frying pan'

d. 'Sauceboat' with three spouts

e. Footed jar

Fig. 100. Cycladic vessels of Syra

high drum into which the body of the vase fits. Generally painted decoration.

2. *The footed jar with cylindrical neck* (Fig. 100e). This shape is not uncommon in the Cyclades, but it has a special shape in Syra. It always has a high foot, and shoulders which slope upwards to a short neck. At the top of the neck is the mouth with a slightly protruding lip.

These jars as a rule are decorated mostly round the collar and the shoulders, but sometimes the ornamentation descends as low as the suspension lugs so as to cover the greater part of the body.

3. *The 'frying pan'* (Fig. 100c). Of all the vessels found at Syra, the most original and curious is known as the 'frying pan'. It is generally in the form of a disc with a rim round it like a frying pan. The shape of the short handle varies with different specimens.

Much discussion has taken place over the purpose of this vessel. Some scholars have suggested that filled with water it served as a looking glass. Others are inclined to think that it is a libation vessel, but perhaps when we cannot find some practical every-day use for a Bronze Age vessel we are too inclined to attribute some ritualistic use for it, particularly in the service of the dead. Perhaps on the other hand the scholars are right, for in this machine age it is difficult for our matter-of-fact minds to appreciate the superstitions of man in a primitive world where ritual played a more fundamental part than it does in our world today.

We who live in this age of automation can hardly guess at the mystic superstitions that governed almost every act of a people fearful to observe the proper ritual to placate the forces of unknown chance. We have only to read the account of his travels in the Cyclades by J. T. Bent to see how the observance of the proper rites governed the lives and deaths of the Cycladic peoples so lately as 1885, observances no doubt descended relatively unchanged since the Bronze Age or even earlier.

These 'frying pans', mostly found in the Cyclades, have been discovered in Amorgos, Andros, Naxos, Sikinos and Paros, but the great majority come from the graves of Syra. Some early ones have been found at Aghios Kosmas near Phaleron in Attica. In Euboea, too, they are fairly common, but most of these are without ornament. It has been suggested by some that those found in other places are copies of the ones made in Syra. Others are of the opinion that while peculiar to the Cyclades, those from Syra are of a more developed style than those in the other islands.

Pyxides and frying pans from Syra are covered with incised and stamped motifs. These include triangles, concentric circles, spirals and ships.

4. *The sauceboat.* This vessel of the conventional shape is found in Syra

as well as in the other islands of the Cyclades, but an unusual as well as graceful shape has been found there which has three spouts (Fig. 100d).

5. *Animal vases* are rare with painted as with incised pottery. A delightful example of a painted vase has been discovered in the shape of a bear holding a basin with a hole in it.

In addition to incised and stamped decoration, quite a number of vases from Syra have a painted decoration, and these two forms of ornamentation seem to be contemporary. The painted decoration is purely linear, made up of rectilinear and curvilinear motifs. It is strange that concentric circles which are so common in contemporary stamped ware are not found on painted vases. Apart from ships, no naturalistic motifs were used.

Syra must have been fortunate in having a large number of vase decorators during the Middle Cycladic period, so much so that she probably owed much of her prosperity to their products.

THE MIDDLE CYCLADIC PERIOD 1900–1600 BC

Besides Phylakopi in Milo, a dozen or more settlements of varying size and importance flourished during the successive stages of the Middle Cycladic period, though not all seem to have been based on Early Cycladic sites. These include Amorgos, Andros, Delos, Keos (Zea), Kimolos, Kythnos (Thermia), Mykonos, Naxos, Paros, Siphnos, Tenos and Thera (Santorin). Nevertheless it is at Phylakopi that the bulk of the pottery of the Middle Bronze Age belongs, and it was the potters of Milo who were foremost in creating a distinctive Cycladic style.

It is characteristic of Middle Cycladic settlements that in two respects they are always conveniently sited: they are either on or near the sea with a convenient anchorage at hand, and near by they have some good agricultural land. They would thus have been self-supporting.

It is not certain when the potters' wheel came into use in the Cyclades. Some authorities seem to have assumed from the roundness of the pots that the slow wheel at least must have been used in very early times, but the remarkable skill used by certain primitive people today without the use of any sort of wheel shows that it is easy to be misled into thinking that great regularity of form implies the use of a potter's wheel when this is not the case.

Moreover, a quantity of pottery is made to this day in Crete, Cyprus and the Peloponnese without the use of the potter's wheel.

A peculiar feature of the early pots with linear decoration is the impressions on the bottom of many of them, made while the clay was still soft from an interwoven rush mat. Some archaeologists have suggested that the vase was placed upon a mat so that it could be turned or moved more easily than if it had been placed directly upon the ground. Sometimes, however, the impressions are those of leaves, and it would seem more likely that the pots were placed upon a mat or on leaves while they were drying.

Vases of the Middle Cycladic period have flattened bases, not round like a gourd. Where a vase has a ring base it is an indication that it is comparatively late in the period. Sometimes the lower ends of the handles are stuck through a hole in the side of the vase and protrude on the inside. In the case of open vessels such as cups and bowls, the join is smoothed over, but in the case of narrow-necked jugs it is left projecting inside.

MINYAN WARE. In the chapter dealing with the Middle Helladic Era (see page 146), we described the vessels known as Minyan Ware found on the mainland of Greece. Just as Minyan Ware continued to be found on the mainland till Mycenaean times, so it has also been unearthed in considerable quantities in Middle Cycladic contexts at Phylakopi, and continued to be found until the beginning of Late Cycladic I.

Grey Minyan ware has also been found in a number of the other islands, namely Paros, Siphnos, Naxos, Keos, Mykonos, Tenos and Syra. Some of this Minyan pottery seems to have been imported from the mainland, but other examples are Cycladic imitations of the mainland ware. The local imitations can be distinguished by the gritty nature of their clay, and by certain eccentricities of colour and profile.

The excavators were of opinion that most of the grey Minyan they found at Phylakopi was imported ware. Although some of it may have been imported from the mainland of Greece, it seems likely that Minyan ware first came to Greece from north-western Anatolia, and since the Cyclades lie on the route, some of the early Minyan ware may have come from there.

It is doubtful if any complete examples of Minyan ware have been found in the Cyclades, but the better fragments found at Milo and Siphnos as well as in Aegina have a red burnished surface.

Middle Cycladic I (Linear Style)

We showed how during the latter part of the Early Cycladic period the vase decorator abandoned the use of incising in favour of brush painted designs, designs in white on a dark background, probably suggested by the use of white gypsum filling in the grooves of the incised patterns. It was not long, however, before this process was reversed by the application of a light slip on which designs could be painted in black.

We pointed out earlier on that in the Middle Cycladic I phase, two different types of painted decoration were applied:

A design in shiny black upon a light slip surface.

A design in matt black upon a light slip surface, with the probability that the styles developed in that order.

Although the shiny paint was meant to be black on a light slip surface, it is frequently found that the black has changed to red through over-firing, and a uniform colour, whether black or red, was seldom attained. As a rule the sheen is very faint while the white slip has taken on a yellowish tinge. This style had its origin in Urfirnis ware, and the designs on many of the pots were inspired by those of the incised ware of the previous Early Cycladic period as Furumark has pointed out (*The Mycenaean Pottery*, pages 217–19). Besides Phylakopi, examples have been found at Paros and Amorgos.

The second style of matt black paint on a light slip surface was possibly evolved because the potters of Milo discovered that the shiny paint did not show up too well upon their coarse and porous clay.

Imitation of Cretan ware in the MC I period could not succeed owing to the less good quality of the Cycladic clay which prevented the glossy paint from ever achieving the brilliance of the Cretan original. So the Cycladic potters abandoned the attempt and confined themselves to producing a light slip ware with dark matt designs, at first in rectilinear and later in curvilinear patterns. Characteristic forms are the shallow milk bowls and the cluster vases or 'Kernoi' with a Cycladic individuality of their own.

The matt paint is of a uniform dead blackness upon a light slip, colder and more chalky than the previous kind. It showed up more clearly than did the dark shiny paint, which owing to the porosity of the Melian clay was never able to obtain the distinctness of outline or the lustre of the Cretan designs.

Although, as we have said, the first painted decoration of MC I was inspired by the rectilinear motifs in use with incised ware of the Early Cycladic period, it was not long after the brush had superseded the graver that the potter adopted a wider range of patterns which differ from those of neighbouring peoples.

Among them were:

A series of chevrons traversed by wide black bands.
Long narrow angles.
Bands of zig-zags.
Lozenges within frames.
Hatched lozenges traversed by a line.

Hatched triangles alternating with boxed triangles.
The same with their apexes pointing alternately up and down.
Rectangles separated by the arms of a cross and decorated with dots.
Swastikas.

Although the patterns of MC I were predominantly rectilinear, this phase also included some early examples of curvilinear tendencies, particularly on pithoi and beaked jugs, as we shall see.

Milo during this period became an exporter of her pottery as well as of obsidian. Evidence of this export trade is forthcoming from Crete, where in contemporary deposits of their native lustrous ware, fragments of porous clay sherds with a pale slip and lack-lustre dark designs have been found which are evidently from Milo. Examples have also come to light in Keos, Tenos and Naxos.

With the adoption of painting instead of incising as a means of embellishment, so a number of new forms of vessels made their appearance in MC I. Among them were:

1. *The beaked jug* (Fig. 101b) which was one of the most characteristic Cycladic vessels of this period – but not of the graceful form into which it evolved later. It may not be so graceful, but there is nevertheless something in its onion-shaped, low-bellied body that strikes the eye as of a vessel infinitely old; and one wonders what primitive man slaked his thirst from its depths as he poured his wine or water out of the narrow, trough-shaped spout pointed up in the air like the beak of a bird.

2. *The Cycladic Prochous* (Fig. 101a) is another variety of jug distinguished from the beaked jug by its wide leaf-shaped spout. The word prochous means jug or ewer, but it is convenient to use the Greek word instead of the English to distinguish the two varieties.

In both cases the handle, which is thick and round, joins the body to the back of the neck as if to tilt the spout up into the air. The ornamentation consists as a rule of a series of bands encircling the neck and shoulder, with a pattern of some sort below the lowest band. One of the most common of these patterns is of a ring of pendants which may represent a garland or a necklace hanging on the breast, with sometimes a flower in the middle, and petal-shaped pendants at the sides.

Although this early curvilinear pattern may suggest a garland or a necklace, it is evidently evolved from simpler rectilinear patterns which are to be found on the earlier beaked jugs of this phase.

But there was no sharp division in early Cycladic art between rectilinear and floral motifs, for the artist of the period often caught at a suggestion to mingle linear and naturalistic elements in his designs.

Only with the rarest exceptions are the jugs of this period round

a. Cycladic prochous
Milo

b. Beaked jug with black decoration
Phylakopi

c. Spouted bowl
Phylakopi

d. Kernos with black linear design
Milo

e. Amphora
Phylakopi

Fig. 101. Middle Cycladic I vessels

bottomed like a gourd. It is a characteristic that they are all flat bottomed, which indicates perhaps that the houses of this period were furnished with tables, unlike those of the Early Cycladic period when, since the vessels were almost all fitted with suspension handles, we may suppose that house furniture was very scarce.

3. *The pithos* of this period is of two principal forms:

a. One with a mouth surrounded by a flat rim (Fig. 102a), and a body that swells as it descends to a low belly and a rounded base. It has low ledge-handles with string-holes low down at the broadest part of the jar. It has a slight neck above the rim, which is intended for holding a lid. On each side of the rim are holes for tying the lid on. It has matt-painted rectilinear decoration consisting of a series of chevrons traversed by wide bands.

In the majority of pithoi of this period the design did not descend below the level of the handles, but in this particular type, a fringe of loops sometimes hangs below the lowest band below the handles, the same motif that is so common on beaked jugs of the same period.

Some good examples of this type are found in the museum at Aegina, for Aegina seems to have been a stage of transmission at this period for certain vases from the Cyclades to the mainland of Greece. This type of Aegina ware is common to both Middle Cycladic and Middle Helladic periods.

b. The other characteristic pithos shape of the period has high rounded shoulders and tapers towards the base (Figs. 102b and c). The alternation of broad and narrow chevrons on the former example deserves to be noted. It is one of the devices that occurs on much later Mycenaean pottery.

4. *The amphora* (Fig. 101e) of very simple outline, low neck or neckless, and short vertical handles, which join the lip to the shoulder. In some cases a small spout was fitted. This shape is a development of the more primitive type of jar with neither handles nor spout found at Milo and Amorgos. Of the two best known, one is covered with discs and the other shows a bird engaged in pulling a worm out of the ground. The appearance of this quaint bird is important as it shows that the way was being prepared for a greater freedom of decoration, for such animal and human forms could not be confined within the rigid schemes of division which were characteristic of the rectilinear style.

5. *The cup*, of which several types have been found. The simplest was the cup with no handles. The commonest examples of this form are little ones where the only kind of decoration is two or three round spots just below the rim.

The patterned handleless cups are larger, wider across the top, and with slightly convex sides (Fig. 102d). The cups with handles are of an

a. Pithos (A)
Phylakopi

b. Pithos (C)
Phylakopi

c. Pithos (B)
Phylakopi

e. Spouted jar with
black linear decoration
Phylakopi

d. Cup
Phylakopi

f. Mug
Phylakopi

Fig. 102. Middle Cycladic I vessels continued

entirely different form and are really more in the shape of a beer mug
(Fig. 102f). A modification of this mug has a trumpet-shaped foot.
Examples of these have been found at Siphnos and Syra but not at
Phylakopi.

The patterns are arranged in bands of the simplest linear type, like
those of incised ware, except that occasionally they have rows of simple
festoons and arcs above or below the central band.

6. *The kernos* or *cluster vase* (Fig. 101d) is a composite vessel in which
one or more rings of small cups are mounted upon a central stem. Kernoi
have been found at Phylakopi in Milo, and in Crete. From the number
found in the Phylakopi cemetery it is evident that the kernos was a
common article of tomb furniture. They do not seem, however, to have
been made exclusively for sepulchral use, for others have been found in
houses. They may have been used for holding flowers or for religious
rites, or as multiple oil-lamps, or to contain offerings to the dead or to
a divinity.

The kernos is of great antiquity, but its production seems to have
ceased when the rectilinear style of decoration went out of vogue. Very
large numbers of them have been found, and the kernos is a vessel of
peculiarly Cycladic type. All are decorated in the dark-on-light technique,
mostly with zig-zag patterns. These kernoi have sometimes eight, eleven,
nineteen, twenty or even as many as twenty-five small vases. They are
often found in tombs in Crete, and one found at Mallia near Herakleion
has no less than forty-one small vases.

7. *The spouted bowl* (Fig. 101c) forms one of a long series of which the
earlier members are characteristic of the dark-on-light rectilinear style
of the Middle Cycladic I phase. It has a sharply incurved rim with a small
trough-spout projecting from it, and exactly opposite a suspension-handle
which is always horizontal. The decoration normally consists of simple
vertical lines or chevrons or triangles in groups on the rim. Below this, the
bowl is undecorated or in some cases covered with a red burnished slip.

8. *The spouted jar* (Fig. 102e). We leave to the last a majestic spouted
jar found at Phylakopi. It does not conform to any special class of vessel
although it bears a certain family resemblance to the duck vase with its
vertical shoulder-spout, its conical top and arched handle.

Its painted decoration belongs to the early rectilinear style of MC I.
Its general shape corresponds to that of some of the larger and more
striking shapes of the stirrup jars of a later date.

Middle Cycladic II (Curvilinear Style)

As we mentioned earlier (page 238), to the Middle Cycladic II phase has
been assigned matt painted dark-on-light ware with curvilinear designs.

a. Beaked jug with 'breasts'
Lerna

b. Beaked jug with 'breasts'
Probably from Phylakopi

c. Shallow cup with
internal decoration
Phylakopi

d. Shallow cup with
external decoration
Phylakopi

e. Shallow bowl
Phylakopi

Fig. 103. Middle Cycladic II vessels

Vessels of this MC II style of decoration seem to have been made almost entirely at Phylakopi, whence they were exported to the other islands and to the mainland of Greece, although some similar ware has also been found in Thera and Amorgos.

The basic motif in the decoration of this pottery was the spiral or the circle, from which a variety of curvilinear patterns was evolved. Among the many motifs that the vase painter used during this MC II phase were parallel wavy lines, large discs, tridents, hatched lozenges, four-leafed rosettes, hatched pears, plain leaves and leaves with hatchings and other fillings, but the commonest motif is unquestionably the spiral in a great variety of forms (Fig. 105).

These patterns seem often to have been inspired by designs on Kamares ware from Crete of the Middle Minoan II period, a certain amount of which has been discovered on the same site. The beauty of Cretan Kamares ware could not fail to strike the attention of all peoples in contact with the Minoans.

No attempt was made by the Cycladic potter to give his ware the varied colouring of the Kamares pottery, but he managed to achieve some diversity of tone by hatching some parts of his motifs, and by adopting greater freedom of design.

It is interesting to trace the motifs on sherds of Minoan ware at Phylakopi which the Cycladic potter used as his model.

Plate XV.2 of *Excavations at Phylakopi in Melos*, for instance, shows the motif on a Cycladic sherd, while Fig. 131 on page 150 of the same work shows the design on a contemporary Kamares sherd from which the Melian potter drew his inspiration (Fig. 104).

Fig. 104. Designs on potsherds from Phylakopi

One cannot say that the Cycladic design was a direct copy of the Cretan, for it is thoroughly Cycladic in character, and in no way achieves the inventive grace of its model.

The Curvilinear style was not the only innovation at this time. Some new vase-types of Anatolian origin made their first appearance. One of these was the beaked jug with moulded 'breasts'. It has not been found in Crete, though it was copied on the mainland from Cycladic models. Another, though rare, was the spouted jar, a type which was already in vogue in Cretan ceramics from the Early Minoan period onwards. A third type was the bowl with one loop handle, which has been found on several Cycladic sites, but has not been found in either Crete or the mainland.

The MC II period was a time when Cretan influence became more evident in Milo, and Anatolian influence was exercised upon the whole Cycladic group of islands. It is possible that there may have been a small influx of Anatolian immigrants into the Cyclades at that time.

The following are examples of vessels of this MC II style with matt black designs on a light ground.

1. *The beaked jug* (Figs. 103a and b). The general shape is common to both MC I as well as to the later phases of the Middle Cycladic period, but the MC II shape is rather more elongated than in MC I and differs markedly by its more graceful shape from the type in use during the earlier phase. Not only is the body more elongated, but the channelled spout, tilted as before up into the air like a bird swallowing water, is thinner and longer to give the impression of a bird's beak. This illusion of a bird's head is heightened by the addition of a raised stud on either side of the spout to look like eyes. Below this head the curve of a girl's throat is suggested by the addition of two small moulded breasts surrounded by dotted circles. These beaked jugs of MC II end in a slightly raised foot, flat or a little hollowed underneath to improve their stability. Jugs of the same shape have been found in the islands of Amorgos and Thera, while a double vase of the same type also comes from Amorgos. The ornamentation of these beaked jugs of MC II is of two kinds.

One consists of horizontal zones of various patterns encircling the upper part of the jug, which might be called the necklace type of decoration. The decoration of these zones bears a close resemblance to Egyptian jewelry. The other has a decorative ornament on the breast below the spout with accessory motifs.

A strange ornament that sometimes appears in the second case is a curious goblin-like creature with staring eyes and a grinning mouth with two rows of sharp teeth (Fig. 105). Perhaps this was the first manifestation of the gorgon's head or 'gorgoneion' that became such a favourite subject of decoration on early Greek vases a thousand years later.

2. *The shallow bowl* (Fig. 103e) is a new shape in Melian pottery. It is very typical of the matt black class of pottery of MC II. It is shallow, with a convex base, but of a curve so slight that the vessel stands perfectly steady. It has two loop-handles rising on opposite sides of the rim. The form is like that of certain large Minoan bronze bowls, and of others

Fig. 105. Middle Cycladic II patterns

found in the shaft graves at Mycenae. Except for a black band a little below the rim, the outside is left plain. Decoration is confined to the inside which is invariably covered with designs. These include a quatrefoil design, a rosette and discs, a rosette and curving petals, as well as circular motifs and lines of spiral chains radiating from the centre of the bowl.

3. *The shallow cup* (Figs. 103c and d). The shallow cups of MC II are of two types, one of which is decorated inside and the other outside. In the first case there is a slight inward curve round the outside of the rim, the base is flat and slightly raised and the handle is flat. Both rim and base are surrounded by a black ring. The insides are decorated with designs similar to those used on the shallow bowls.

In the second case the cups are of the same shape but are decorated on the outside. In this case the inside has a coat of matt red paint in imitation of the glossy paint on the interior of Minoan cups. In only a few cases do these cups have a design both inside and outside.

4. Examples of a *spouted jar*, a bridge-spouted jar, an amphora and a pithos have been found which, from their form or decoration, are attributable to MC II, but such examples are either so extremely rare, or represented only by a few fragments that it is not considered worthwhile dealing with them here.

Middle Cycladic III (Naturalistic Style)

During MC III Phylakopi still carried on an extensive trade as is seen by the wide distribution of her pottery, not only among the islands, but also on the mainland at Athens, Asine and Mycenae.

Aegina also made pottery with a distinctly Cycladic air. Fragments of Cypriot pottery have been found in Milo and Thera while Cycladic sherds have been found in Cyprus which indicates their route to the Levant. Minoan ware from Crete was imported into the islands at this period, although there was as yet no slavish copying of Minoan designs. Rhyta in the form of bulls' and cows' heads found at Phylakopi suggest that there was some observance of Minoan ritual, and from the signs on the pottery, it seems that Linear A script was in use there as in Crete. Phylakopi was not alone, however, in possessing some degree of Minoan culture, for pottery found in Keos, Delos and Thera includes copies of Cretan MM III designs.

Sir Arthur Evans suggests in Vol. I of *The Palace of Minos* that the 'Black and Red' bird vases found in the temple repositories of Knossos probably contained Melian wine which formed a tribute to the ruler of Knossos. 'The volcanic soil of the island', he says, 'is in fact specially favourable to the cultivation of the vine, which may have begun here relatively early.' The same might be said of Thera where much of the pottery consisted of large amphoras and pithoi suitable for the storage and transport of wine.

It was at this period that Crete was at the height of her overseas expansion. Minoan pottery found at Aegina and Kythera, and the adoption of Minoan styles in Argolis, all testify to the power exerted by Crete. And yet from excavations made in the Second Grave Circle at Mycenae, finds have been made proving that pottery from the Cyclades was used at Mycenae even earlier than Minoan ware. It is evident that the Cycladic population as well as the Cretan was actively concerned in trade with the mainland.

We mentioned on page 238 that the Cycladic pottery of MC III fell into two categories:

a. Dark-on-light matt painted ware in naturalistic designs.
b. Dark-on-light matt painted ware in naturalistic designs with highlights of burnished red or brown.

a. In the first of these categories we see an increasing tendency to represent natural objects. The patterns which evolve as a result of this process develop into a peculiarly Melian style.

Some of the decorative elements are taken from vegetable, and others

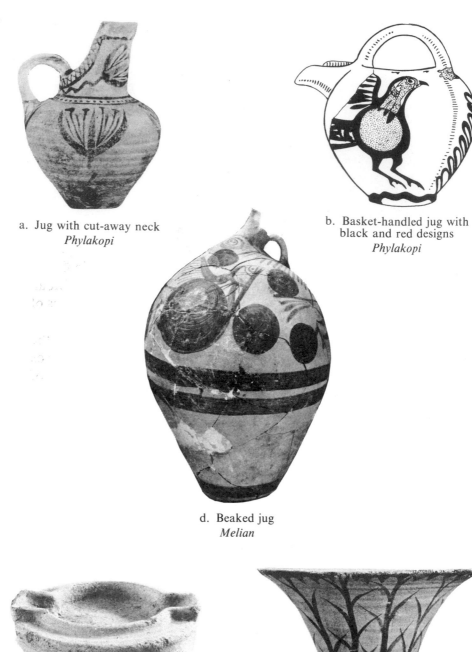

a. Jug with cut-away neck
Phylakopi

b. Basket-handled jug with
black and red designs
Phylakopi

d. Beaked jug
Melian

c. Lamp
Phylakopi

e. Kalathos
Phylakopi

Fig. 106. Middle Cycladic III vessels

from animal life, a number of which seem to derive from frescoes of Minoan type found at Phylakopi. The Cycladic potters did not often borrow their motifs from the vegetable world, but when they did so, both plants and flowers were very much stylised.

The principal vegetable motifs are the daisies with pointed or rounded petals, a favourite device with the Minoans. Another floral device which appears for the first time is the palmette usually hanging downwards. Yet another very stylised floral motif is the lotus palmette with its fan of petals between two curled-over 'falls'. In the animal world, the most popular is the bird, but fragments have been found with strange cat-like creatures in a row round the vase.

Only one example showing the human figure has been found belonging to this period, and that is on a fragment found at Phylakopi belonging to a globular jar with a projecting spout. It represents a man in an attitude of worship. Although the figure bears some resemblance to the figure to which we referred in the chapter on Early Cycladic III, the two figures

Fig. 107. Man in an attitude of worship

are very different. Whereas in the older figure, the body is indicated by two triangles united at their apexes, this one shows more resemblance to nature. Its arms are lifted and bent at the elbows like those of the well-known terra-cotta figures of goddesses in the Museum at Herakleion and like them his fingers are spread in the shape of a fan.

Some vessels characteristic of this naturalistic phase of matt black decoration on a light ground are as follows:

1. *The beaked jug.* There is little to distinguish this jug from that of the MC II curvilinear style except firstly that the base is rather higher and secondly that the decoration is naturalistic – floral or animal. The jugs of this phase still have the moulded 'breasts' and the 'eyes' on the beak.

2. *The shallow bowl.* Several large fragments have been found which are believed to have belonged to the shallow bowl of the same type as that of the curvilinear style of MC II. The decoration takes the form of vegetable motifs and of birds.

3. *The shallow cup.* Again the shape is the same as that of the curvilinear style of MC II, and again the decorative patterns are birds and fish, palmettes and vegetable tendrils.

4. *The panelled cup* (Fig. 108a). The shape of this cup is more like our modern tea-cup, namely one handle, a convex bowl tapering gracefully to a low base. They are called 'panelled cups' because the ornamentation is confined between two vertical lines, and on one half of the cup only, namely the half which is on the right-hand side of the handle and so visible to someone other than the drinker. The interior is given a red wash. The decoration on those specimens which have been excavated include wildfowl flying through reeds, floral designs, palmettes and plant tendrils.

5. *The spouted bowl* which we described in MC I as having a sharply incurved rim with projecting spout and horizontal handle appears in the MC III phase with simple naturalistic motifs round the rim.

b. The second category of Middle Cycladic III in which appear those vessels decorated in dark paint on a light background, with some subsidiary elements of the design in burnished red or brown, is one of the most interesting phases of Cycladic ceramics. This category is generally referred to as the 'Black and Red' class of decoration, for the artist uses two colours instead of one.

At first the red paint plays only a subsidiary part. The main part of the design is drawn in black, while the red is used merely as a dividing band between two friezes, or to fill up a vacant space in, say, the body of a bird. Later on, however, it forms an essential part of the design.

We can illustrate this change in the case of the two beaked jugs illustrated on Fig. 108. Both are decorated with a floral design. In the first case the whole design is painted in black with only the stamens of the flowers painted red. In the second case the main part of the design is red and only the stamens are in black.

The most common occurrence of red in this decorative phase, however, is in the use of large burnished red or brown discs, generally used for the bodies of birds, but also as mere decorative ornaments or for representing fruits (Figs. 106d and 108b).

The use of a round red disc for the body of a bird was not confined to pottery from Milo alone. It seems to have been a wide-spread convention. Examples were found in the shaft graves of Mycenae, which indeed were possibly contemporary with the Melian ones of Middle Cycladic III. The bird was a favourite decorative subject in both Cycladic and Mycenaean pottery of this period, a fondness which may well be traced to Egyptian influence, for lifelike pictures of many varieties of birds appear on the Egyptian monuments. Although Mycenaean and Cycladic art may have borrowed such ideas from Egypt, they treated them more freely.

In fact with rare exceptions, all the birds appearing upon Cycladic

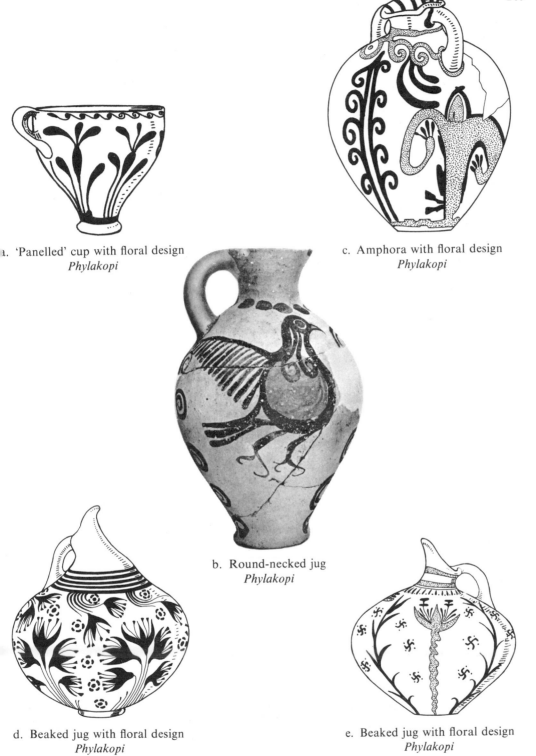

a. 'Panelled' cup with floral design
Phylakopi

c. Amphora with floral design
Phylakopi

b. Round-necked jug
Phylakopi

d. Beaked jug with floral design
Phylakopi

e. Beaked jug with floral design
Phylakopi

Fig. 108. Middle Cycladic III vessels continued

vases of this class of MC III have the same round body represented by a burnished disc. It is the head that identifies the species of bird, whether hawk, duck, or whatever it may be. A number of these 'Black and Red' class vases decorated with birds have been found in the temple repositories at Knossos.

Fish were also a favourite subject for the decoration of Melian pottery during this phase. These animals gave life and originality to the vases after the somewhat rigid and stylised motifs of the preceding period.

We deal below with vase types which particularly characterise this phase of MC III, but before doing so, special mention should be made of the most remarkable piece of painted earthenware discovered at Phylakopi, and certainly the most important example of the human figure decoration belonging to this period. It is known as:

The Fishermen Vase (Fig. 109), now in the National Archaeological Museum in Athens. It forms a cylinder, broken and rather badly burned round the top. The base, though much worn, appears to be nearly complete, for there are traces of a band of paint round the inside of it. From this it may be concluded that it was originally hollow underneath. The sides are very thick. It is not clear what its purpose was, but from the thickness of the sides, the way it tapers towards the top, the moulding round the base, it seems probable that it may have been the pedestal of a lamp. Round the top is a frieze of ivy-leaves, but the principal decorative subject is a procession of four men in line marching to the right holding a fish in each hand, except for one who is hitching up his kilt with his left hand. They are naked except for the characteristic Mycenaean kilt with a flap in front. Their hair falls down over their shoulders in long wavy locks. They walk bare-footed. Although so small, the fishes which they carry, with one exception, look like dolphins.

The dotted band below them probably represents a pebbly beach or path. The fishermen are outlined in black, and their bodies are painted in lustrous paint varying from red to brown.

The drawing shows a great advance in decorative skill during the relatively short time which had elapsed since the primitive representations of the human figure in the previous period. The four bodies are here shown naturalistically and with infinitely more artistic skill than the conventionalised symbols which formerly represented the human body. They have supple limbs, and the solemnity of their march is well suggested by the bending of the left knee and by the way their shoulders are thrown back.

The slim figures of the four men and the fish which they hold are so well drawn that it seems possible that the artist's inspiration may have derived from some Cretan processional frieze in Crete or in Argolis. The

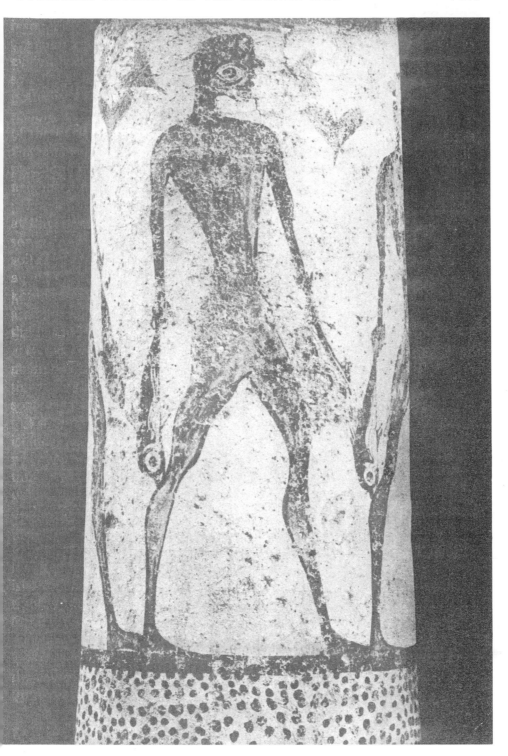

Fig. 109. The 'Fishermen Vase'. Middle Cycladic III from Phylakopi

most primitive features of the drawing are the absence of hands and their Cyclopaean eyes in the middle of the cheek.

It is interesting to compare this procession of fishermen belonging to the Middle Cycladic III period with the procession of soldiers on the well-known Warrior Vase of Mycenaean III C and drawn, therefore, some five hundred years or so later.

Some typical vessels of this dark-on-light phase of MC III with naturalistic designs and red or brown high-lights are as follows:

1. *The round-necked jug* (Fig. 108b). Two nearly complete specimens have been found at Phylakopi. One is painted in black with a red round-bodied bird and outstretched wing; the other has a graceful pomegranate or tulip design on the body, and a loose spiral ornament round the neck.

2. *The beaked jug with bird design* (Fig. 106d). This impressive vessel was found at Knossos, but is evidently Cycladic and Melian. It has a superb swelling outline with tilted beak and swelling throat. The design, confined to the upper part of the jug, shows birds pecking at fruits. The discs forming the fruits and the circular bodies of the birds are of burnished red.

3. *The beaked jugs with floral design* (Figs. 108d and e). These jugs have a curved, sharp-pointed spout, sometimes with a slight swelling on the throat and a small foot: They are decorated with floral designs in the 'Black and Red' style. In some cases the flowers are painted black and the stamens red while in others the flowers are red and the stamens painted in black.

The flowers are not a realistic copy of any one kind of plant, and whether the artist intended to represent a crocus or fritillary or any other individual flower is uncertain. It consists of three sharp-pointed petals enclosing a cluster of stamens.

4. *The jug with cut-away neck and floral design* (Fig. 106a). This type of jug is common in the Early Mycenaean period. It has an upright circular neck with the back part cut right away. The three-pointed crocus is the main decorative motif on several of these jugs.

5. *The basket-handled jug* (Fig. 106b). Two fairly complete examples of this are known. They have basket handles and are decorated with a bird with extended wing facing a foliate design.

6. *The amphora* (Fig. 108c). A complete example of this vessel with mouth pinched in where the tops of the handles join the rim has been found. The flowers may represent a lily with the petals curled outwards, but the tufts of small leaves at the tips of the petals prevent them representing any particular species of flower.

7. *The kalathos* (Fig. 106e). Vases of the kalathos or basket shape were a Cycladic form. The designs are of branching blades of grass or of reeds

painted alternately black and red, or sometimes entirely in red. All the painted vases of this type have a hole in the bottom. They may, therefore, have been intended for use as flower-pots.

8. *The conical filler* seems to have been used in Thera during this phase. These vessels were merely decorated with red burnish in simple patterns.

9. *The Cycladic lamp* (Fig. 106c) found at Phylakopi is a copy of the Cretan lamps of LM I found at Phaestos and Mallia. Few of them really belong to MC III and they are most plentiful in the Late Cycladic period.

THE LATE CYCLADIC PERIOD 1600–1100 BC

The brilliant evolution of Crete in all branches of activity, which was one of the important factors in the development of the Mediterranean civilisation towards the end of the Middle Minoan and the beginning of the Late Minoan I periods, powerfully affected her nearest neighbours, Milo and Thera.

This overwhelming Cretan influence in the early part of the Late Cycladic period seems to have altered the native style of these two islands. They adopted a number of Cretan vase forms and made use of a lustrous paint as well as a number of Minoan ornamental motifs. In this Creto-Cycladic style we find a number of Minoan motifs such as branches, ivy-leaves, water plants, the lily and crocus, as well as the water fowl and octopus.

The result was that the beginning of the Late Cycladic period was marked by a decline in the pre-eminent position formerly occupied by Phylakopi as the creative centre for the Cycladic style of pottery. The local Melian pottery lost its own distinctive style and became increasingly Minoan in character.

Thera also adopted a style inspired by Minoan pottery at the beginning of LC I, a period which for her did not last long, for it seems that the settlements on that island were submerged by volcanic eruption soon after the end of it. From then onwards, this unfortunate island ceased to produce any more pottery for the remainder of the Bronze Age.

During LC I, however, the Melian and Theran potters improved the standard of their work due to Cretan influence. It is not possible to say whether this was due to Cretans living in the islands or due to local vase painters inspired by Minoan productions. The latter seems the more likely, for the vases made in the island workshops show certain differences from their Cretan prototypes. Moreover, research is now in progress by analysing the different regional clays of Greece to help in solving problems of this sort.

T

With the other islands it was different. None of the vase painters of Amorgos, Paros, Naxos, Siphnos or Syra seem to have adopted the naturalistic style of Crete; and as for the remoter islands such as Sikinos and Pholegandros, they continued to produce undecorated and even incised ware.

After the submission of Milo and Thera to Cretan influence, the spirit of invention declined in their own workshops. With the shrinking of its own native industry, the inhabitants of Milo satisfied their requirements by importing pottery from Crete, to judge by the large amount of Cretan ware and Cretan fragments among the native remains. Whereas at the beginning of LC I the bulk of pottery was Melian, in its later stages it was entirely displaced by imported ware.

Then towards the end of LC I we observe the decline of Cretan influence and the rise of the mainland power of Mycenae. During the Late Cycladic I and II periods, the amounts of Minoan ware and Mycenaean ware imported into the Cyclades seem to have been about equal, but in Late Cycladic III the Minoan pottery was almost completely ousted by Mycenaean.

In Myc. III B Greece was culturally at a zenith. It was the century that included the Trojan War and the great personalities of Agamemnon, Achilles, Nestor and the other Homeric heroes.

Myc. III C and consequently Late Cycladic III C is dated between 1200 and 1100 BC. This is the century of the Dorian invasions, the century of the destruction of Mycenae and Tiryns, the end of the Mycenaean civilisation and the end of the Bronze Age.

It is not easy to make a distinction between either local or imported pottery of the Late Cycladic I and the Late Cycladic II periods, nor is it easy to distinguish between imported Mycenaean III A and III B ware.

Before disappearing completely, the Phylakopi workshops turned once more to the production of pottery of its early style to make ware of linear decoration, and in the upper layer among Mycenaean fragments, some bits of local ware have been found that bear witness to the fact that the geometric rectilinear style of decoration was inherent in the spirit of the Cycladic vase painters.

In assigning shapes and decoration to the Late Cycladic period, we shall, therefore, adopt the following chronology:

LATE CYCLADIC I AND II (1600–1400 BC)
a. Local ware (LC I and II).
b. Imported Late Minoan I and II ware.
c. Imported Mycenaean I and II ware.

LATE CYCLADIC III A AND B (1400–1200 BC)

a. Imported Late Minoan III ware.

b. Imported Mycenaean III A and B ware.

LATE CYCLADIC III C (1200–1100 BC)

a. Imported Mycenaean III C ware.

b. Local ware – rectilinear style.

Late Cycladic I and II 1600–1400 BC

LOCAL WARE (LC I AND II). Although Phylakopi in Milo was beginning to recede from her position as the creative centre of a distinctive Cycladic style pottery, we still owe the greater part of the available information on Cycladic ware during LC I and II to specimens recovered from Phylakopi.

Until the volcanic eruption soon after LC I, Thera contributed a certain amount of local ware, and the pots and fragments in the Thera museum form a fairly homogeneous collection. Unfortunately these specimens are inadequately labelled as to their place of origin, and they do not really justify by originality of style or shape or decoration any very special attention. As regards the technique of local ware from Thera, the paint employed was a not very lustrous brownish-red or black paint. On some vases white paint has been added in the manner of LM I. On the whole, the Theran pottery of this phase came under the influence of both Crete and Milo.

As regards locally made pottery from Phylakopi, the most typical of this period is generally decorated in red and black, with red as the predominant colour and details picked out in black. As the red was not inherently very lustrous, many of the pots were burnished all over in imitation of the Minoan lustrous ware of LM I and II.

The typical vessels of this LC I and II period include:

1. *The trough-spouted jug and jar* (Figs. 115a and b). Many examples of this type have been found both in Milo and Thera. It is one of the most characteristic Minoan vase-forms of the LM I period as also of the corresponding Mycenaean period. The earliest type had no moulded rim round the opening, as if the top of the vase had been sliced clean off. Then comes a type with a broad flat rim which is a common variety.

Next, a piriform type with a small rounded rim and again a further development shows the beginning of a neck, which again in later examples becomes more pronounced and, like several other examples, is distinguished by a vertical handle at the back in addition to the two usual side-handles (Fig. 115b). The majority of these vessels are

276

a. Pedestal vase
   Phylakopi

c. Strainer
   Phylakopi

b. Conical filler
   Phylakopi

d. Cup with high foot
   Phylakopi

e. Hemispherical cup
   Phylakopi

f. Hemispherical cup
   Phylakopi

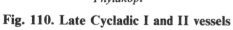

Fig. 110. Late Cycladic I and II vessels

decorated with a broad frieze of running spirals, which usually have a disc surrounded by dots in the centre of each spiral.

An interesting point is the method adopted by the vase painter to fill up the triangular spaces, one above and one below, between each pair of spirals. The first method was to insert a small triangle (Fig. 115d). Next the triangle was attached to the outer line of the spiral. This in turn develops into the pattern

Fig. 111. Patterns to fill triangular spaces

Another pattern which evolved out of the inserted triangle was

Fig. 112. Patterns to fill triangular spaces continued

Yet another device for filling in the triangular space was the use of two flexible stalks with ivy-leaves that fill up the corners.

Fig. 113. Patterns to fill triangular spaces continued

In some cases we find a double row of spirals and the space between them is filled with a spray of stamens.

Fig. 114. Patterns to fill triangular spaces continued

Some fragments of these bridge-spouted jars show floral patterns including grass-fronds.

2. *The pedestal vase* (Fig. 110a). This curious vessel consists of a tubular stem with wide-spreading circular bowl. This bowl has a large central boss with a hole in it. With the petal-like decoration of the top it gives one the impression of a marigold on a stalk, with the dotted boss like the centre of the flower.

The hole in the central boss allows liquid poured into the bowl to escape through the tube below. There is a small ledge handle below the rim on each side of the bowl. Some vessels of this type have a decoration of running spirals inside the bowl.

We have no information as to the purpose of these pedestal vases. They originated in Crete. If they were used for making libations the lower part could have been fixed into the ground while liquid was poured into the bowl and so escaped into the earth.

3. *The basin* (Fig. 115c). A number of large bowls or basins were found at Phylakopi belonging to this period. They are roughly elliptical. A good example is plain on the outside, but richly decorated inside in lustrous red with large running spirals, grass-fronds and ivy-tendrils.

These large basins have a broad rim ornamented with dashes. Most of them are decorated with spiral designs, but other smaller ones have been found with fishes swimming round the inside and on one fragment an octopus – a very rare subject in local Melian pottery. A row of studs runs round the outside just below the rim, indicating that the vessel is probably of metal origin.

4. *The strainer* found at Phylakopi (Fig. 110c) is fairly similar in shape to the ones found in Crete at Gournia belonging to the LM I period. It has a globular body with a wide rim. The body has four handles, two large horizontal and two small vertical ones. This globular body has a high hollow pedestal foot and a sieve bottom. The body is ornamented with a sort of leaf pattern while the pedestal foot is decorated with two cross-hatched bands, each with plain bands above and below. A strainer of similar shape comes from Thera.

5. *The handled cup* of this period is represented by several types:

  a. A cup with a single handle and a high foot. It is almost a handled goblet (Fig. 110d).

  b. A hemispherical cup with no distinct rim ornamented with spiral, foliate or horizontal zoned decoration (Fig. 110e).

  c. A hemispherical cup with a slightly defined outcurved rim. The decoration is a close one, and has a great variety of motifs.

  d. A hemispherical cup with a rim that slopes sharply upwards and outwards (Fig. 110f). It is most often decorated with a broad running spiral.

The above cups generally have a stud of clay where the handle joins the rim to imitate a rivet. In a few cases the rim is very slightly pinched so as to suggest, rather than actually to form, a spout.

6. *The conical filler.* Several examples of this vessel have been found at Phylakopi (Fig. 110b), but they are in no way so well shaped or decorated as their Cretan equivalent. The profile which is very irregular

a. Trough-spouted jug
Phylakopi

b. Trough-spouted jar
Phylakopi

c. Basin
Phylakopi

d. Trough-spouted jar
Phylakopi

e. Trough-spouted jar
Phylakopi

Fig. 115. Late Cycladic I and II vessels continued

curves inwards towards the lower end. In most cases the decoration consists mainly of zones of spirals, rows of leaves and zig-zag vertical lines.

IMPORTED LATE MINOAN I AND II WARE. A large quantity of imported
Late Minoan I and II ware has been found at Phylakopi, but most of it
unfortunately is very fragmentary, so that although the designs can be
recognised and generally reconstructed, it is not so easy to determine to
what kind of vessel they belong. The result is that although it has been
possible to recognise certain sherds as belonging to amphoras, jugs, cups,
bowls, conical fillers or alabastra, no special novelties have been discovered either in the matter of shape or decoration. Small quantities of
this ware have also been found in Keos, Naxos, Delos and Thera.

IMPORTED MYCENAEAN I AND II WARE. Again the bulk of imported
Mycenaean I and II ware found in the Cyclades comes from Milo and
Naxos, with small amounts also from Keos and Delos. By comparing the
finds with pottery on the mainland, it seems likely that most of it was
made in the Peloponnese. Again, virtually the whole of the pottery found
was in a fragmentary condition, to such an extent that in some cases it
has even been difficult to decide whether a sherd is of Minoan or Mycenaean origin.

Late Cycladic III A and B 1400–1200 BC

The fall of Knossos, the destruction of the Cretan palaces, and the collapse of the Minoan Empire occurred about 1400 BC. The power of
Mycenae, seen to be rising during LC II, came to its peak during LC III A.
Whatever the cause of the fall of Knossos, the event resulted in the disappearance of Cretan contacts with nearly all the Cyclades. On the other
hand, considerable quantities of Myc. III pottery has been found in a
number of the islands.

At the same time there seems to have been a decline in the native
energy of the Melian people. It is likely that one of the immediate causes
of this decline was the decay of the obsidian industry which for centuries
must have been the chief source of prosperity in Milo. Weapons had been
manufactured on a large scale, but for some time there had been a gradually increasing substitution of bronze for obsidian in the manufacture of
arrow-heads as well as in that of other weapons. The result led to the
gradual but sure decline of the town of Phylakopi, whose chief source of
prosperity since time immemorial had been the possession of the unique
obsidian quarries and a great trade all over the Mediterranean world.

At the same time we see the remains of a palace built at Phylakopi
which is not Cretan in style but more in the style of the mainland

buildings. We are led to the conclusion that while the bulk of the population of Milo remained unchanged, the people who designed and built the new palace were Mycenaean, perhaps part of a general wave of emigration from the mainland in a spirit of colonisation on the part of a vigorous and energetic race.

IMPORTED LATE MINOAN III WARE. The fall of Knossos and the collapse of the Minoan empire, with the consequent cessation of trade between Crete and the islands, is seen in the fact that Minoan ware of this period imported into the Cyclades has only been found up to now in Milo, Amorgos and Kimolos in small quantities. Even that is of so fragmentary a nature that the only shapes recognisable from the available sherds are some kylikes, a few bowls, a stirrup jar and a conical filler.

IMPORTED MYCENAEAN IIIA AND B WARE. Meanwhile the mainland power of Mycenae was growing, and we find that the amount of Myc. III A and B pottery imported into the Cyclades was far greater than the amount of Myc. I and II during the Late Cycladic I and II periods. It has been found not only in Milo and Naxos, Keos and Delos as in the previous period, but also in Amorgos, Kimolos, Kythnos, Paros, Seriphos, Siphnos and Tenos.

A certain amount of ware was made locally, but as most of it is fragmentary, while the designs are so Mycenaean in character, that it is not always easy to decide whether a sherd is of local make or imported Mycenaean.

It does not seem worthwhile to go into any sort of detail regarding the types of vessels found in the Cyclades at this time, for the shapes are those typical of the Myc. III A and III B and described under Mycenaean ware. They include kylikes, stirrup jars, three-handled jars, alabastra, spouted jars, tankards, conical fillers, bowls and jugs. A fairly comprehensive list is given in *B.S.A.*, LI (1956).

Late Cycladic III C 1200–1100 BC

IMPORTED LATE MYCENAEAN IIIC WARE. In the last Cycladic phase, that of LC III C, excavation reveals a general decline of culture and the dissolution of the mainland power.

Myc. III C pottery has been found only in Amorgos, Delos, Milo, Naxos and Paros. Much of this appears to have been locally made, although it still resembles the mainland type. It is quite clear, however, that the once powerful Mycenae had lost direct control over the islands, and it is probable that for this reason there is no mention of them in the Homeric Catalogue. Trade between them had virtually ceased.

A local ceramic style reappeared in Milo, but among the few sherds that have been recovered we see scenes of weapons and war that show evidence of the events that were bringing about the final disappearance of the Mycenaean Empire. They mark the end of Cycladic ceramic art.

CHAPTER SIX

The Dorian Invasion

1200–1100 BC

We have already seen how the Mycenaean civilisation and power were declining at the beginning of the twelfth century (Myc. III C) upon the mainland of Greece. This decline does not seem to be attributable entirely to the onset of old age. It was at this time that Egyptian inscriptions record unrest in the Aegean, and a southward movement of the 'Peoples of the Sea'.

The fifteenth and fourteenth centuries BC had seen the birth or rise in Asia, Africa and Greece of powerful empires: the Babylonian, the Assyrian, the Egyptian and the Achaean confederacy on the mainland and islands of Greece.

Then during the twelfth century the apparent stability of these powers was abruptly shaken. A great series of invasions by barbarous hordes broke forth from obscure regions of Europe and Asia. Greek legend has preserved the memory of events connected with the arrival of the Dorians – 'the return of the Heraclidae'.

The sons of Heracles, a demi-god honoured by most of the Dorian cities, were taking possession once again of the lands of their father after a long exile in Doris in central Greece.

Excavations in Macedonia have uncovered, together with implements of iron, the traces of a sudden change of civilisation. A new people of apparently Nordic origin made their appearance in the Vardar valley which they left again shortly afterwards to penetrate as far south as Dodona (Yannina) in Epirus and the foothills of Mt. Ossa in Thessaly.

A linguistic map of Greece proper suggests a racial stream moving southwards. It shows in the neighbourhood of the path of the stream some traces of a north-western tongue to which Dorian belongs, and even a disturbance of the older tongues which cannot be explained otherwise than by the sudden immigration of a new race.

We have no means of determining the exact date of the invasion nor the period of its duration. It cannot have begun before the twelfth century BC and it must in fact have begun before the beginning of the eleventh if we can rely upon the Iron Age discoveries as belonging to that period. It would seem to have corresponded approximately with the Myc. III C period.

The country of origin of the invaders seems to have been in the valley of the Danube which rolls right across the Balkans from west to east, a few hundred miles north of Greece, before flowing into the Black Sea. It was there that these warlike tribes had learnt to make and to use weapons of iron. On reaching Greece the invaders followed two routes, one to the east and one to the west of the Pindus range. The western group, passing through Epirus about 1140 BC, and down the west coast of Greece, reached the Gulf of Corinth about 1120 BC which they crossed at Naupaktos and landed in Elis, famous in classical times for its great religious centre at Olympia.

The eastern group, leaving the Pindus range to the west, followed the east coast southward and entered the plains of Thessaly by way of the Vale of Tempe. Still pursuing their southward route they reached the Gulf of Lamia, and here they seem to have split up into two smaller groups. One of these made its way by land to the Gulf of Corinth which they crossed to land on the north coast of the Peloponnese; the other seems to have gone by sea, down the channel between Euboea and the mainland, and finally disembarked in Argolis to the east of Corinth.

Argos, sheltering under the great natural fortress of Larisa, served as a base from which they could dominate the surrounding country. The region round Corinth was easily subdued, while the capture of Epidaurus opened the way to the island of Aegina. Even the great Achaean fortresses of Mycenae and Tiryns were overcome, and the centre of power was transferred to Argos, which became queen of the Argive plain. Megara itself, gateway to the east, fell to the invaders, but somehow they were prevented from persevering further in this direction, and Attica escaped their occupation.

Moving still further south they gained Sparta which became the Dorian capital of Laconia and within three generations they had reached the southernmost point of the Peloponnese.

After the mainland came the turn of the islands: Milo and Thera, Crete and Rhodes. For a time their situation and their comparative poverty afforded the islands a relative immunity from the invaders, but the many links which had been forged between them and the mainland during centuries of peace and prosperity were broken. It was too hazardous for the innumerable vessels which formerly thronged the Aegean seas to brave the passage through dangerous waters once the Cretan navy was no longer there to ensure their safety.

The Dorian invasion was a disaster for the Achaeans. Their Mycenaean civilisation was crushed. For them it was the final catastrophe. Their citadels of Mycenae and Tiryns went up in flames. The palace of Knossos in Crete was once more destroyed, never to rise again. Iron took the place of bronze, and Mycenaean art, as a living thing, ceased to exist.

The results of the Dorian invasion of the twelfth century bear no resemblance to the Achaean invasion of Crete two hundred years earlier. The Achaeans, who had already experienced Cretan influence on the mainland, although they allowed it to decline, preserved a certain continuity of their Minoan heritage. The Dorians coming from the wilds of Macedonia, entirely destroyed it.

The human race has need, it seems, of a periodical blood-bath and a descent into the grave. The Dorian invasion meant the return of barbaric codes, of savage chieftains, and of a land made a prey to insecurity. What to the Achaeans had been beautiful they found an abomination. Time is not granted to empires any more than to men to learn from past errors. The artist can improve his masterpiece if he finds it imperfect, but nature prefers to start again from chaos itself, and this horrible waste is what we call the natural order. It took two or three centuries for the artistic spirit instinct in the Greek race to blossom afresh.

What was the origin of the name Dorian?

During their stay in northern Greece they had been known as Macedonians, but to the Mycenaeans they appeared to have come from Doris, a small district just north of Delphi, which was their last halting place before they invaded the Peloponnese. Dorians, therefore, was the name which seems to have been given them by the victims of their invasion.

It can be readily appreciated that the movement of peoples resulting from the Dorian invasion was not limited to the mainland of Greece. The bays of Thessaly and the Peloponnese served as points of embarkation for the displaced populations, while the islands and the coasts of Asia Minor stood ready to receive them, with the result that the civilisation of all Asia Minor was transformed.

After the early confusion occasioned by the evacuations had subsided, the Greeks expelled from their country displayed a remarkable sense of unity. This was partly due to language, partly to religion. The rise of Greek communities upon the coasts of Asia Minor, sustained by the development of communications along the maritime routes linking them to the mainland of Greece, aroused a strong communal Greek sense in face of the barbarians against whom they had to defend themselves.

Side by side with this sense of racial unity, however, two developments occurred which tended to keep the Greeks constantly at odds with one another. One of these was their sense of independence in the creation of their small city states. The old Bronze Age powers of the Aegean had disappeared or were in a state of dissolution. Knossos and Mycenae became heaps of ruins, but the successors of these powers had lived long enough in contact with them to have absorbed much of their culture, with the result that the small city states of Greece which arose from the ruins, though simpler than their predecessors, preserved much of their cultural heritage.

The other development was the direct result of the Dorian invasion which split the Greek world into two hostile camps, the Dorian (which included Sparta) and the Ionian (which included Athens), and it was this antagonism which stamped the Hellenic world of the post-Mycenaean period, and culminated in the Peloponnesian War.

Nevertheless the link forged by their common tongue and common religion rose superior to the sense of local separatism, and those speaking the Greek tongue took the name of Hellene. The origin of the name is lost in obscurity. It originally belonged to a tribe in Thessaly, and Hellas – which in very early days was limited to a region of Thessaly – came in time to mean all of what was inhabited by Greeks of whatever race: Ionians, Achaeans (who became Aeolians in Anatolia), or Dorians. Another link was to unite them still further. They invented for themselves a common writing.

What happened to the long tradition of pottery which had developed all through the Minoan and Mycenaean Ages? The invaders were probably a nomadic people at first, living in tents or huts and using wooden utensils. They may have had superior weapons, but in arts and crafts they were inferior to the race they conquered. They brought no distinctive painted pottery with them, although such crude ware as they did bring bears affinities with the pottery of the Danube valley.

Here we are in a quandary. With so radical a conquest we should have expected an immediate change in material products. But recent excavations have shown that there was no sharp change in pottery style. The Mycenaean style slowly decayed, and in Athens at all events, the excavations in the Kerameikos cemetery have unearthed a sequence of styles in which sub-Mycenaean (1100–1000 BC) merges into Protogeometric (1000–900 BC) and so evolves into the Geometric (900–700 BC).

Attica was virtually untouched by the Dorian invasion, with the result that many Achaeans from neighbouring parts and from the Peloponnese sought refuge there. Found among the earliest débris left by the invaders in Macedonia and on sites in the Ionian islands is pottery with the compass-drawn concentric circle as a decorative feature – the most characteristic feature of Protogeometric ornament. It marked the first signs of the new style.

NOTE ON CONICAL WINE FILTERS

Since the draft of this book has gone to press, the author and Mr C. P. Greaves of Market Drayton, Shropshire, a maker of wines for many years, have examined together at Herakleion and Knossos the vessels which have hitherto been described as Conical Fillers or Conical Rhytons to consider their purpose.

The author is of the opinion that these vessels are conical wine filters, an assumption which is supported by S. M. Tritton in his book, *The Practice of Wine Making*, in which is described and illustrated a 'Valentine's Flask'.

This is a vessel similar in shape and size to the Minoan vessels in question. In it is placed charcoal or other suitable material. New cloudy wine is poured into the top of the flask until the filtrate runs clear and bright.

This method of clarification is quicker and sounder than any other, and in commercial practice is used mechanically by vintners throughout Europe.

Mr Greaves pointed out that the large conical flask borne by the Minoan 'cup-bearer' in the fresco at Knossos has lines running down its length. These, he believes, would represent grooves or tongues to allow air to escape when the vessel was fitted into the mouth of the wine jar which was to receive the filtrate.

He feels that the smaller conical vessels found in such numbers in the Minoan excavations in Crete, where wine has been made for thousands of years, might well have been used for filtering new wine at feasts or for ritual purposes.

There would, therefore, seem to be a case for calling these vessels Conical Filters rather than the names hitherto used for them.

Bibliography

American Journal of Archaeology (*A.J.A.*). Concord, N.H.

Annual of the British School at Athens (*B.S.A.*). London.

Annuario della R. Scuola Archeologica di Atene. Rome.

Archaeologia. Society of Antiquaries of London. London.

Asine. See O. Frödin.

Banti, L. See Pernier, L. and Banti, L.

Blegen, Carl W. *Korakou: A Prehistoric Settlement near Corinth*. Boston, Mass. 1921.

> *Prosymna*, Vol. I: text.

> > Vol. II: plates and plans. London. 1937.

> *Troy and the Trojans*. London. 1963.

> *Zygouries*. Cambridge, Mass. 1928.

Boardman, J. *The Cretan Collection in Oxford*. Oxford. 1961.

Bolletino d'Arte del Ministero della Publica Istruzione. Rome.

Bosanquet, R. C. and Dawkins, R. M. *Unpublished Objects from Palaikastro 1902–1906*. B.S.A. Supplementary Paper No. 1. London. 1923.

Bossert, H. T. *The Art of Ancient Crete*. London. 1937.

Boyd-Hawes, H. *Gournia*. American Exploration Society. Philadelphia. 1908.

British Museum, Catalogue of the Greek and Etruscan Vases in, Vol. 1, Part I. *Prehistoric Aegean Pottery*, by E. J. Forsdyke. London. 1927.

Bulletin de Correspondance Hellénique. Ecole Française. Athènes.

Bury, J. B. *A History of Greece*, 3rd edition. London. 1951.

Caskey, J. L. 'The Early Helladic Period in the Argolid', *Hesperia* 29. Cambridge, Mass. 1961.

Chadwick, J. *The Decypherment of Linear B*. Cambridge. 1961.

Chapoutier, F. and others. *Mallia*, Vols. I onwards. 1928 onwards. Paris.

Childe, V. Gordon. *New Light on the Most Ancient East*. London. 1934.

Corpus Vasorum Antiquorum of the Museums containing collections of Bronze Age Greek pottery.

Demargne, P. *Aegean Art*. London. 1964.

Desborough, V. R. d'A. *The Last Mycenaeans and their Successors*. Oxford. 1964.

Dussaud, René. *Les civilisations préhelléniques dans le bassin de la Mer Egée*. 2ᵉ édition. Paris. 1914.

Encyclopaedia Britannica.

Evans, Sir Arthur. *The Palace of Minos*, Vols. I–IV. London. 1921–1935.

> 'The Prehistoric Tombs of Knossos', *Archaeologia* 59. London. 1906.

> *The Shaft Graves and Beehive Tombs of Mycenae*. London. 1929.

> 'The Tomb of the Double Axes', *Archaeologia* 65. London. 1914.

> *Scripta Minoa*, I. Oxford. 1909.

and J. L. Myres. *Scripta Minoà*, II. Oxford. 1952.

Evans, Dr Joan. *Time and Chance*. London. 1943.

Forsdyke, Sir John. *Minoan Art* (Herz lecture to the British Academy). 1929.
            Greece before Homer. London. 1956.

Frankfort, H. *Studies in Early Pottery of the Near East*. 1927.
            Royal Anthropological Journal Nos. 6 and 8. London. 1924 and
            1927.
    and Pendlebury, J. D. S. *The City of Akhenaten*, Part II. London. 1933.

Frödin, O. and Persson, A. W. *Asine*. Stockholm. 1938.

Furness, A. *The Neolithic Pottery of Knossos*. *B.S.A.* London. 1953.

Furtwängler, A. and Loeschke, G. *Mykenische Thongefässe*. Berlin. 1879.
            Mykenische Vasen. Berlin. 1886.

Furumark, Arne. *The Chronology of Mycenaean Pottery*. Stockholm. 1940–1941.
            The Mycenaean Pottery. Stockholm. 1941.

Glotz, G. *The Aegean Civilisation*. London and New York. 1925.

Goldman, H. *Excavations at Eutresis in Boeotia*. Cambridge, Mass. 1931.

Greece. Hachette. Paris. 1964.

Hall, Edith H. *The Decorative Art of Crete in the Bronze Age*. University of
            Pennsylvania. Philadelphia. 1907.
            Early Painted Pottery from Gournia, Crete. University of Penn-
            sylvania. Philadelphia. 1905.
            Excavations at Sphoungaras in eastern Crete. University of
            Pennsylvania. Philadelphia. 1912.

Hall, H. R. *Aegean Archaeology*. London. 1915.
            The Civilisation of Greece in the Bronze Age. London. 1928.
            The Oldest Civilisation of Greece. London. 1901.

Hammond, N. G. L. *A History of Greece*. Oxford. 1959.

Hampe, R. and Winter, A. *Bei Töpfern und Töpferinnen in Kreta, Messenien und
            Zypern*. Bonn. 1962.
            *Bei Töpfern und Zieglern in Suditalien, Sizilien und
            Griechenland*. Mainz. 1965.

Hawes, H. B. and C. H. *Crete the Forerunner of Greece*. 1916.

Hazzidakis, J. *Tylissos, Etudes Crétoises*. Paris. 1934.

Hesperia – Journal of the American School of Classical Studies at Athens.

Hutchinson, R. W. *Prehistoric Crete*. London. 1962.

Illustrated London News. London.

Jouquet, P. *Les Premières Civilisations*. Paris. 1950.

The Journal of Hellenic Studies (*J.H.S.*). London.

Karo, G. *Die Schachtgräben von Mykenai*. Munich. 1930.
            Greifen am Thon. Baden-Baden. 1959.

Lane, Arthur. *Greek Pottery*. London. 1948.

Mackendrick, P. *The Greek Stones Speak*. London. 1962.

Makeprang, M. B. 'Late-Mycenaean Vases'. *A.J.A.* 42. Concord, N.H. 1938.

Marinatos, Sp. and Hirmer, M. *Crete and Mycenae*. London. 1960.

Matz, F. *Kreta, Mykenai, Troja*. Stuttgart. 1956.
            Crete and Early Greece (Art of the World Series). London. 1962.

Montelius, Oscar. *La Grèce Préclassique*. Stockholm. 1924 and 1928.

Monumenti Antichi – Reale Accademia dei Lincei. Rome.

U

Mosso, Angelo. *The Dawn of Mediterranean Civilisation*. London. 1910.

Mylonas, G. E. *Ancient Mycenae*. London. 1957.

Palmer, L. R. *Mycenaeans and Minoans*. London. 1965.

Pendlebury, J. D. S. *The Archaeology of Crete*. London. 1939; reprinted 1967.

Pernier, L. and Banti, L. *Il Palazzo Minoico di Festos*. Rome. 1935–1951.

Perrot, G. and Chipiez, C. *Histoire de l'Art dans l'Antiquité*. IV. La Grèce primitive. L'art Mycénien. Paris. 1914.

Phylakopi in Melos, Excavations at, conducted by the British School at Athens. B.S.A. Supplementary Paper No. 4. London. 1904.

Pottier, E. *Vases antiques du Louvre. Salles A–E*. Paris. 1897.

Schliemann, Heinrich. *Mycenae*. London. 1878.

  Orchomenos. Leipzig. 1881.

  Tiryns. Leipzig. 1886.

Seager, R. B. *The Cemetery of Pachyammos, Crete*. Philadelphia. 1916.

  Pseira, Crete. Philadelphia. 1910.

  Mochlos, Crete. Boston and New York. 1912.

  Vasiliki, Crete. Philadelphia. 1906.

Stobart, J. C. *The Glory that was Greece*. London. 1921; new edition 1964.

Stubbings, F. H. *Mycenaean Pottery from the Levant*. Cambridge. 1951.

Taylour, Lord William. *Mycenaean Pottery in Italy*. Cambridge. 1958.

  The Mycenaeans. Cambridge. 1964.

Ventris, M. and Chadwick, J. *Documents in Mycenaean Greek*. Cambridge. 1956.

Vermeule, E. *Greece in the Bronze Age*. Chicago. 1964.

Wace, A. J. B. 'Chamber Tombs at Mycenae', *Archaeologia* 82. London. 1932.

  Mycenae, An Archaeological History and Guide. Princeton. 1949.

Winter, Adam. *Keramische Zeitschrift*. Vols. 8 and 9. 1956 and 1957.

Xanthoudides, S. *The Vaulted Tombs of Messara*. Liverpool. 1924.

Zafiropulo, J. *Histoire de la Grèce à l'Age du Bronze*. Paris. 1964.

Zervos, Chr. *L'Art de la Crète Néolithique et Minoenne*. Paris. 1956.

  L'Art des Cyclades 2500–1100 BC. Paris. 1957.

Zervos, Chr. *L'Art de la Crète Néolithique et Minoenne*. Paris. 1956.

  L'Art des Cyclades 2500–1100 BC. Paris. 1957.

Index